CO-ATX-675

FLORIDA STATE
UNIVERSITY LIBRARIES

DEC 20 1994

TALLAHASSEE, FLORIDA

∘ Adding Counters
didn't really agree
orginal prgm

Mercenaries and Lyndon Johnson's "More Flags"

Mercenaries and Lyndon Johnson's "More Flags"

The Hiring of Korean, Filipino and Thai Soldiers in the Vietnam War

by ROBERT M. BLACKBURN

McFarland & Company, Inc., Publishers
Jefferson, North Carolina, and London

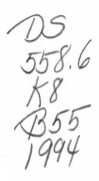

DS
558.6
K8
B55
1994

British Library Cataloguing-in-Publication data are available

Library of Congress Cataloguing-in-Publication Data

Blackburn, Robert M., 1942–
    Mercenaries and Lyndon Johnson's "more flags" : the hiring of
Korean, Filipino and Thai soldiers in the Vietnam War / by Robert
M. Blackburn.
        p.   cm.
    Includes bibliographical references and index.
    ISBN 0-89950-931-2 (lib. bdg. : 50# alk. paper) ∞
    1. Vietnamese Conflict, 1961–1975 — Korea.   2. Vietnamese Conflict,
1961–1975 — Philippines.   3. Vietnamese Conflict, 1961–1975 —
Thailand.   4. Johnson, Lyndon B. (Lyndon Baines), 1908–1973.
I. Title.
DS558.6.K8B55   1994
959.704'34 — dc20   93-42174
                                                                          CIP

©1994 Robert M. Blackburn. All rights reserved

Manufactured in the United States of America

McFarland & Company, Inc., Publishers
  Box 611, Jefferson, North Carolina 28640

Table of Contents

List of Tables

List of Acronyms
and Abbreviations

AID	Agency for International Development
CINCPAC	Commander-in-Chief, Pacific
DMZ	Demilitarized Zone
DOD	Department of Defense
FRG	Federal Republic of Germany
FYI	For Your Information
GOP	Government of the Philippines
GVN	Government of Vietnam
GRC	Government of the Republic of China
JCS	Joint Chiefs of Staff
MACV	Military Assistance Command, Vietnam
MAP	Mutual Assistance Program
MASH	Mobile Army Surgical Hospital
MIA	Missing in Action
NSC	National Security Council
NSF	National Security File
OSD	Office of Strategic Development
PHILCAG	Philippine Civic Action Group
PHILCON	Philippine Contingent
POW	Prisoner of War
PSYWAR	Psychological Warfare
R&R	Rest and Relaxation
ROK	Republic of Korea
SEATO	Southeast Asia Treaty Organization
SVN	South Vietnam

Johnson Administration Officials in the "More Flags" Program

BALL, GEORGE W.
Undersecretary of State; resigned in September 1966.

BELL, DAVID E.
Administrator, Agency for International Development, the State Department.

BLAIR, WILLIAM M., JR.
Ambassador to the Philippines, 1964–1967.

BOWMAN, R.C.
Aide to National Security Advisor McGeorge Bundy.

BROWN, WINTHROP G.
Ambassador to Korea, 1964–1967.

BUNDY, MCGEORGE
Special Assistant to the President for National Security Affairs; resigned in February 1966.

BUNDY, WILLIAM
Assistant Secretary of State for Far Eastern Affairs and co-chair with John McNaughton of the National Security Council Working Group.

BUNKER, ELLSWORTH
Ambassador to South Vietnam, April 1967–May 1973.

CLAXTON, ALLEN E.
Budget Examiner, Bureau of the Budget.

CLIFFORD, CLARK
Advisor to Lyndon Johnson, 1963–1968; chairman of the Foreign Intelligence Advisory Board; appointed Secretary of Defense in 1968.

COLBY, WILLIAM E.
Head of CIA Far East Division.

COOPER, CHESTER
White House aide to Lyndon Johnson.

FORRESTAL, MICHAEL
Aide to National Security Advisor McGeorge Bundy and chairman of the Vietnam Coordinating Committee.

HUGHES, THOMAS L.   Director of Intelligence and Research
                            at the State Department.

KINTNER, ROBERT E.   Lyndon Johnson's Chief of Protocol.

KOMER, ROBERT W.   Special Assistant to President Johnson,
                            1966–1968; appointed Ambassador
                            to Turkey in 1968.

LODGE, HENRY CABOT   Ambassador to South Vietnam,
                            August 1963–June 1964 and July
                            1965–April 1967.

MCNAMARA, ROBERT   Secretary of Defense until 1968.

MCNAUGHTON, JOHN   Co-chair with William Bundy of the
                            National Security Council Working
                            Group.

MARTIN, GRAHAM A.   Ambassador to Thailand, 1963–
                            1967.

PORTER, WILLIAM J.   Ambassador to Korea, 1967–1971.

READ, BENJAMIN H.   Executive Secretary, Department of
                            State.

ROSTOW, WALT W.   Counselor to the State Department
                            and chairman of its Policy Planning
                            Council until 1966; succeeded
                            McGeorge Bundy as National
                            Security Advisor in 1966.

RUSK, DEAN   Secretary of State.

SULLIVAN, WILLIAM   Special Assistant to Secretary of State
                            Dean Rusk.

TAYLOR, MAXWELL D.   Chairman of the Joint Chiefs of Staff
                            until appointed Ambassador to
                            South Vietnam in July 1964; re-
                            signed this post in July 1965 to serve
                            as a Special Consultant to President
                            Johnson, 1965–1969.

THOMSON, JAMES C.   Aide to National Security Advisor
                            McGeorge Bundy.

WHEELER, EARLE G.   Chairman of the Joint Chiefs of Staff,
                            1964–1970.

WRIGHT, MARSHALL   Aide to National Security Advisor
                            Walt W. Rostow.

ZWICK, CHARLES J.   Director, Bureau of the Budget.

Introduction

In almost any American accounting of the casualties suffered in the Vietnam War, one figure receives primary consideration — more than 58,000 American men and women lost their lives there.* Only rarely mentioned are the tens of thousands of Vietnamese, both North and South, who also lost their lives in that war. And not mentioned at all are the 5,241 dead suffered by other free world countries that also fought in South Vietnam, side-by-side with American troops, from 1962 through 1973.† These troops fought and died, but few American accounts of that war bother to cite their contribution. This lack of acknowledgment for the supreme sacrifices of 5,241 youths can be seen as an even more grievous injustice when one considers the fact that most of these men fought and died in South Vietnam so that Americans would not. They served, while being paid by the United States government, as mercenaries in service to America.[1]

Although it is used herein with full knowledge of its strong, even inflammatory implications, the term *mercenary* as used to describe most§ of the allied combat troops that fought in South Vietnam does not originate with this study. This descriptive label, with all its negative connotations, has a long history. Various politicians, journalists, and scholars — during the period of American

---

Determining the exact death toll, as is the case for all wars, becomes a frustrating exercise. There is no agreed-upon set of criteria, for example, on whether such an accounting should include those still listed as Prisoner of War or Missing in Action. Further, some would have the figure include those whose deaths months or years later are attributable to the wounds they received in combat. See Appendix A for one accounting.

†*The free world countries which sent ground combat troops to South Vietnam and their totals killed in action were Republic of Korea 4,407, Australia and New Zealand 475, Thailand 350, Philippines 9.*

§*Reasons why the Australian and New Zealand troops are not considered mercenaries are given in Chapter 6.*

involvement in South Vietnam and afterward — have repeatedly made use of the term when referring to the free world troops fighting with the United States in South Vietnam:

> Defense Secretary McNamara says that these South Korean combat soldiers are not mercenaries.... It would be interesting to note what synonym for "mercenary" the Secretary of Defense would choose to use to define the status of these ... soldiers[2];

"Such 'allies' are to mercenaries ... what an 'incursion' is to an invasion — mainly the same thing"[3]; and, "Vietnam resembled Renaissance Italy in many ways with its French and Spanish mercenaries. Not only was Vietnam long and angular ... but the mercenaries were there also."[4] Declarations that mercenaries were used in Vietnam is not a new phenomenon.

Nevertheless, although it has long been an acknowledged fact that the United States hired military units from several allied nations to fight as a U.S. mercenary force in Vietnam, there still exists no research into the subject.* Not only has there been no substantive inquiry into the subject of their hiring and use, no attempts have been made even to examine the definitional parameters of the word *mercenary*.† There has been no research, furthermore, into why so many free world soldiers came by some to be labeled mercenaries, or into the American foreign policy that brought these allied soldiers to South Vietnam in the first place.§[5] As a consequence, a detailed study of President Lyndon Johnson's "More Flags" program, how and why it became the responsible agent for America's hiring of mercenary troops for service in the Vietnam War, is long overdue.

Many writings refer to the Montagnard (in Vietnam) and Meo (in Laos) as being mercenary forces; since these people were, however, native to the areas in which they fought, they do not fulfill the definitional requirements for the term mercenary. *While persons of many nationalities and ethnic groups fought for many sides during the war, this study concentrates only on the hiring by the United States of military units from allied nations.*

†*See Chapter 8 for a detailed examination of the various definitions and concepts of this term.*

§*The encyclopedias, dictionaries, and almanacs of the Vietnam War do not mention the word.*

Chapter 1

Lyndon Johnson
and "More Flags"

The official U.S. State Department title for the American program of obtaining allied aid for South Vietnam was "The Free World Assistance Program." "More Flags" is, nevertheless, the label most often attached to the program. Occasionally, the program is cited as the "Other Flags" or "Many Flags" program.

As presented to the American public in the spring of 1964, the sole purpose of the "More Flags" program of President Lyndon Johnson was to obtain free world aid for the beleaguered nation of South Vietnam. Johnson's use of the program to pursue this publicly stated goal allowed him, however, the opportunity to achieve a more important, and more covert, objective. To Lyndon Johnson, the primary purpose of the More Flags program, when first inaugurated, was to serve as a visible symbol of free world support for his Vietnam policies. Notably, when first conceived, the hiring of mercenaries to fight in South Vietnam was not one of the More Flags program's original goals.

The program's original objective to pursue only non-combat–related aid for South Vietnam did not, however, survive even the first year of its existence. Even before Johnson sent American ground combat troops into South Vietnam in March 1965, less than a year after the More Flags program's inception, the program's purposes had already been redefined to allow for the procurement of free world troops to fight, and die, in Southeast Asia. The More

1

Flags program had become, even before the United States began sending its own combat troops to South Vietnam, the device through which America would hire mercenary troops.

Before any attempt is made to document and examine the More Flags program, it is necessary to look at Lyndon Johnson's role in its genesis. Rooted as More Flags was in Johnson's own political philosophies, the "why" of the program can only be understood by first attempting to understand the political personality and ideology of Lyndon Johnson. Just as Lyndon Johnson's actions made the Vietnam War "Johnson's War," Johnson's reason for establishing the More Flags program, and his continuing personal commitment to the program throughout his presidency, made the More Flags program, Johnson's program.

Few presidents in recent history have generated so much controversy, and perhaps none so many biographies, as Lyndon Baines Johnson. Even so, it is doubtful that anyone has yet rendered the complete account. The man had such a variegated personality that to call him complex would be an understatement. It is because of the multifaceted nature of Lyndon Johnson that any examination of a particular area of his persona requires a narrowing of focus. Such is the case for a detailing of Johnson's role in the More Flags program. To avoid becoming mired in extraneous details, it is perhaps most useful to examine only two very narrowly defined areas of the Johnson personality: his political personality as it pertained to the implementation of foreign policy decisions, and the effect his personal political ideology had on his determination of what should be America's responsibilities to, and role in, South Vietnam and Southeast Asia.[1]

Upon ascending to the presidency after John F. Kennedy's assassination, Lyndon Johnson brought to the office not only a finely tuned political acumen, but also a long and impressive list of legislative skills. During the many years he served in both the House of Representatives and Senate, Johnson may well have become "the most accomplished legislative strategist in American history."[2] When John F. Kennedy was assassinated, very probably no man in the United States was better prepared than Lyndon Johnson to exercise the purely political and governmental duties that are integral to the administration of the presidency. Yet these skills, great as they may have been, ultimately proved both inadequate and flawed when applied to the defining foreign policy problem of his administration, Vietnam.

A significant element of the decision making process through which Johnson developed his South Vietnamese and Southeast Asian policies can be seen, in retrospect, as resulting from techniques he developed to achieve legislative success as a Senator. It was here that Johnson perfected the style and methods that resulted in the form of political manipulation known as the "Johnson Treatment."[3] A mannerism as complex as the man who developed it, the "Johnson Treatment" blended the intensity of Johnson's personality with his political ideology until the two became all but inseparable. Neither a character trait nor a political maneuver, however, constituted the core concern of the "Johnson Treatment." The base foundation for his treatment of political associates was Lyndon Johnson's obsessive desire for consensus, compromise, and coalition building. An absolute need for public affirmation of his actions served as the driving force behind Lyndon Johnson's application of the "Johnson Treatment."

While this mastery of the art of consensus and coalition building in the pursuit of domestic political goals may have made him the acknowledged "master of the Senate"[4] during the 1950s, as president in the 1960s he found it a skill difficult to implement in the field of international diplomacy. Even one of Johnson's closest friends and advisors would admit:

> The real tragedy of President Johnson was the failure to realize that the usual results of the application of power, domestically in our own country, did not indicate that the application of an analogous force, internationally, would similarly result in changes being brought about.[5]

The finely honed domestic skills which had served him so well in the Congress now proved particularly less than adequate when used in attempts to resolve the inherited problems of America's involvement in South Vietnam. No matter the successes achieved in the legislative branch of the United States, in Southeast Asia, the "master manipulator had finally undertaken a political juggling act that was beyond even his greatest skill."[6]

Although South Vietnam, indeed the entire Southeast Asian region, had been a continuing source of controversy and conflict for every American president since Franklin Delano Roosevelt, the region constituted only one of many foreign policy problem areas Lyndon Johnson faced immediately on assuming the presidency in 1963. Nevertheless, while Johnson could understandably spare little time for the problems of the Southeast Asian region during the weeks immediately after Kennedy's assassination, it was not, as some have suggested, because he "cared even less than Kennedy for the problems of Vietnam."[7] When Johnson was finally able to turn his full attention to Vietnam, after first addressing the more immediate post-assassination fears of the American society, his considerations reflected a long history of involvement and interest in the problems of Southeast Asia dating back to the period of French occupation of Indochina.*

Even with the French withdrawal from Southeast Asia after 1954, Johnson's position as Senate Majority Leader obliged him to further develop his knowledge of the region. As the Democratic leader in the Senate, Johnson was constantly involved in the development and implementation of the Eisenhower Administration's efforts to establish and support the newly formed Republic of Vietnam.

In addition to his involvement with the events of the region during his tenure in the Senate, Johnson also learned more about Southeast Asian problems when he visited Saigon in 1961 as Kennedy's vice president. While the ostensible purpose of the Johnson mission was to assure South Vietnamese President Ngo Dinh Diem that the recent change in American presidents did not mean a change in America's support for Diem's government, the mission also served to benefit Johnson directly. Johnson took the opportunity afforded by the trip to gain firsthand knowledge of the problems then besetting the country and the region. Even with Johnson's extensive background and knowledge, subsequent events would prove, however, that his interest in the region would not

---

*The French, during the 1954 siege at Dien Bien Phu, urgently petitioned the United States government to commit American sea and air forces to the struggle. President Eisenhower called the various Congressional leaders, including then Senate Minority Leader Lyndon Johnson, to the White House to advise him, but ultimately decided not to honor the French request. See Chalmers M. Roberts, "The Day We Didn't Go to War," The Reporter, 14 September 1954, 31–5.

guarantee that his later decisions as president would be well considered.

Several events during his 1954–1961 involvements in U.S.-Vietnamese affairs can be seen as foreshadowing indicators of actions Johnson would take as president. In 1954, Johnson, as an astute politician, could not help but note that President Eisenhower partially predicated his decision not to accede to the French request on the decisions of France's other allies, particularly Great Britain. Although the French government particularly sought U.S. assistance during this period, they had also requested combat troops from their other allies. These nations, however, adamantly refused to become militarily involved in France's colonial problems. As a direct consequence of the decisions made by France's other close allies, President Eisenhower also chose not to involve the United States in a military action in Indochina. Eisenhower's determination that American troops should not fight alone in Southeast Asia later served as a major consideration when Johnson began reshaping the More Flags program into a vehicle to hire mercenary troops for service in Vietnam. Eisenhower did not consider it politically expedient for him to commit Americans to fight alone in Indochina, and neither would Lyndon Johnson.

Just as Eisenhower's 1954 decision served as one indicator of Johnson's future actions, Johnson's 1961 trip to South Vietnam provided another. In a private discussion with Diem during this visit, Johnson discreetly suggested that, if Diem were to make a personal request of President Kennedy, the U.S. would seriously consider sending American combat forces to South Vietnam. While nothing immediately came of Johnson's suggestion — Diem pointedly "displayed no interest"[8] in pursuing the idea — the fact it was made is important. At the very least, his suggestion to Diem demonstrates that Johnson, as early as 1961, accepted the possibility that American combat troops would serve in Vietnam, a possibility that would become reality in 1965.

America's problems in Southeast Asia were not the only ones Johnson inherited from John F. Kennedy when he assumed the presidency. In addition to Kennedy's cabinet level officers, also coming with the office was J.F.K.'s entire personal and executive staff, the team of officials most responsible for America's Southeast Asian policy positions. While Johnson may have had his doubts about the abilities of some of these men, two senior cabinet officers, Secretary of Defense Robert McNamara and Secretary of State Dean Rusk, did have his full trust and confidence: "At the Cabinet level he leaned immediately on Robert McNamara [and] . . . Dean Rusk, a fellow Southerner."[9] Still, while he might lean on the two Kennedy Administration holdovers, Johnson was not one to defer to anyone in formulating American policy toward South Vietnam. Consequently, when Robert McNamara was afforded the opportunity, during a speech at the Forrestal Award Dinner in Washington, on 26 March 1964, to give the first comprehensive presentation to the American people of what would be the Johnson Administration's Southeast Asian and South Vietnamese policy,*[10] his speech showed clear evidence of Lyndon Johnson's personal contributions. McNamara may have made the presentation, but the content of the speech reflected Johnson's own ideas and ideology, and it had Johnson's official support and authorization.[11]

In his Forrestal Award speech, McNamara delineated almost the entire spectrum of the professed reasons for America's involvement in South Vietnam. At the core of this message lay Lyndon Johnson's own personal political ideology, one conceived and built on ideas formed in another time and for another place. This ideology, when coupled with his firm belief that the president of the United States alone was responsible for making U.S. foreign policy,[12] motivated Johnson to implement an international diplomacy that, by the 1960s, had become obsolete, for he believed in

> such twentieth-century national characteristics as risking major wars, standing up for principles no matter what, expecting good to come ultimately from waging apparently just wars, and expecting history to reward the wartime president. To him, the crusade in Vietnam strikingly resembled Truman's in Korea, Roosevelt's for the Four Freedoms, and Wilson's to fight a "grim and terrible war for democracy."[13]

Lyndon Johnson, by the time he came to the presidency, did not realize that many of the basic principles of the American foreign policy he held in such high esteem had already become untenable. Formed as it was during years of Depression, World War, and Cold War, U.S. diplomacy by the early 1960s effectively pursued only two goals: the need to confront the Soviet Union and to prevent the export of its communist ideology. With this myopic orientation, American foreign policy was ill prepared to meet the challenge of the breakup, in the mid- to late–1950s, of the world's colonial powers and the subsequent formation of dozens of new countries. By the beginning of the sixth decade of the twentieth century, then, a new foreign order required, if not a new American foreign policy, at least a basic reformulation of existing policy. This, sadly, was not to be. Both John F. Kennedy and Lyndon B. Johnson believed in and fully supported the existing American policy positions. By their continued tenacious adherence to the practices established and implemented by their predecessors, both Kennedy and Johnson amply demonstrated, as one foreign observer observed at the time, that they simply did not fully "comprehend the kind of forces that [were] loose outside the United States in the 1960's."[14]

Simply stated, the Kennedy and Johnson diplomatic world of the early 1960s was not the same diplomatic world of Truman and Eisenhower. It had undergone fundamental changes, yet "Neither Kennedy nor Johnson realized the extent to which their own experiences and the anti–Communist mood in postwar America had straitjacketed their thinking about foreign affairs."[15] As had Kennedy before him, Johnson perceived the United States as the last bastion of the free world's defense against a global and unified communist threat.[16] This was no longer the case:

> If up to 1961 communism still seemed monolithic in Asia and Europe . . . after 1961 these perceptions were wrong and dangerously out of date. If up to 1961 containment of China on the early 1950's model still made sense, after 1961 the model was . . . out of date. . . . If up to 1961 U.S. nuclear military power was still essentially hegemonic and U.S. economic resources for large-scale dispensation abroad were largely unimpaired, after 1961 they were not. If up to 1961 the U.S. social order still seemed stable, after 1961 . . . the portents of a breakdown were visible.[17]

Neither Kennedy nor Johnson, nor the able men they chose as their advisors, recognized this emerging new world order and since they "did not perceive these changes, . . . U.S. policy was ill-prepared to cope with them."[18]

An indicator of both Kennedy and Johnson's dated foreign policy beliefs can be seen in the fact that both men maintained an absolute belief in the validity of the "domino theory" of communist conquest. This theory, accepted as official American foreign policy dogma in 1950,[19] maintained that all Southeast Asia would fall to the communists like a row of dominoes if South Vietnam fell. It should be noted, however, that Kennedy and Johnson were not alone in their conviction that the domino theory was a realistic predictor of events. The theory also constituted a policy absolute for many senior statesmen in both presidents' administrations, a list that included both Secretary of State Rusk and Secretary of Defense McNamara. In a joint report to President Kennedy in 1961, the two cabinet officers forcefully assured him that if he allowed South Vietnam to fall, it would be "a near certainty that the remainder of Southeast Asia and Indonesia would move to a complete accommodation with communism, if not formal incorporation with the communist bloc."[20] Further, after Lyndon Johnson assumed the presidency, McNamara made sure the new president received the same appraisal of the perceived danger: "Unless we can achieve this objective [prevent the fall of South Vietnam] . . . almost all of Southeast Asia will fall under Communist dominance."[21]

It would be easy to excuse Kennedy, Johnson, and others for their dogged adherence to the principles of the domino theory if the theory had, at the time, no detractors. There was, however, a growing body of thought and study even in the early 1960s that served to question the validity of the domino theory's basic precepts. Noted scholars were observing that the automatic "if-then" scenario on which the theory was based just did not agree with the real world political environment of the time.[22] Nevertheless, it was not until 1968 that someone in the Johnson Administration, in the person of newly appointed Secretary of Defense Clark Clifford, began to express doubts on the basic validity of the domino theory: "I could not free myself from the continuing nagging doubt . . . that if the nations living in the shadow of Viet Nam were not now persuaded by the domino theory, perhaps it was time for us to take another look."[23] Unfortunately, by this time it was too late.

Lyndon Johnson's formulation of America's Vietnam policy, of which the More Flags program was only a part, thus came about as a direct result of his belief in two political maxims that were no longer applicable to the world existing when he assumed the presidency. In the first incidence, Johnson thought he could easily transfer to the international arena the selfsame political tools he had designed and perfected for use on the domestic political scene. Furthermore, he then sought to use these tools to perpetuate a 1940s and 1950s Cold War diplomacy which, by the beginning of the 1960s, had already demonstrated its inapplicability to the new world order then emerging.

Still, Lyndon Johnson cannot be assigned full blame for America's actions in South Vietnam. By 1963, American foreign policy decisions affecting the nations of Southeast Asia already had a twenty year history spanning four presidential administrations. They did not become fully developed only during Lyndon Johnson's tour of duty, but had slowly matured over time, from a commitment of economic aid, to the presence of American men and women serving in harm's way. It is not surprising, then, that by the time Lyndon Johnson took office, he would view America's role in, and responsibilities to, South Vietnam and Southeast Asia as representing more than just a base commitment of money, men, and materiel. To Lyndon Johnson and many of his personnel, the good name and honor of the United States were now at stake, so much so that a commitment of American combat troops became warranted.

With this decision to escalate the war, a decision taken with the aid of what Johnson thought were proven and trusted tools and men, a debate developed over whether his actions were taken in a just cause or not. This remains a continuing dispute that shows no immediate sign of resolution. After decades of disagreement and dissension, it should not be expected that any study of a single facet of the problem, such as this examination of Lyndon Johnson's More Flags program, would serve to resolve the controversy. One can hope, however, that studies such as this, because of their contributions to the overall body of knowledge, can contribute to an ultimate explanation and understanding of America's involvement in the Vietnam War.

Chapter 2

"More Flags": The First Year

The birth of the More Flags foreign policy of the United States occurred at a presidential news conference on 23 April 1964. Lyndon Johnson, in response to a question about the content of possible future American assistance to the Saigon government, acknowledged that while he "anticipated" that the United States would send more aid, he hoped

> we would see some other flags in there, other nations as a result of the SEATO meeting, and other conferences we have had, and that we could all unite in an attempt to stop the spread of communism in that area of the world, and the attempt to destroy freedom.[1]

Although the final task of formally establishing the More Flags program as a U.S. policy fell to Lyndon Johnson, his actions amounted only to a continuation of efforts begun some years earlier. Kennedy Administration officials first began studies on the feasibility of obtaining free world aid for South Vietnam soon after taking office in 1961.[2] Despite a perceived need for the development of such a program, Kennedy officials never implemented a government policy position on the subject.*[3] Nevertheless, Secretary of State Dean Rusk, seeing an unfulfilled need, kept the idea alive. In

---

The commitment of combat forces to South Vietnam, by the United States or its allies, was a frequent component of these early discussions. The continuing controversy over this subject may have contributed significantly to the Kennedy Administration's choosing not to implement a More Flags type program.

early April 1964, he broached the subject anew with President Johnson. In a suggestion to the president, Rusk maintained that the United States could significantly assist the Saigon government by "Engag[ing] more flags in South Vietnam."[4]

While there is no documentation indicating that Johnson, prior to the Rusk suggestion, ever independently considered the idea of involving America's allies more actively in the South Vietnamese imbroglio, given Johnson's political philosophy it is very likely that the idea had at least occurred to him. Since all available evidence shows Johnson's establishing speech as coming after the Rusk memo, credit must be given to Secretary of State Rusk for originating the idea for the More Flags program. Nevertheless, whatever may have been the original genesis of either its name or its purpose, the More Flags program became Lyndon Johnson's own personal project from the moment of its formal inception and it remained so until the last moments of his tenure in office. For, in the More Flags program, Johnson had found the means through which he could achieve the international consensus for America's Vietnam policy he so fervently desired.

The More Flags program received formal recognition as official U.S. foreign policy on 1 May 1964, just one week after Johnson's press conference, when Secretary of State Rusk informed all of America's worldwide embassies that:

> The United States Government has decided to call upon other nations of the Free World to express their support for the Vietnamese Government and provide evidence of that support in the form of practical and material contributions to the Vietnamese Government.[5]

Rusk's cable to his embassies, in addition to being the formal declaration of the More Flags program as official U.S. policy, also contained several other key components. Primary among these was a description of the program's goals and a detailing of the means and methods which the State Department would use to direct the program's implementation.

As established by the Rusk message, the program's primary goal was to obtain nonmilitary aid for South Vietnam from as many free world nations as possible. From the very beginning of the More Flags program, however, the State Department intended for this objective only to serve as a public mask for the program's activities. As Rusk explained in his message, More Flags would have another even more important goal, a goal that would receive much less public attention:

> The nature and amount of the contributions being sought are not for the present as significant as the fact of their being made. The basic objective is to have Free World Governments display their flags in Viet Nam and indicate their recognition of the fundamental nature of the struggle there.[6]

The Johnson Administration thus considered More Flags, from its inception, as being primarily an instrument through which the United States could obtain an international consensus for its Vietnam policy. Only secondarily would its efforts be directed towards obtaining allied support and assistance for the Saigon government in its battle against communism.

Rusk's 1 May message to his embassies also included a list of free world aid then being sent to South Vietnam (see Table 1).

Table 1

Free World Assistance to the Republic of Vietnam as of 1 May 1964

Country	*Type of Assistance*
Australia	30-man military advisor-training mission; livestock and veterinary experts; construction materials; under the Colombo Plan — railway cars, construction and agricultural equipment, condensed milk
Canada	Wheat; an entomologist
France	Loans and import-export credits; educators and technical experts
West Germany	Machinery and equipment for an engineering and trade school; educators and engineers
Japan	Construction materials, equipment, and technical help for a dam; general consumer goods

Country	Type of Assistance
Malaya (Malaysia)	Scout cars; training in Malaysia in jungle warfare for the Vietnamese military; a 12-man training-advisory team
New Zealand	A surgical team; woodworking machinery; veterinary equipment
South Korea	Karate instructors for the military
United Kingdom	Advisory mission on counterinsurgency and police operations; loans; equipment for medical, mining, and engineering schools; English language teachers

Source: Message, Rusk to AmEmbassies, 5/1/64, "Vietnam Memos, Vol. VIII, 5/64," Item No. 110, pp. 4–6. NSF Country File–VN. LBJ Library.

While the inclusion of this list might seem perfectly innocuous on the surface, a closer analysis reveals a much more significant reason for its addition to the document. As a direct consequence of Lyndon Johnson's desire for an international consensus in Vietnam, Rusk's list served to establish the precedent that the most important indicator of the More Flags program's success would be the total number of aid-contributing nations, not the content of their aid packages. To Rusk, and by extension the State Department, the most important factor was that an allied nation sent aid, any aid, to South Vietnam, because by so doing that country, *ipso facto*, showed it supported the U.S. position there. Further, a country's reasons for sending aid to Vietnam also mattered very little in Rusk's accounting. Conveniently overlooked in the 1 May message was the fact that the listed aid packages were projects already undertaken and thus could not be considered as resulting from the More Flags program. Even further yet, the reasons why several of these listed nations sent their aid in the first place, had little, if anything, to do with American Vietnamese policy.* Despite all this, Rusk still cited

*Aid coming from Japan at this time resulted from a World War II reparations agreement signed with South Vietnam. France was simply continuing the aid it had been sending since ending its colonial control of the area. Although Japan would later send aid as a result of More Flags entreaties, France, which criticized the U.S. presence in South Vietnam throughout the 1960s and 1970s, never responded to any American More Flags request. France did, [continued]

all aid from all nine countries as aid sent "in recognition of the fundamental nature of the struggle"[7] in South Vietnam, and in support of U.S. policy positions in Southeast Asia.

One source of listed aid, that from South Korea, was even fallaciously included. Not only were the South Korean karate instructors not then in South Vietnam, but the Saigon government had not even sent Seoul a formal request for aid.[8] It would be September 1964 before the first Korean aid to South Vietnam would arrive, notwithstanding the U.S. State Department's assertions to the contrary. Washington would finally admit to the actual timetable involved, but not until December 1968.[9]

Rusk's message to his embassies thus misstated the reasons why one-third of the listed free world nations sent their aid. Future State Department listings of aid-contributing countries, taking their cue from Rusk's original presentation, would continue this propensity to misrepresent.

To Rusk and the Johnson Administration, since all aid sent to South Vietnam was to serve as proof of international approval of America's Vietnam policy, all contributed aid had to receive a thorough and complete press coverage. Washington thought that complete press coverage of a contributing nation's aid commitment would assist them into bringing more recalcitrant nations into the program. Rusk thus made sure that his message provided full instructions to his overseas personnel on this important aspect of the More Flags program. Every American embassy was ordered to insure that all allied aid to South Vietnam no matter its size or composition, "be thoroughly publicized.... We want this obligation to be publicly acknowledged and action indicative of that acknowledgement publicly undertaken in the near future."[10] It remained the policy, throughout the entire history of the More Flags program, that free world aid, even token aid, would receive the widest possible media publicity.

The Rusk message ended with one last significant order, addressed specifically to the American ambassador to South Vietnam*:

however, continue sending aid to all of their former Southeast Asian colonies, including North Vietnam.

*The United States ambassadors who served in South Vietnam during the lifetime of the More Flags program were Henry Cabot Lodge, 1 August [continued]

Ambassador Lodge should inform General Khanh [the junta leader of Vietnam] of the nature of the action being undertaken and seek his assurances that all such offers of assistance from Free World Nations will be appropriately and gracefully received and seriously considered by the Government of the Republic of Viet Nam.[11]

From the very beginning of the More Flags program, requests for aid to South Vietnam would originate from Washington, not from Saigon, and Saigon would, or could, do little but go along with Washington's actions.

There is no record of what the various Vietnamese government officials personally thought of the More Flags program. The South Vietnamese government's official position was to accede to the new policy position Washington had taken on their behalf. Less than two weeks after Secretary Rusk began the More Flags program, the Saigon government began efforts to fulfill its role in the new program. In the first Vietnamese action undertaken under the auspices of the new program, Vietnamese Foreign Minister Dr. Phan Huy Quat sent individual letters to the leaders of each North Atlantic Treaty Organization (NATO) member, asking that they "bring assistance to SVN [South Vietnam] in this critical period."[12] Although the success of these letters remained questionable at best, since the Republic of Vietnam had no diplomatic standing with NATO, just the fact of their being sent helped to assure the State Department that Saigon would follow Washington's lead.

Washington's uncertainty over the level of support the South Vietnamese would give More Flags proved a valid concern. As it turned out, Dr. Quat's almost immediate response to Secretary Rusk's suggestion that South Vietnam begin requesting aid from other free world nations proved the exception rather than the rule. From the outset of the program, South Vietnamese government efforts in pursuing free world aid proceeded at an aggravatingly slow pace, at least by State Department standards. Even after the More Flags program had been in operation for over two months, the government of the Republic of Vietnam still had not even determined exactly what allied aid they wanted or needed. Further, Saigon also

1963–28 June 1964 and 31 July 1965–5 April 1967; Maxwell D. Taylor, 1 July 1964–30 July 1965; Ellsworth Bunker, 5 April 1967–11 May 1973.

had no definite idea of which free world countries were amenable to sending aid and which were not. The end result was that all requests for free world aid to South Vietnam continued to come from Washington despite the State Department's desire to have Saigon originate these requests. Two U.S. State Department messages, transmitted in tandem on 10 July 1964, offer examples of both South Vietnamese foot-dragging in requesting free world aid and Washington's actual role in the process. In the first message, sent at 6:52 P.M., the State Department ordered its mission in Saigon to begin working with the South Vietnamese government in developing a specific aid request list: "We believe best way out of present and potential problems would be for Mission to coordinate closely with GVN [Government of Vietnam] in preparing individual country tailored lists."[13] Since the Saigon government did not seem particularly motivated to produce such a list on their own volition, the U.S. government would push them into doing so.

At almost the same moment that the State Department was asking its Saigon embassy to begin working on a prospective aid request list, at 6:53 P.M., Washington transmitted a message to most of its worldwide embassies that contained a completed South Vietnamese aid request list. Although Washington officials had made up the list, the State Department still sought to maintain the facade that all aid requests originated in Saigon: "GVN has finally issued QTE shopping list UNQTE of possibilities for third country aid."[14]

It did not take long for the Saigon government's reluctance in requesting free-world aid to draw the wrath of Secretary of State Rusk. On 13 July 1964, Rusk displayed his impatience in a message to Maxell Taylor, the newly appointed Ambassador to South Vietnam. In this message, Rusk charged Taylor with the responsibility of pushing the Vietnamese leaders harder because "it apparant [sic] several countries may be hiding their reluctance to contribute behind fact they have not received such direct requests from GVN."[15] In Taylor's next-day reply, he assured Rusk that the problems were being worked out, and that the "GVN effort on third country aid will now go into high gear." After putting the onus for the delays on Vietnam's junta leader: "Getting [General Nguyen] Khanh's signature had been a major obstacle for two weeks,"[16] Taylor went on to inform Rusk of other steps the South Vietnamese

were taking to fulfill their role in the More Flags program including
the

> construction of suitable mounting to display flags of all par-
> ticipating nations in square at important crossroads (Le Loi and
> Nguyen Hue) in downtown Saigon. General motif will be similar
> to flag display in front of UN.[17]

In a closing comment, Taylor observed that Vietnamese government activities for the More Flags program were "now moving at this
end as rapidly as sound planning and GVN personnel limitations
permit."[18]

South Vietnamese actions, however, at least in 1964, never
seemed fast enough to satisfy Washington. Although Rusk's charge
to Ambassador Taylor did result in a minimal amount of Saigon
government activity toward requesting free world aid—within a
week of Taylor's message to Rusk, General Khanh wrote personal
letters to the heads of 20 countries[19]—such actions were at best
sporadic. Washington had to continue pressuring the Saigon government throughout the remainder of 1964 to present a "better GVN
representation abroad,"[20] and "to prepare formal requests for aid"[21]
from the free world countries. Nevertheless, despite repeated requests,[22] it would not be until sometime in 1965 before South Vietnam would finally comply with Washington's repeated requests for
such a list, or even, for that matter, to establish a bureaucratic
mechanism for the processing and receiving of the free world aid
that began arriving as a result of Washington's requests.

By 15 June 1964, Rusk felt that he had enough responses to his
1 May telegram to draft a status report on the More Flags program
for President Johnson.[23] In this report, Rusk detailed the not too encouraging responses of 21 countries to the State Department's More
Flags appeals. Of the 21 mentioned countries, three (Norway,
Netherlands, and Pakistan) flatly rejected sending any aid at all,
and six (Belgium, Iran, Denmark, Greece, Italy, and Spain) were
only listed as agreeing possibly to send aid. One country, Turkey,
was mentioned but no aid was formally requested of it. Rusk's
memo to President Johnson could report only that 11 free world nations were participating in his More Flags program. Moreover, even
that small number was misleading, as eight of these 11 were already

listed in Rusk's 1 May 1964 message.* After six weeks of intense
diplomatic activity, Secretary Rusk could report that only three new
countries (Nationalist China, or Taiwan, Thailand, and the Philippines) had entered the program. Although Rusk sought to assure
the president that the "overall response to our requests for aid to
Viet Nam has not been discouraging," Rusk's report did not sit well
with President Johnson. Penned to the cover letter to the report is
Johnson's curt evaluation of the report: "There is still not enough
progress."[24]

Rusk's 15 June status report reflected a strong indication that
American allies viewed the More Flags program with little enthusiasm. Such a demonstrated lack of interest was, however, not
because of a lack of State Department time and energy applied to
the program. The cables to and from George McGhee, the U.S.
Ambassador to West Germany, provide a good example of the intense pressures Washington was exerting on behalf of the More
Flags program. In several messages from Bonn to Washington,
McGhee reported on the many disappointing meetings he had held
with the West German Foreign Minister, trying to talk the Germans
into increasing their More Flags contributions.[25] Rusk's reply to
McGhee's messages to Washington on the fruitless outcome of these
meetings gives ample evidence of the diplomatic pressures being
applied worldwide for the More Flags program. In his cable,[26] Rusk
acknowledged Bonn's complaint about the "unusually large
number of requests" made of the Germans for aid, but he reminded
McGhee that the number of requests only reinforced how important
the Johnson Administration viewed the More Flags program: "We
wish to underline Departmental and *other high-level Washington interest* [emphasis added] in subject of third country aid to
Viet Nam."[27] Continuing, Rusk reacquainted Ambassador McGhee
with the official State Department rationale for the More Flags program: "the main idea . . . is to show Free World solidarity with
Vietnamese in their struggle against Communist aggression,"[28] but
the telegram made it clear that this purpose did not constitute the
More Flags program's only, or even primary, goal. Towards the end

---

*Of the nine countries mentioned in Table 1, only France's aid contribution
was omitted from this report. Korea's fallacious contribution of karate instructions was, however, included.*

of his telegram, Rusk added an "FYI Only" comment that better il-
lustrated Washington's true rank ordering of priorities: "FRG
[Federal Republic of Germany] support for our stand in Viet Nam
will serve to show French that even their close European ally and
neighbor supports the U.S. in Southeast Asia."[29] To Rusk, while it
may be true that the aid West Germany sent to Vietnam demonstrated their "solidarity" with the Saigon government, solidarity
remained subsidiary to a West German "support for our stand"
there.

It became evident to some Johnson Administration personnel
very early in the More Flags program implementation period that
the program was in serious trouble. To these men, if More Flags
were to have any chance of success, President Johnson himself
would have to become personally involved. To this end, Undersecretary of State William Sullivan sent a memo to Johnson's National
Security Advisor McGeorge Bundy on 24 June suggesting that President Johnson should consider assisting directly in the prosecution
of the program:

> [I]t may therefore be necessary for the President to put in writing
> [in telegrams to U.S. Ambassadors] an indication of the importance
> which he attaches to these third country contributions and the
> necessity that the U.S. Mission bend over backwards to accommodate
> them . . . [and thus to] pin upon the ambassadors personally the
> responsibility for obtaining these contributions.[30]

Sullivan's suggestion evidently struck a responsive chord in the
White House for, on 2 July 1964, Lyndon Johnson transmitted such
a letter to all American missions located in the countries targeted
for the More Flags program.[31]

The greater part of Johnson's letter of 2 July represented little
more than a pep talk to his representatives overseas as Johnson used
most of the message to restate America's official Vietnamese policy
positions as they pertained to the More Flags program. The grist of
the letter, however, lay in its closing comments. It was here that
Johnson not only formally charged his embassy heads with the responsibility to more actively seek a higher level of More Flags participation, but he removed any doubts there may have been about
the high level of importance he personally attached to the program:

"I know of no other task imposed upon you in your current assignment which to my mind, precedes this one in its urgency and its significance."[32] It is very probable — given all the problems American diplomacy was experiencing at the time with such countries as the Soviet Union, Cuba, and China — that Johnson simply made this statement for effect. Nevertheless, even if this were the case, the comment still stands as a very strong indicator of the high level of importance Johnson attached to the program.

President Johnson's personal appeal on behalf of the More Flags program, however, produced no major changes in the number of free world nations choosing to participate in the program. Johnson's actions and entreaties notwithstanding, because of the unpopularity of the war in most foreign countries, U.S. embassy personnel could do little to convince most of America's allies to become involved in America's problems in South Vietnam. As more and more of America's allies rejected Washington's More Flags requests, demonstrations of State Department frustrations began to surface. In an August 1964 memo to President Johnson, Secretary of State Rusk ruefully noted that despite "fact that GVN sent letters to 34 countries requesting aid there has been no great progress since last status report."[33]

In an in-house report, Thomas L. Hughes, the Director of Intelligence and Research for the State Department, presented an even more telling indication of the More Flags program's limited level of success:

> A number of Asian and western European countries are providing or have agreed to give assistance to South Vietnam. Little if any is likely to be forthcoming from Africa and Latin America. For the most part, contributions have taken the form of small-scale grants of economic and technical assistance and represent in most cases a continuation or increase in programs that have been in existence for some time. Most countries have been reluctant to provide military assistance, and where it has been given it has been of a largely token character.... There has been little evidence of enthusiasm for a more direct involvement, particularly in the form of military aid, and willingness to provide additional assistance has come largely as a response to US urging. Only Nationalist China and, to a lesser extent, South Korea have shown an interest in developing on their own a greater degree of military cooperation with Saigon, including

indications of a possible willingness to make available ground forces
for use in South Vietnam.[34]

The Hughes report constituted the most detailed evaluation to date
of the progress of the More Flags program. In it, Hughes not only
surveyed Washington's efforts towards each of the 34 specifically
targeted countries, but he evaluated the futile American efforts
toward eliciting regional support from African, Arabian, and Latin
American countries. While the Hughes summary did not specifically state that the More Flags program was failing, its content left
few doubts in anyone's mind that the Johnson Administration was
faced with a failing foreign policy.

By 11 December 1964, the State Department could only report
to the president that a scant 15 of America's worldwide friends and
allies were then sending assistance to South Vietnam,* and of these
15, only six were offering significant help (South Korea, Australia,
New Zealand, the Philippines, Thailand, and Nationalist China).
As for the possible participation of the rest of the free world nations,
the State Department summarily dismissed the possibility of their
future participation with one succinct sentence: "The actual and anticipated contributions from other countries doesn't amount to very
much."[35] The More Flags program was obviously not coming close
to achieving the expectations Lyndon Johnson had of it. If the program were to succeed, something more would have to be done.
More Flags had to change.

The first intimations of a modification in the More Flags program's originally stated goals came in a 3 December 1964 cable from
President Johnson to Henry Cabot Lodge, America's ambassador to
South Vietnam. Johnson, in a sentence added to the last page of this
message, hinted at what the future would hold as far as the basic
intent, purpose, and character of the More Flags program were concerned: "We propose to seek the *military* [emphasis added] and
political cooperation of the governments of Thailand, the Philippines, Australia, New Zealand, and the United Kingdom."[36]

---

*This tally, however, now included aid sent from Switzerland. As with the pre-
viously discussed French aid, which is also included in this list, Switzerland's
aid, coming from a neutral party, should not be counted as being More Flags
inspired.

Further evidence that President Johnson contemplated making changes of a military nature in the More Flags program is also found in letters drafted by White House officials for Johnson's signature. Each of these letters, addressed to the heads of government of Australia, New Zealand, and the Philippines, three of America's Southeast Asia Treaty Organization (SEATO) allies, contained a Johnson appeal for each leader to increase his country's aid commitments to South Vietnam.[37] In two of these letters however, to Australian Prime Minister Robert Menzies and President Diosdado Macapagal of the Philippines, the appeal for additional aid also included a specific request for a military commitment. Of the three leaders, Prime Minister K.J. Holyoake of New Zealand alone was asked only to increase the level of his country's nonmilitary aid. While the More Flags program's original purpose, to seek nonmilitary aid for Vietnam, would continue as a component of the program throughout the remaining years of the Johnson presidency, after December 1964 this humanitarian purpose would never again be the primary goal of the program. After this date, noncombat aid fell behind military related aid, and later, combat troops, in Johnson's rank ordering of importance for the More Flags program.

With President Johnson directing his personal attention to only a few of America's allies, the responsibility of informing America's worldwide missions of More Flags' new orientation fell to the State Department. This change in the program toward an active pursuit of military aid — the State Department still refrained from formally requesting actual combat troops at this time — did present some very difficult problems for the American overseas missions. From May through December 1964, American efforts to obtain free world aid for South Vietnam had succeeded in achieving only marginal success. Very few U.S. allies sent any aid at all, and those that did rarely made more than a token commitment to the South Vietnamese. Now, with Johnson's new direction for the More Flags program, U.S. embassy officials found it even more difficult to gain an aid commitment from their host countries. Instead of working to convince these allied leaders to send just aid, which constituted essentially nothing more than a financial commitment, America's overseas diplomats now had to also try to talk the free world leaders into committing part of their military forces to the struggle in South Vietnam. Because of the new direction for the More Flags program, not only were America's free world allies presented with a highly charged political issue, but the economic costs of their accession would climb. If the revised version of the More Flags program were to succeed, the U.S. had to find a way by which those free world nations that did support America's Vietnam policy could afford the increased financial costs of sending a military aid package to Vietnam.

It soon became evident that a change in the More Flags program's goals also required a concomitant change in the means by which the program would be prosecuted. On 15 December 1964, the State Department supplied this needed change when it notified America's allies that the United States would pay the entire cost of any free world military aid commitment to South Vietnam (see Table 2). If Lyndon Johnson, using ideological arguments and diplomatic pressures, could not convince other countries to adopt America's Vietnam policy as their own, he would now attempt to bribe them into doing so.

Table 2

Authorization for United States Financing of Free World Military Aid Committed to South Vietnam

> *From: JCS*
> *To: USCINCSO*
> *CINCSTRIKE/USCINCMEAFSA*
> *USCINCEUR*
> *CINCPAC*

Info:	*White House*	*State*	
Secret	*Noform JCS*	*002919*	*J-3 sends*

Subject: Increase of Third Country representation in Vietnam.

1.   Decision highest authority here to exert all feasible pressures for increased third country representation in Vietnam. As consequence US now prepared to defray all costs for units which are made available, i.e., pay and allowances, transportation, operating costs.

Source: Message from National Military Command Center, 12/15/64, "Vietnam Memos, Vol. XXIV, 12/19-25/64," Item No. 170. NSF Country File-VN, Box 11. L.B.J. Library.

This new element in the More Flags program created a diplomatic maelstrom over the next several weeks. The State Department flooded the White House with telegrams sent to and received from American embassies throughout the world detailing the actions taken in regards to Washington's new directive. Nevertheless, a reorientation of the More Flags program, even when coupled with new economic incentives, did not automatically guarantee an increase in the number of free world participants in the program. A week after the United States agreed to pay the total costs of all free world military aid sent to Vietnam, the Commander in Chief, Pacific (CINCPAC), the commanding officer of all U.S. military forces in the Pacific, notified Washington that the success of the new policy would not be essentially different from the old policy: "No assistance of the type envisaged in Ref A [the 12/15/64 message] is likely to be offered by Malaysia, Indonesia, Laos, Burma, Thailand and Japan. Korea, China and the Philippines could be expected to make contributions."[38] Although the White House promised to keep "the heat on"[39] in its pursuit of free world military aid, the initial results of the new More Flags policy of buying other nation's aid were not promising. Not one previously uncommitted country chose to buy into the program.

As 1964 drew to a close, Secretary Rusk reconfirmed the high priority of the More Flags program and further legitimized its new direction in an end-of-the-year cable sent to America's worldwide diplomatic posts: "The type of assistance particularly desired would comprise non-combat, small-size military units."[40] The stage was now set, and forces set into motion, for the More Flags program to take the next step; to begin hiring Third World combat troops as an American mercenary force in South Vietnam.

Despite the More Flags program's noted lack of success in 1964, the Johnson Administration continued to press its overseas missions for action on behalf of the program throughout the early months of 1965. As a spur to their orders to continue pushing the program, a reaffirmation of President Johnson's undiminished personal interest in the program was cabled to all U.S. embassies in January and March of that year: "President continues to place very high priority on obtaining broadest possible Free World support for South Viet-Nam,"[41] for instance, and "This continues to be an objective on which the President continues to place a very high priority."[42] Even Lyndon Johnson also expended a large amount of personal effort on the program's behalf:

> In 1965 he [President Johnson] began pulling every lever at his command—the SEATO treaty, diplomatic pressure, personal entreaties, and the disposition of U.S. foreign aid—to broaden the allies' involvement in South Vientam. [He was] eager to avoid going it alone.[43]

The Herculean efforts by all involved did little to change the More Flags program's success ratio. On the program's first anniversary, in May 1965, the State Department, in a country by country assessment (see Table 3), had to significantly stretch the facts in order to present the program to the president in as positive a light as possible. While Secretary Rusk's statement in his cover letter to the report intimated that the program had achieved some appreciable degree of success—"Thirty-eight Free World nations are providing or have agreed to provide aid to Viet-Nam"[44]—the program's true measure of success actually amounted to something much less.

Table 3

Free World Assistance to the
Republic of Vietnam as of 26 May 1965

Country	Type of Assistance
Australia	Direct military assistance of one infantry battalion, 100 combat advisors, and a 73-man air force unit with aircraft. Also, an 8-man military surgical team; engineers and technical experts; school textbooks; tools; construction materials; in–Australia training for Vietnamese; consumer goods; a radio station
Belgium	Medicines for flood relief
Brazil	Coffee and medical supplies

Country	*Type of Assistance*
Canada	A medical professor; construction materials; in–Canada training for Vietnamese
China [Taiwan]	An 80-man agricultural team; a 16-man military psyops team; an 8-man electrical power mission; a 10-man military surgical team; in–Taiwan training for Vietnamese; electrical power stations; seeds and fertilizers; school textbooks; construction equipment and materials
Denmark	Flood relief assistance
Ecuador	Medical supplies
France	Economic and technical experts; loans, credits, and grants; educators; in–France training for Vietnamese
Germany	Civilian medical personnel; 30 ambulances; credits and loans; construction equipment and material; educators; in–Germany training for Vietnamese
Greece	Medicine
Guatemala	Medicine
India	Cloth for flood relief
Iran	Petroleum products
Iceland	Red Cross aid
Israel	Pharmaceutical supplies
Italy	A 9-man military surgical team; in–Italy training for Vietnamese
Japan	Personnel to build a power dam; a 6-man medical team; medical goods; 20,000 transistor radios; 25 ambulances; an electrical transmission line; monetary grants from a World War II reparations agreement
Korea	A 130-man Mobile Army Surgical Hospital; a 2,200-man Engineering Task Force; 10 karate instructors
Laos	Flood relief aid

Country	Type of Assistance
Malaysia	In–Malaysia training for Vietnamese and counterinsurgency materials
Netherlands	Medical supplies
New Zealand	A 25-man army engineer detachment; a 6-man military surgical team; grants and loans; in–New Zealand training for Vietnamese; an English language professor
Pakistan	Flood relief aid
Philippines	Military and civilian medical teams; a military psywar detachment
Spain	Medicines, medical supplies, and blankets through the Spanish Red Cross
Switzerland	Microscopes
Thailand	A 17-man military air detachment; construction materials; in–Thailand training for Vietnamese
Turkey	Turkish Red Crescent Society contribution to the Vietnamese Red Cross
United Kingdom	A 6-man advisory mission; medical, laboratory, and printing equipment for various schools and government departments; in–England training for Vietnamese; an English language professor

Source: United States State Department, *World Sitrep on Free World Assistance to Viet-Nam,* 5/26/65, "Vietnam Memos, Vol. XXXIV, 5/65," Item No. 311a. NSF Country File-VN, Box 17. L.B.J. Library.

An analysis of the 26 May 1965 document reveals that the actual number of countries listed as then sending aid, and those having once sent aid, totaled only 29 (in addition to the United States). The remaining eight nations (Argentina, Austria, Costa Rica, the Dominican Republic, El Salvador, Honduras, Luxembourg, and Nicaragua) had only agreed to a possible aid commitment at some future date. Still, 29 contributing countries would seem to indicate, at least on the surface, that the More Flags program had begun to succeed. A careful examination of the evidence, however, belies this supposition.

Of the 29 nations, the aid from at least ten, and possibly as many as 14, nations constituted humanitarian relief assistance. These nations sent their aid to South Vietnam as a compassionate response to the devastating monsoon flooding of the previous winter and spring and not as a reaction to any More Flags request. Secretary of State Rusk nonetheless conveniently tacked their aid onto the More Flags list of contributing nations. A prime example of this padding of the aid list was the inclusion of Pakistan's aid. Not only did Pakistan have a long history of criticism for America's policies in the Southeast Asian region, it had also repeatedly rejected every More Flags entreaty emanating from Washington.[45] With such a background of opposition, it is obvious that Pakistan's aid to South Vietnam constituted only a humanitarian gesture and was not an affirmation of the U.S. position in Vietnam. The State Department would later, in fact, admit to President Johnson that the Pakistani aid came in response to the flooding and not in support of More Flags.[46]

A close examination of all the facts thus reveals that from one-third to one-half of the nations listed by Rusk on his 26 May accounting constituted spurious inclusions. Further, there exists strong evidence suggesting that a few of the remaining aid contributing countries sent their aid for reasons other than as either a show of support for the South Vietnamese cause or in support of the American policy there—that they sent aid to Saigon only because the United States bought and paid for it:

> As general principle donor countries will be strongly urged to meet as much of cost of their aid as possible, particularly expenses within donor countries and transport. U.S. will be prepared on case by case basis to consider financing these costs or portion thereof, if necessary to prevent aid offer from being withdrawn.[47]

It is not possible to know for sure how many countries succumbed to the tempting lure of being able to gain the good graces of the United States at no financial cost to themselves. Reason and common sense, however, prompt the belief that at least a few of the contributing countries should fall into this category.

The State Department list of 26 May 1965 thus presents a rather bleak picture of the More Flags program on the first anniversary of its implementation. After a full year's efforts, Washington could count only 13 nations actually sending aid to South Vietnam in support of their fight against communism. Of the 13, only five (the Philippines, Italy, Iran, Thailand, and Nationalist China) were added since May 1964 (see Table 1). While it may be true that success can sometimes be denoted by small gains, such is not the case with the few gains made by the More Flags program. With the high expectations accorded the program on its inception, and with all the effort put into the program's prosecution, the More Flags program, in its first year, has to be viewed as a failed American foreign policy.

The failure of the More Flags program in obtaining aid from as many free world countries as possible became something of a moot point however, after 9 March 1965. With the introduction of American combat forces into Vietnam, the primary focus of the program shifted from a simple solicitation of aid to one concentrating on recruiting troops. From the moment the first Marines waded ashore at Da Nang, the More Flags program became the mechanism through which the United States would make "an energetic effort to recruit other nations to fight with the U.S. forces in Vietnam."[48] After 9 March 1965, the More Flags program and Lyndon Johnson's pursuit of mercenary troops to fight in support of American foreign policy goals became irrevocably linked.

Chapter 3

The Republic of
Korea Commitment

The largest contingent of free world troops, approximately 50,000 men at its height,* sent to fight with and for the United States in South Vietnam came from the Republic of Korea (ROK). Because of the large size of their commitment and the conditions of their service, of the five free world troop-contributing nations, these Korean units became the troops most frequently accused of being American mercenaries,† of being "Seoul's hired guns."[1]

Charges that the Korean combat troops were serving in South Vietnam as a mercenary force, and not simply as South Korea's answer to a Vietnamese request for assistance, began to surface almost as soon as the first ROK troops landed in South Vietnam. These mercenary changes came, however, from critics who had little more than ideological and emotional arguments to support their allegations. Confirmation that the ROK units, and certain other allied troop units that followed them into Vietnam, were actually U.S.-paid mercenaries, could only come with the declassification of official United States government documents from the period. With the current availability of these declassified documents, it is

---

*See Appendix B for a year-by-year accounting of all allied military troop strengths in South Vietnam.

†An examination of the basic concepts and definitions of the term mercenary is found in Chapter 8.

now possible to prove that the Republic of Korea furnished the United States with mercenary troops to fight in South Vietnam. Further, these newly released records also provide a serendipitous feature. Not only do they specify the Korean mercenary role, but they describe in detail exactly how the U.S. government used the More Flags program as the agent for buying all allied mercenary troops for service in South Vietnam. It thus becomes necessary to carefully examine the South Korean military involvement in the Vietnam War as a prerequisite to the understanding of America's use of allied mercenary troops in that conflict.

The South Korean involvement in America's war in South Vietnam did not begin with a commitment of mercenary troops there. The South Korean government in Seoul had, in fact, already sent two separate, non–combat related detachments to Vietnam before the first ROK combat troops arrived. Indeed, Seoul's initial aid commitment to South Vietnam of ten tae kwon do karate instructors* and a Mobile Army Surgical Hospital (MASH) unit constituted one of the first free world assistance packages negotiated under the auspices of America's More Flags program. Nevertheless, even this first Korean aid commitment can be viewed as little more than a necessary first step in the Koreans' later deployment of combat troops to Vietnam, for it was these first U.S.-Korean discussions that produced the two precedents that established the parameters for all future Korean assistance programs to South Vietnam.

South Korea's opening move at the beginning of the U.S.-Korean negotiations established the first of these precedents when Seoul presented its aid offer to Washington, not to Saigon. This simple act established, for all future Korean aid sent to South Vietnam, the continuing procedure whereby Korean and U.S. negotiators decided between themselves what aid Korea would send and only informing Saigon what that aid would be after-the-fact.

A Washington-Seoul determination of the composition of Korea's aid packages sent to Vietnam did not mean, however, that the South Vietnamese government had no say in the matter. In fact,

---

*As discussed in Chapter 2, the U.S. listed the ten karate instructors as having arrived prior to May of 1964, although this aid did not actually arrive until September of that year. See Appendix C for a chronology of all Korean troop commitments to South Vietnam.

the State Department went out of its way to ensure that the South Vietnamese government would have a say in even the most arbitrarily determined aid decisions. Even though Saigon would have no direct role in determining what aid they would receive, because of Washington's insistence that all diplomatic formalities be strictly observed—meaning no aid would be sent without Saigon's making a formal request for that aid—the Vietnamese could reject the Korean aid if they wanted. As a consequence, after the United States and Koreans determined, in negotiations conducted between May and early July 1965,[2] what the Koreans would send to Vietnam, the State Department would not allow its automatic shipment to South Vietnam. Washington held up the shipment of this aid until the South Vietnamese had been instructed to request the aid: "The Korean Amb to Saigon . . . [must be] instructed to seek formal GVN request for such assistance."[3] As an independent country, the Republic of Vietnam could have refused the Korean offer. As a client state of the United States, however, they were in no realistic position to do so. The South Vietnamese government thereby dutifully sent a formal request to the South Korean government in late July 1965, asking for the predetermined ROK aid package.

A determination of what assistance Korea would initially send to Vietnam also served to set an indirect precedent that would have unexpected ramifications. While Seoul's dispatch of taekwondo instructors and a MASH unit to Vietnam constituted a large commitment when compared to what most other countries sent in response to More Flags entreaties, it still amounted to much less than the Koreans wanted to send. Even before More Flags began operations, and long before President Johnson began seeking allied troops to fight in South Vietnam, South Korean government officials had repeatedly petitioned the U.S. for permission to send combat troops there. Apologists, from within and without the government, for America's use of Korean troops in Vietnam, use this evidence to support the assertion that later ROK combat contingents did not constitute an American mercenary force. They argue that this early offer of ROK combat units, proffered long before their first aid commitment, proves that Korea sent its combat units to Vietnam simply in response to another Asian country's request for help, and not as a mercenary force. The logic underlying this argument does not, however, hold up under close scrutiny. In the real world of international diplomacy, the South Korean offers of troops amounted to little more than political posturing by the Korean government. What the South Korean government said they wanted to do was not necessarily what they had the physical capabilities to do. Further, the United States government recognized this. A report written by Thomas L. Hughes, the State Department's Director of Intelligence and Research, took note of the large gap which existed at the time between the Seoul government's troop offer and its actual economic and physical capabilities:

> The South Koreans think in terms of direct military intervention in the struggle, and, from time to time, they have talked of an expeditionary force of two or more divisions. It is obvious that a force of this size could not be committed or maintained without large-scale United States assistance and that the South Koreans' plans have not been refined, even on a contingency basis, to cover many problems which action on this scale would raise.[4]

A White House memo to President Johnson, submitted four months after the Hughes report, evaluated the Korean offers of combat units in an even more straightforward manner, succinctly putting the offers into their proper context: "The Koreans have not only been willing to send military help to Viet-Nam, but are even anxious to do so, providing we pay the bill."[5]

Nevertheless, the Korean petitions to send combat troops to Vietnam did succeed in generating a certain amount of discussion among various State Department officials as early as March 1964.[6] Even with the serious consideration given the matter, however, during this early period of the More Flags program the State Department had no choice but to reject the petitions. At this time, the program still operated on the premise that the aid needed in Vietnam did not involve combat troops. As a consequence, when South Korean President Park Chung Hee, or his Foreign Minister Lee Tong-wan, would make their periodic offers of troops for duty in South Vietnam, the State Department tendered polite refusals, such as "We have told our Embassy that they should give no encouragement to the Koreans on this point"[7] and "we do not see any suitable role at this time for ground units from Korea."[8]

The initial More Flags negotiations with South Korea to obtain aid for South Vietnam served also to point out a basic inconsistency of purpose in the program. Instead of pursuing only its publicly stated humanitarian goals and purposes, the U.S.-Korean negotiations revealed that the More Flags program suffered from a mix of competing, and sometimes mutually exclusive, purposes. On the one hand, in adhering to the program's originally stated objectives, State Department officials maintained that the only Korean aid really needed in South Vietnam was non-combat related aid such as field hospital units and signal corps support.[9] On the other hand, and still in the name of the More Flags program, these same officials also actively solicited a South Korean commitment of military advisors to serve in the field in South Vietnam.[10] To the State Department, these apparently dichotomous positions were reconciled through an assumption that there somehow existed a qualitative difference between military advisors and combat troops.* Washington officials continued in this belief despite the clear intimation, presented in Ambassador Henry Cabot Lodge's 9 May 1964 request for ROK advisors, which pointedly suggested that the two concepts were essentially the same thing:

> I note that . . . ROK contribution would be limited to support units. It seems to me that the contribution of truly significant value would be of advisers and selected military personnel who would share in the really dangerous work. I understand that the ROK has well qualified personnel for the type of work where our men are getting killed and wounded. Why not use a few of them here?[11]

Although Secretary of State Rusk initially acceded to Lodge's suggestion by instructing him to "Request Seoul in subsequent

---

*Apparently, the Washington view was that advisors only became involved in combat operations as a result of their accompanying the South Vietnamese forces — they did not generate or provoke the actions themselves. On the other hand, combat troops were those that instigated, directed, and executed actions on their own. Semantics aside, one only has to compare the casualty data for the American "advisors" in Vietnam with that for the "combat troops" there to see how little real difference there was between the two groups: In 1964, the 23,300 American advisors in Vietnam suffered 1,179 casualties, a ratio of five casualties per 100 advisors. In 1965, the 161,000 American combat troops in Vietnam suffered 4,726 casualties, a ratio of just under three casualties per 100 troops. In Vietnam, a soldier was safer serving in a combat unit rather than as an advisor.

contacts urge ROK contribution of special forces advisors,"[12] the State Department eventually decided that the use of ROK advisors was not feasible because not enough Korean troops knew how to speak Vietnamese.[13]

Even though the State Department eventually dropped the idea of using the More Flags program to obtain Korean advisors for Vietnamese service, their mere consideration of the action boded ill for the future of the More Flags program. Once it became acceptable for More Flags to request advisors to engage in combat operations in Vietnam, it became much easier to take the next step and use the program to introduce combat troops.

From the very beginnings of the Korean assistance programs to Vietnam, be it either the aid they actually sent or their offer of combat troops, the motive for that aid had little to do with the Koreans' wanting to help a sister nation in its fight against communism. In fact, South Korean diplomatic requisites in 1964 insured that all Korean policy positions made with respect to South Vietnam would have, at their base, Korean government relations with the United States as their principal element. Simply stated, all Korean aid sent to Vietnam, be it actually sent or only suggested, was engendered because South Korean government officials wanted to ingratiate themselves with the United States government in general and President Johnson in particular. Aid sent from Seoul to Saigon thus came about as a direct result of Korea's "alliance relationship with the United States,"[14] which sought to further strengthen the security ties South Korea felt it needed with the United States,[15] and not because the Koreans felt any particular kinship for the South Vietnamese government, people, or cause. This early tailoring of Seoul's diplomatic relations with Vietnam to fit American policy needs would later play a determining role in U.S.-ROK relations when Lyndon Johnson changed the focus of the More Flags program to include the hiring of combat personnel.

If Washington had not recognized that Korea's periodic 1964 offers of combat troops were made for effect, the U.S. rejections of these offers might have presented some diplomatic problems for the State Department. However, since both sides understood exactly what ends the offers sought to achieve, the rejections created no strains on relations between the two countries. In fact, during the first few months of the More Flags program, only four persistent problems restricted any State Department request for South Korean aid to Vietnam. Three of these restrictions — Korea's inability to provide enough skilled personnel, their inability to fund them, and the lack of Vietnamese-speaking Koreans — have already been mentioned. While these personnel, funding, and language problems did cause the State Department some concern through November 1964, they were at least solvable problems. Such was not the case, however, with the fourth major constraint, Vietnamese pride. The loss of face that the South Vietnamese experienced from accepting aid rendered by another Asian nation constituted a continuing irritant to South Vietnamese self-esteem throughout the period of Korea's involvement in the Vietnam War. While U.S. diplomats and officials would periodically note this as a sore point with the South Vietnamese, the Americans did little to alleviate their discomfort. Vietnamese sensibilities received only the most marginal consideration in Washington's pursuit of its own Southeast Asian objectives.

With President Johnson's 1964 change in the More Flags program, allowing it to solicit military units participating in noncombat activities, U.S. and South Korean negotiators met again in early December 1964 to decide the contents of Seoul's second aid package to South Vietnam. Since both the Korean and American officials entered into these negotiations knowing that the Seoul government would agree to almost any American request, these proceedings were expected to be little more than a *pro forma* exercise. One serious difficulty still remained, however. The language problem, which had already prevented the deployment of a detachment of ROK military advisors, also served to seriously inhibit any ROK troop deployment to Vietnam. After some discussion, the negotiators from the two countries decided that the problems inherent to the Koreans' inability to speak Vietnamese could be minimized if they made the next Korean assistance package to South Vietnam a self-contained military engineering unit.[16] State Department officials reasoned that a completely self-contained unit, operating independently inside Vietnam, would experience only limited day-to-day contact with the Vietnamese and thus the language problems would be minimized.

At the completion of the negotiations, President Johnson sent a message to ROK President Park on 19 December 1964,[17] formally requesting the predetermined Korean engineering unit. Notably, even though the request was for a military engineering unit, with security to be provided by an army infantry company—units which would operate in a zone of intense combat activity within South Vietnam—the Johnson Administration still refused to classify the ROK contingent as a combat unit. Washington still wanted to maintain the illusion that all More Flags aid was strictly nonmilitary. As a consequence, when President Park, in replying to President Johnson's request for the engineers, once more offered to send two ROK combat divisions to Vietnam, Washington yet again politely refused the offer.[18]

While Washington and Seoul were negotiating this increased Korean aid commitment to South Vietnam, it never seemed to occur to either country to include members of the Saigon government in their discussions. In an amazing display of insensitivity, not only did the United States government neglect to inform the Saigon government of their negotiations with the South Koreans for the engineering detachment, but Vietnamese government leaders were not even informed of similar U.S. efforts then being made to obtain other free world military assistance for Vietnam.[19] Only after the U.S. and Korean actions became public knowledge with the South Korean cabinet's approval for the dispatch of the ROK detachment on 29 December 1964, a vote reported in the Korean newspapers, did Washington deign to ask the government of Vietnam to submit a request for the Korean engineers.[20] Though no documents are available which mention whether or not the South Vietnamese took umbrage at the American actions, an intimation that the slight did not go unnoticed is found in Saigon's delay in formally requesting the South Korean engineers. Despite Johnson's 19 December request for the ROK engineers, and the Korean cabinet's 29 December 1964 approval of their deployment, the State Department still found it necessary to notify President Johnson on 5 January 1965 that the "GVN has not yet requested additional Korean assistance."[21] There is no official record of the actual date of Saigon's formal request for the ROK engineers. Nevertheless, since the Korean National Assembly voted on 12 January 1965 to authorize deployment of the ROK engineer detachment to Vietnam, an action they could not make without first receiving a Saigon request, it can be assumed that the request came sometime between 5 and 12 January 1965.[22]

Throughout the negotiation period and the wait for Korean

National Assembly authorization, the Johnson Administration had few doubts that their agreements with President Park would be honored. Though the ROK engineering unit deployment required a third party acquiescence, the Korean Assembly authorization, even this detail did not particularly concern the U.S. government as it was known that President Park's political party controlled a solid majority of the votes there. Park's opposition in the Assembly, however, even though they did not have the votes to stop the deployment, did succeed in attaching a significant restriction to the deployment bill. In an attempt to prevent the Korean engineers from becoming too directly involved in actual combat operations, the restriction mandated that the engineering unit could not "fire unless attacked . . . [and] could not fire on or pursue the enemy outside the area delineated for Korean operations."[23] Because of these restrictive rules of combat enforced on the ROK detachment, the unit soon became commonly known as the "Dove Unit."

Even though the Korean engineers deployed to Vietnam would only perform in an essentially noncombat role, the South Korean government's very act of deploying a 2,000-man unit outside Korean national boundaries made it a lot easier for it to later consider, then commit, ROK combat troops there. The negotiations involved in getting the Dove Unit sent to Vietnam also presented the State Department with its first exposure to a Korean concern that would later play a significant role in their obtaining an ROK combat unit sent to Vietnam.

Unlike the financing of the Korean government's dispatch of its karate instructors and MASH unit to Vietnam, which came directly from the Korean national budget, Washington officials recognized early in the Dove Unit negotiations that Korea did not have the ability to fund the costs for a 2,000-man engineering detachment: "Pressing ROKG to defray substantial costs for units made available [the Dove Unit] would be fruitless."[24] The State Department determined however, that a simple matter of money should not interfere with Korea's making a further More Flags commitment to South Vietnam. After all, from the beginning of the negotiations for the Dove Unit, the Johnson Administration's "major purpose"[25] in requesting the Korean engineers was to fill an American need, not obtain needed aid for the South Vietnamese. Consequently, State Department officials fully accepted the fact that if the Dove Unit were to be deployed to Vietnam, the United States would have to finance the majority of the costs involved.

Washington's willingness to finance the costs involved with deploying the Dove Unit to Vietnam presented the State Department with a major public relations problem. State Department officials worried that the large amount of American financing involved in this agreement, if it became known, would produce substantial negative reactions in the American citizenry. Thus, in order that the Dove Unit be perceived as an entirely Korean financed aid package, the State Department insisted, from the beginning of negotiations, that all details be kept secret from both the American public and media.[26] State Department officials would later, in the 1969 U.S. Senate hearings, attempt to justify the United States financing of the Korean Dove Unit's deployment:

> The fundamental basis on which these troops were sent to Vietnam was that their dispatch should not significantly degrade the security of Korea ... and that it should not impose a significant economic burden.... The Koreans did not have the necessary financial resources but they gave what they had — excellent and highly motivated manpower.[27]

This was, however, not the case in 1965. At that time Washington went out of its way to present to the world the fiction that the Korean government was paying the majority of these costs out of their own budget. Like so many other examples of the public picture presented of the More Flags program, the State Department's presentation of the facts behind Korea's Dove Unit contribution sought only to obscure and misrepresent.

Because of this desire to hide the Johnson Administration's financial involvement in the deployment of the Dove Unit, extreme measures were taken to present a public picture of significant ROK budget expenditures for the unit. Despite these attempts at obfuscation, however, a close examination of the record reveals how little the Koreans actually paid for the Dove Unit's service in Vietnam. While the public record does show the South Korean government paying the expenses for the unit, the not-so-public record shows how those expenses came from American clandestine arrangements that funneled American monies into the ROK treasury.

It was the American taxpayer who ended up paying a majority of the costs for Korea's Dove Unit service in South Vietnam.

To maintain the pretense of substantial Korean funding of the Dove Unit, the United States resorted to several indirect methods of funneling money to the Korean government. A principal method involved the use of PL-480 foodstuffs, an Agency for International Development (AID) "Food for Peace" program. The original intent of PL-480, as mandated by the United States Congress, was that AID use the program as a "food for development program, under which [U.S.] agricultural commodities are donated to least developed countries for . . . sale with the foreign currency proceeds being used for . . . economic purposes."[28] The program, however, as used in the More Flags program, served a much less humanitarian goal, and certainly a legally questionable one. The U.S. government provided PL-480 rice and other bulk foods to the Korean government with the understanding that, when the foodstuffs were sold inside South Korea, the Korean government would then use the proceeds to help meet their Dove Unit expenses.

There is currently only one declassified example of the Johnson Administration's using the PL-480 program in conjunction with the Korean commitment to More Flags: "At State's suggestion, we gave him [South Korean Ambassador Kim Hyun Chul] small White House Christmas gift in form of advance notice that the Koreans will get the PL-480 agreement."[29] This message, though innocuous on the surface, does nevertheless serve to tie the PL-480 program to the Dove Unit negotiations when events happening elsewhere are also considered. There is substantial documentation showing that the United States used the PL-480 program to help the Philippine government fund its PHILCAG detachment, their More Flags contribution (see Chapter 4). And since the same State Department officials handled both the Korean and Philippine funding negotiations, it is a reasonable assumption that if PL-480 was being so used in the Philippines, it would likewise be true for South Korea.

In addition to the direct monetary returns realized from the State Department's PL-480 program, Korea's budget also received substantial financial assistance through a Department of Defense (DOD) administered program. One of the principal methods through which the DOD helps an allied country develop and maintain its armed forces is by furnishing aid through the Mutual

Assistance Program (MAP). Through this program, the Department of Defense, using U.S. taxpayer dollars, purchases whatever military supplies and equipment it perceives an allied military needs to upgrade its armed forces, then it donates this materiel to that allied nation. It is expected, however, that when the donor nation's military reaches a given level of readiness, or their national economy becomes stronger, the financing of these MAP purchases would incrementally transfer to the allied nation's national budget. In respect to South Korea, because of the favorable economic and military conditions existent there, the U.S. DOD had intended for a $100 million MAP transfer to take place in 1965. The Koreans, not the United States, would then assume the responsibility of purchasing the $100 million worth of equipment. Because of the Dove Unit negotiations, this transfer did not, however, take place: "In January 1965, the United States announced its intention to postpone the implementation schedule of the MAP transfer program in return for the dispatch of South Korean . . . forces to Vietnam."³⁰ Although the MAP transfer delay added no monies directly to the Korean budget, the action did allow the Koreans to use funds for the Dove Unit that they would otherwise have had to spend on military procurement. The MAP transfer delay was thus the equivalent of a $100 million cash grant from the United States to South Korea, as it allowed the Koreans, for one $100 million expenditure, both to gain the military supplies they needed and also to fund the Dove Unit.

If, even with the PL-480 sales and the MAP postponement, the Korean government still found it could not afford to fund the Dove Unit's deployment to South Vietnam, Washington had two other plans standing by to furnish even more money to the Koreans. The first of these plans was concerned with the Korean government's ability to fund the transportation costs of getting the Dove Unit to South Vietnam and necessary equipment and services it required once it got there: "All Defense articles and services that cannot be provided by donor nation from its available resources will be funded out of worldwide MAP."³¹ The second plan involved the South Korean funding of their personnel's pay and allowances.

Getting the Dove Unit to South Vietnam involved one expense that the United States felt the Koreans should fund entirely out of their own budget, personnel pay and allowances. It was felt that, since Korea had to pay their military personnel salaries anyway, whether they were sent to Vietnam or not, the United States should fund only those extra costs that Korea would incur in the deployment: "We . . . propose that we ask ROKG to bear only those expenses which do not involve additional budgetary expenditures."[32] In spite of this expressed desire, however, and since Lyndon Johnson desperately needed more allied participation in the More Flags program, the State Department was prepared, if they had to, to fund even these costs: "In some exceptional cases AID may have to finance this [the pay and allowances] . . . if Washington finds this to be necessary to keep the offer from being withdrawn."[33] This funding did indeed become necessary.

Although the pay scale for the South Korean military did not become an issue in the U.S.-Korean negotiations for the Dove Unit, questions over the amount of overseas allowances for the Korean soldiers serving in Vietnam did: "We have again approached [ROK] officials in effort to persuade them to restrict payment of overseas allowances . . . to one dollar per man per day."[34] Even with the U.S. agreement to fund an overseas allotment schedule that was greatly in excess of the total pay for most of the Korean armed forces (see Table 4), the Korean negotiators still worked to get more. Having already promised their troops an overseas allotment figure substantially in excess of what the Americans were willing to fund, the Koreans dug in their heels and refused to budge.[35] Although State Department negotiators objected strenuously, their dissent amounted to little more than protestations made for the record. Lyndon Johnson wanted the Dove Unit in Vietnam and he was willing to have the U.S. taxpayer absorb almost any amount to get it there. As a consequence, after all was said and done, the United States not only agreed to fund the monthly basic pay for the Dove Unit personnel through the various indirect and *sub rosa* methods already detailed, but also agreed to fund, in a more direct fashion, the Korean-dictated overseas service allowances (see Table 5).

With the Johnson Administration's agreement to fund, either directly or indirectly, the pay and allowances for the 2,000-man Dove Unit, the precedent was set for it later also to do the same for the much larger ROK combat divisions. The U.S.-ROK funding arrangements for the Dove Unit also achieved yet another outcome that may not have been fully recognized at the time. With the

Table 4

ROK Military Monthly Basic Pay

(In U.S. Dollars; figures are
for pay scale effective 1 July 1969)

Pay Grade (Officer)	Monthy Pay	Pay Grade (Enlisted)	Monthly Pay
0-10	361	Warrant Officer	85
0-9	300	E-7	61
0-8	242	E-6	54
0-7	217	E-5 (Career)	27
0-6	194	E-5	8
0-5	156	E-4	2.60
0-4	119	E-3	2.10
0-3	91	E-2	1.80
0-2	60	E-1	1.60
0-1	47		

Source: U.S. Congress. Senate. Committee on Foreign Relations. *Republic of Korea: Hearings on United States Security Agreements and Commitments Abroad*, 91st Cong., 2d sess., Part 6, 1970: 1572.

Table 5

ROK Overseas Duty Daily Allowances as of 1 March 1965

(In U.S. dollars; amounts were
in effect from 1 March 1965 to 1 July 1966)

Officers	Amount	Enlisted	Amount
Colonel	6.50	Master Sergeant	2.50
Lieutenant Colonel	6.00	Sergeant 1st Class	2.00
Major	5.00	Sergeant	1.50
Captain	5.00	Corporal	1.20
1st Lieutenant	4.00	Private 1st Class	1.00
2nd Lieutenant	4.00	Private	1.00

Source: U.S. Congress. Senate. Committee on Foreign Relations. *Republic of Korea: Hearings on United States Security Agreements and Commitments Abroad*, 91st Cong., 2d sess., Part 6, 1970: 1569.

American funding of the South Korean pay and allowances, the Korean More Flags commitment to Vietnam moved from being an assistance program only to being a mercenary operation.

There is probably no way to determine exactly how much U.S. money the various funding methods pumped into the Korean national budget to offset their Dove Unit expenses. No unqualified statement is therefore possible that the Koreans paid little or none of the financial costs for sending their Dove Unit to Vietnam. Nevertheless, the available evidence does show that the ROK contribution was minimal at best. The funding of the Korean Dove Unit does undeniably show, however, the lengths to which the Johnson Administration would go in order to obtain third country military aid for South Vietnam. Unfortunately for the U.S. taxpayer, matters would only get worse.

As long as ROK personnel committed to South Vietnam totaled fewer than 130 men—the numbers of the karate instructors and MASH unit personnel—the Korean government did not feel it necessary to justify or explain their Vietnam aid to either the Korean people or to the international community of nations. When the Korean government began considerations on deploying a 2,000-man military unit to South Vietnam, however, justifications became very necessary. After all, the Korean government could not just ignore the fact that their sending the Dove Unit to South Vietnam constituted the first time Korea had sent a military unit outside its borders since the nineteenth century. Over the years since the event, while various Korean politicians and scholars have offered many opinions for the deployment, the most commonly mentioned motives still essentially parrot the official government rationale of the time. According to President Park and the members of his government, the Korean troop commitment was seen as a partial payment of a Korean debt of honor, payback for the aid Korea received during the Korean War. Also mentioned by these government leaders, but seen as coincidental to the debt of honor aspect of the aid, was that their deployment of the Dove Unit also resulted in enhancing Korean prestige in the eyes of the international community of free-world nations.[36]

As would be expected from two listings separated by decades, there are some differences between the official Korean government justifications of the time, and the litany of reasons for the troop commitment surfacing from subsequent scholarship. The two listings do, however, have one major component in common. Both lists of reasons for the Korean deployment of the Dove Unit either fail to list the financial rewards South Korea received from the United States as a justification for that deployment, or, if it is mentioned, the American economic assistance is presented as being of only secondary importance. Even Seoul's publicly stated position for sending Korean troops to Vietnam does not mention what payments the government received for their deployment:

> We felt that keeping Vietnam secure from Communism was closely related to Korea's security. The dispatch of our troops would encourage the people of Vietnam in their struggle against Communism. It was a way of repaying those 16 free nations which came to our military aid during the Korean War.[37]

Korean President Park's characterization of the Dove Unit as a payment on a debt of honor also allowed him to minimize any in-Korea political opposition to the move. Because of Park's use of this justification for deploying the Dove Unit, even President Park's main political rival, Kim Chun-yon, openly supported the unit being sent to South Vietnam: "The government decision would be tantamount to repaying a moral obligation this nation owes to the free world."[38] Such justifications aside, made as they were for public consumption, the fact remains that unless the United States paid the bill, no member of the Dove Unit would have set foot in South Vietnam.

The main elements of the Dove Unit began arriving in South Vietnam on 16 March 1965, but they had hardly settled into their new home when negotiations started on the introduction of Korean combat troops into Vietnam. Although Washington knew as early as December 1964 that a U.S. request for ROK combat forces would soon be forthcoming,[39] official negotiations between U.S. and Korean officials for these troops did not begin until May 1965.[40] Even before these official discussions began, Johnson Administration officials already knew exactly what the Koreans would be asked to send. In an April 1965 meeting held between Secretary of Defense McNamara, members of the Joint Chiefs of Staff (JCS), and U.S. Ambassador to Saigon Maxwell Taylor, the United States decided that the next Korean aid package should consist of a "regimental combat team (4000 men or so) . . . with the possibility that at a later phase the ROK force might be expanded to a division."[41] A scheduled May 1965 Washington visit by President Park necessitated, however, a delay in the start of any formal U.S.-Korean negotiations on this newest South Korean commitment to the More Flags program.

Prior to Park's Washington trip, Secretary of State Rusk had every reason to expect that Washington's request of Korean combat forces would receive quick approval by the Korean leader. This feeling came partly from the long history of Korean offers of combat forces, but also because of a January 1965 comment by the Korean Ambassador to the United States that Park was willing to do almost anything that President Johnson requested.[42] While Park's positive reception of the request both substantiated the ROK ambassador's observation and fulfilled Rusk's expectations, the ROK troop commitment discussions held during the Park visit still produced their share of surprises, particularly surprises of an economic nature.

With the negotiations for the Dove Unit serving as a guide, American officials fully expected that the commitment of an ROK combat unit would require substantial U.S. financial concessions. Expecting this, Johnson staffers tried to warn him before his meetings with Park that the Koreans "hoped to use the question of further troops in order to pry major additional concessions out of the U.S. Government."[43] Nevertheless, even while expecting that the United States would have to pay a high cost for the ROK troops, it is doubtful the Johnson Administration officials fully expected that the end cost would come with such a large number of zeros attached to the figure.

On 18 May 1965, at the conclusion of their two days of meetings, the two presidents issued a joint communique outlining the subjects discussed between the two leaders. While much of this communique was devoted to describing in very general terms the American economic commitments Johnson made to President Park, the subject materials discussed by the two presidents did not originate in their meetings. Many of the economic components of the communique simply reflected U.S.-Korean agreements negotiated weeks before Johnson and Park ever met. Essentially, the two days of meetings between the two presidents only served to validate existing decisions, as most of the communique's content and much of its wording had already been worked out by lower level Washington and Korean officials prior to 1 May 1965.[44]

One significant aspect of the 18 May document was that in none of its wording will one find even an insinuation that the American assistance offered to Korea constituted partial payment for planned ROK troop increases in Vietnam: "There has never been any suggestion . . . of any bargaining in connection with the dispatch of a division to Vietnam."[45] In fact, ROK troop increases to Vietnam are nowhere mentioned in the communique. Nevertheless, after President Park returned to South Korea, the communique's financial concessions, both explicit and implicit, constituted the base of discussion in the formal negotiations to get a South Korean combat division sent to South Vietnam. The communique established the parameters for the negotiations, but the negotiations established the price America would pay for the division.

Despite the Johnson-Park meetings and President Park's long history of wanting to send an ROK combat division to Vietnam, when formal negotiations finally began for the troops, the U.S. and Korean negotiators were not concerned with only executive branch political considerations. President Park alone could not send an ROK combat division to South Vietnam; such a move also required Korean National Assembly authorization. Because of this, while the negotiators could use the Park-Johnson agreements as the framework for their discussions, they had also to incorporate specific Assembly needs and requirements into the dialogue: "There has been . . . increasing pressure from DRP [the Korean National Assembly] members . . . for the assurances referred to above [additional ROK requested concessions], as a condition to favorable action on the request for a division."[46] As State Department officials discovered to their dismay, with their South Korean counterparts having to satisfy both President Park and Korean Assembly requirements, the negotiation process became much more contentious and intense than expected.

American officials, from the very start of the discussions, found themselves negotiating from a severely weakened position, as everyone involved in the process knew how much President Johnson wanted an ROK combat division committed to Vietnam. As a direct consequence of the Koreans' having this knowledge, it was the

Koreans, not the Americans, who set the negotiations' agenda. In their opening proposals in the discussions, Korean officials submitted a substantial, and to the State Department, totally unreasonable, ten item "wish-list"[47] dealing with four general concerns: (1) Korea's need for a firm recommitment of all U.S.-Korea treaty and military obligations, (2) financial benefits accruing from a rescinding of all present and future MAP transfers, (3) the need to modernize the entire ROK armed forces, and (4) U.S. financial assistance for the entire Korean domestic economy.[48] From the moment the Koreans introduced their "wish-list," its items became the principal points of discussion in the negotiations.

The introduction of the Korean "wish-list" as the basis for their deploying an ROK division to Vietnam, regardless of whether the Americans agreed to it, did accomplish one result of interest to researchers. The list belied the Korean government's public avowal that they were sending their troops to Vietnam in payment of a debt of honor. With eight of the ten items in the "wish-list" demanding substantial economic concessions from the United States, it became evident that monetary gain, not honor, motivated the Koreans' offer of a combat division.

On seeing the Koreans' list of demands for the first time, the response of the State Department negotiators bordered on the incredulous: "I told them . . . that their bill was completely unreasonable and there was no chance whatever of the U.S. agreeing to it."[49] Despite such feelings of outrage, the end results of the negotiations were, however, all but preordained. With Lyndon Johnson's desperate desire to obtain the ROK troops, and with the Korean National Assembly refusing to compromise on the agenda of demands, the Koreans got almost everything they wanted:

> Despite optimistic and unqualified statements by the president and PriMin . . . it was the unanimous judgement of the country team [U.S. embassy staff in Seoul] that the situation is so uncertain that we could not afford to risk any further withholding of the authority [to grant the concessions].[50]

After only two months of negotiations, the United States agreed, as payment for the deployment of an ROK combat division to South Vietnam, to the following:

1. There would be no United States or ROK military force reductions in Korea without prior consultation with the Korean government.

2. Concrete assurances would be given to Korea that the American defense of Korea would not be affected by any present or future American actions in Vietnam.

3. MAP funds would be increased for Fiscal Year (FY) 1966 by $7 million, with that amount to be used to fully equip three ready reserve infantry divisions in Korea.

4. The FY 1966 and 1967 MAP transfers would be suspended.

5. All ROK forces in Korea would be modernized in fire power, mobility, and communications.

6. The United States would procure as much military related supplies as possible, materiel needed in either Korea or Vietnam, from South Korean suppliers.

7. Korean civilians would be hired, whenever possible, to work in Vietnam, principally in construction projects.

8. The United States would provide all subsistence, equipment, training, logistical support, construction, and transportation for all ROK troops in Vietnam including the Dove Unit.

9. Per diem overseas allowances would continue to be paid at established rates to all ROK military personnel in Vietnam.

10. American exports of food stuffs to Korea would increase with the increase to be offered at reasonable costs.

11. The United States would provide $150 million in development loan funds to be used for projects inside South Korea in addition to whatever funds would be required at a future date for mutually agreed on development projects.

12. U.S. support for economic development projects would continue at a scale equal to or exceeding the level of current financial support.

13. The United States would provide employment and welfare relief for needy people in Korea.

14. The United States' technical assistance and training grants to Korea would continue, at present levels or higher.[51]

For their part, State Department officials managed to obtain only one major concession from the Koreans. One of the Korean negotiators' original ten "wish list" demands had the United States helping the South Korean government fund an across-the-board pay raise for the entire Korean armed forces. The State Department negotiators were able, however, to talk their Korean counterparts into agreeing that the budgetary savings Korea would realize from American financial concessions, such as from the MAP deferments, would serve as the American contribution to their military pay increase.[52]

No group or individual has yet attempted a determination of the total costs the United States government ended up paying for this first ROK combat division. A few attempts have been made, however, to detail the direct costs incurred by the United States in sustaining the ROK forces inside Vietnam. There are also a very few studies that attempt to examine how much the American largess directly benefited the South Korean national economy. As might be expected in studies relying on two different data bases, figures for the cost to the United States to support the ROK division vary greatly, ranging from about $43 million[53] a year to $106.7 million.[54] Newly revealed documentation suggests that even this $106.7 million figure is far too conservative. It is thus impossible to determine with any reasonable degree of accuracy exactly how much money the United States expended in its purchase of this first ROK combat division sent to Vietnam. But a consideration of the costs involved was of little concern to Lyndon Johnson and the members of his administration. To them, any amount the United States had to pay constituted both a justifiable expense and sound policy as it allowed foreign troops to serve, and to die, in the place of American soldiers in Vietnam, and for a comparatively low cost. To the Johnson Administration, hiring ROK soldiers thus saved the United States "a great deal in blood and treasure."[55]

And hiring these ROK troops to serve in Vietnam did result in U.S. troops' not having to do so. Proof of this assertion is found in a Military Assistance Command, Vietnam (MACV), July 1965 message to the Commander in Chief, Pacific Command (CINCPAC), that states in unequivocal terms that if the Koreans did not send a division to Vietnam by 1 November 1965, the United States would have to deploy an American division there.[56] When the Korean government was informed that their troops were needed in Vietnam sooner than expected, Seoul expedited the deployment schedule for its division. As a result, even though the decision to send the ROK Capital Division, also called the Tiger Division, was not finalized until late May 1965, the South Koreans managed to begin deploying an entire division to South Vietnam in just four months (see

Appendix C). The arrival of an ROK division in Vietnam thus directly resulted in an American division's staying in the United States, at least for a while.

When the ROK Tiger Division arrived in Vietnam, it became the fourth allied combat unit fighting there. Already deployed were military units from the United States, Australia, and New Zealand.* The ROK division was, however, since the South Korean government refused to deploy them without first being paid, the first purely mercenary allied military unit committed to Vietnam — but they would not be the last.

When Lyndon Johnson began deploying U.S. combat forces to Vietnam on 8 March 1965, he knew, if he were to maintain the image that the United States was not acting unilaterally there, that this move required other free world nations to also commit troops. It quickly became evident, however, that the majority of America's allies did not think that Lyndon Johnson's problems in South Vietnam warranted their becoming militarily involved. Only Australia and New Zealand, of all America's allies, chose to voluntarily commit their troops to Vietnam. Johnson had to do something if he was to continue representing to the American people that his policies had international support. The purchase of mercenary troops, starting with the South Korean Tiger Division, allowed Johnson to do this.

America's purchase of South Korean troops did not take into account the desires of the South Vietnamese government, on whose part the United States ostensibly obtained these troops. In its obsession with maintaining the facade of international support, the Johnson Administration spent little time worrying whether Vietnamese interests were coincidental with their own. As a consequence to these feelings, the U.S. government did not even think to include South Vietnamese government officials in the U.S.-Korean negotiations over the deployment of the ROK division to their country. Saigon's exclusion from the discussions was deemed necessary by the U.S. State Department. After all, Washington officials well knew that the Saigon government was opposed to additional Korean troops' being sent to their country: "the Vietnamese show no desire for additional Asian forces since it affronts their sense of pride."[57]

*See Chapter 6 for a detailing of the Australian and New Zealand military commitments.

The decision that an ROK combat division would be sent to South Vietnam was a *fait accompli* by the time the U.S. State Department notified the Vietnamese government and counseled them to formally request the troops: "Vice FonMin Mun Tok-chu [Korea's Vice Foreign Minister] repeated today his request that US urge GVN make formal request for 'one infantry division' from ROKG."[58] While it was all but impossible for Saigon to reject these ROK troops, Vietnamese government officials nevertheless managed to indicate their lack of enthusiasm for the Korean troop deployment in perhaps the only way they could. Saigon postponed making a formal request for the ROK division as long as possible, delaying until 21 June 1965 before sending Seoul a request for their troops.[59] A cursory examination of the record will thus show that the Saigon government did formally request ROK troops; the facts behind that request however, belie both U.S. and Korean assertions that Korea sent its troops only because Vietnam sincerely wanted them and actively pursued them.

With the deployment of the 20,000-man ROK Tiger Division, South Korea became the largest free world contributor of combat troops, save for the United States, in South Vietnam. Still, this one division was not enough to satisfy Johnson Administration needs. With the planned massive increase in the U.S. troop commitments to South Vietnam in 1966—more American combat troops, over 200,000, were sent to Vietnam in 1966 than in any other single year of the war—Washington's search for foreign troops to fight there became even more frenetic. The Tiger Division had not even completed its arrival in Vietnam when Washington notified Seoul that "additional forces [would be] required in 1966."[60] By the time the last Tiger Division contingents came ashore in Vietnam, on 16 April 1966, negotiations for the commitment of a second ROK division had already begun in earnest.

The U.S. effort to obtain an increase in the South Korean troop commitment to Vietnam began with a request for a second ROK division on 8 January 1966, which was followed by 29 January acquiescence to that request by Korean President Park.[61] These opening formalities, however, only succeeded in establishing the possibility of deploying another ROK division to Vietnam. The details for such a move still needed to be worked out by lower level officials, and it became evident early in the discussions that the

United States could not obtain a second ROK division by simply duplicating the Tiger Division agreements. The Americans found that their Korean counterparts, in their January and February meetings, felt that the Korean troops then serving in South Vietnam were being "heavily underpaid and poorly treated,"[62] and they fully intended to redress the situation.

After the first month of preliminary discussions, held from mid–January to mid–February 1966, negotiating officials from both countries could report very little tangible progress to their superiors. It was evident that another element was needed to give impetus to the stalemated negotiations. As fortune would have it, such a stimulus was on hand, the Vice President of the United States, Hubert Humphrey.[63]

Lyndon Johnson, after the completion of his February 6–8 meeting in Honolulu with then Vietnamese Premier Nguyen Cao Ky, had ostensibly assigned Humphrey the responsibility of briefing America's Pacific allies on the decisions arrived at in Honolulu. At least this was the reason Johnson released to the American public. L.B.J. had, however, given his vice president other, more covert, instructions. Humphrey was instructed to use his travels to obtain more allied combat troops for South Vietnam, whatever the cost.[64] Humphrey therefore, on his arrival in Seoul in late February, was able to assure the Koreans that, if they sent a second division to Vietnam, both the Korean government and the troops themselves would receive very favorable concessions from the United States. With Humphrey's timely intercession, the negotiations were able to get moving again.

The very fact that the Johnson Administration deemed it necessary to have the Vice President of the United States relay these assurances signaled a recognition that a fundamental change had taken place in the negotiations. In all prior negotiations, both the United States and Korea recognized that the central issue involved was Korea's diplomatic and military relationship with the United States. To this end, in the early negotiations, American concessions that strengthened Korea's ties with the United States took priority over all else. The economic aspects of these concessions, though important and not to be depreciated, nevertheless remained a secondary concern. By the beginning of the negotiations for the second ROK division, however, the rank ordering of these two concerns had switched. Korean officials now considered accrued economic benefits as the most important determinant of whether South Korea would send more of its soldiers to South Vietnam. It thus fell to Vice President Humphrey to assure these officials that all ROK troops serving in Vietnam, either now or in the future, would receive fair, just, and proper compensation from the United States government.

State Department officials knew, even before the United States made its January request for a second ROK division, that they would probably have to make substantial financial concessions to obtain the division. But the opening discussions of January and February did not help the U.S. officials very much in determining what those financial concessions might be. While these early discussions did verify that the new ROK demands leaned heavily on economic concerns, they still did not give American negotiators a firm grasp of exactly what the Koreans wanted for their division. It thus became the vice president's responsibility to present the Koreans with a list of what Washington was willing to concede, and work out the specifics from there. Consequently, Humphrey told the Koreans that, in addition to the large amounts of U.S. aid then already being furnished the Koreans, the United States was willing to increase the levels of domestic aid sent to South Korea, to increase its pay and allotment schedules to all ROK troops serving in South Vietnam now or in the future, and to increase the opportunities for South Korea's domestic manufacturing plant to compete for a larger percentage of America's Vietnam War procurements.[65]

Vice President Humphrey's intercession into the negotiations worked. In the negotiations that followed his visit, discussions that received a further impetus when Saigon formally requested a second ROK division on 28 February 1966,[66] the U.S. negotiators finally gained a firm idea of what exactly they would have to pay to get the additional ROK division deployed. On 4 March 1966, the U.S. Ambassador to Korea Winthrop G. Brown sent a letter containing the official U.S. government concessions to Korean Foreign Minister Lee Ton-won, a letter that figuratively opened up the U.S. Treasury to the government and people of the Republic of Korea.

The actual contents of Ambassador Brown's letter still have not been relesed for public scrutiny. Although the letter was supposedly released to a U.S. Senate subcommittee in 1970, even this august body did not receive the actual letter. What the Senate subcommittee received, and printed, was a South Korean newspaper article written from a supposedly leaked copy of the letter. Some suspicions still remain, therefore, that not everything contained in the actual letter has been revealed. Even so, what the published account of the "Brown Letter" does disclose is a Lyndon Johnson–authorized financial bonanza for almost every segment of the South Korean economy. As a direct result of President Johnson's need to maintain a charade, Ambassador Browns' letter committed the United States to:

1. Provide for the complete equipping of three South Korean army divisions and expedite the modernization of seventeen other army divisions and one marine division;

2. Provide all equipment and financing for the additional forces to be deployed by the government of the Republic of Korea to the Republic of Vietnam;

3. Equip and provide the training and financing for a total replacement of comparable units in South Korea organized to take the place of the additional forces deployed in South Vietnam;

4. Contribute to filling all the requirements determined to be necessary for the improvement of Korean anti-infiltration capability;

5. Provide the necessary equipment to expand the South Korean production capabilities for increased ammunition production within Korean national boundaries;

6. Provide communications facilities in South Vietnam for the exclusive use of the Koreans which would be capable of maintaining communication between the Korean government and its forces in South Vietnam;

7. Provide the Republic of Korea all of the net additional costs incurred for the deployment of additional Korean forces in South Vietnam as well as for the mobilization and maintenance in Korea of one reserve army division, one brigade, and their support units;

8. Suspend the MAP transfer program for as long as there were substantial Korean forces in Vietnam; and also, procure in Korea, for the use of Korean forces, the items of supplies so suspended in FY 1966 and FY 1967;

9. Procure supplies, services, and equipment in Korea insofar as practicable and also direct selected types of procurement for United States and Republic of Vietnam forces to South Korea in cases in which South Korea has the production capability;

10. Procure in Korea as much as Korea could provide in time and at a reasonable price any goods purchased by AID for use in its projects

for rural construction, logistics, pacification, relief, and so forth, in the Republic of Vietnam;

11. Provide, to the extent permitted by the Republic of Vietnam, expanded opportunities for Korean contractors to participate in the various construction projects undertaken by the United States government or by United States contractors in the Republic of Vietnam, and other services, including employment of skilled Korean civilians in the Republic of Vietnam;

12. Expand American technical assistance to the Republic of Korea in the general field of export promotion;

13. Provide, in addition to the $150 million AID loans already committed, additional AID loans as needed to support the economic development of the Republic of Korea; and

14. Provide Korea with $15 million worth of program loans in 1966 to be used for the support of Korean exports to Vietnam and other development needs.[67]

If, at the beginning of their troop commitments to South Vietnam, the South Korean government could arguably claim that economic gains were not a major reason for their having sent troops to assist the Vietnamese,[68] by 1966 this was no longer the case. By this date, obtaining financial rewards for their troops' services had become almost the sole South Korean motive.

A notable omission from the Brown Letter is any reference to an increase in U.S. funding of the Korean overseas allotment scale. Although Vice President Humphrey had included this item in his list of potential concessions, Ambassador Brown did not feel it necessary to include pay and allowance schedules in his letter because the Korean allotment scale had already received substantial increases (see Table 6). The necessity of a U.S. increase in the overseas allowance schedule had been one of the few points of agreement between the U.S.-Korean officials during the first few weeks of negotiations. Negotiators from both sides felt that without an overseas allowance increase all further discussions would be moot as this was necessary to guarantee the recruitment of sufficient troops to man a second ROK division: "Minister Kim [Korean Foreign Minister] stated that the prospect of increased allowances was, among other things, an important element in attracting volunteers."[69]

After receiving the Brown Letter guarantees, the Korean

Table 6

ROK Overseas Duty Daily Allowances
as of July 1966

(In U.S. dollars; amounts were authorized on 18 January 1966)

Officers	Amount	Enlisted	Amount
Lieutenant General	10.00	Warrant Officer	3.50
Major General	8.00	Master Sergeant	2.50
Brigadier General	7.00	Sergeant 1st Class	2.00
Colonel	6.50	Staff Sergeant	1.90
Lieutenant Colonel	6.00	Sergeant	1.80
Major	5.50	Corporal	1.50
Captain	5.00	Private 1st Class	1.35
1st Lieutenant	4.50	Private	1.25
2nd Lieutenant	4.00		

Source: U.S. Congress. Senate. Committee on Foreign Relations. *Republic of Korea: Hearings on United States Security Agreements and Commitments Abroad,* 91st Cong., 2d sess., Part 6, 1970: 1570.

government moved quickly to authorize deployment of a second ROK division to South Vietnam. On 30 March 1966, the Korean National Assembly voted to send the 9th ROK Infantry Division, the White Horse Division, to Vietnam. However, since the 9th Division did not have the same impetus for rapid deployment that the Tiger Division had, their first elements did not begin arriving in Vietnam until late September 1966. Except for a 1967 deployment of a marine battalion, which only brought the 9th Division up to its full strength, the Koreans made no further increases in their troop levels in Vietnam for the remainder of the war.

The increased numbers of Korean troops directly engaged in combat in South Vietnam, coupled with the concomitant increase in American financial costs, still did not satiate Lyndon Johnson's desire for even more troops. The political debates within South Korea against further troop deployments, however, had become so intense by late 1966 that President Park was forced to concede the virtual impossibility of any further ROK troop commitment to Vietnam in the near future.[70] Thus, when President Johnson sent, in August 1967, his blue-ribbon presidential mission of Maxwell Taylor and Clark Clifford to Seoul to solicit even more Korean troops, they came away empty-handed. That the Koreans would reject the entreaties of the Taylor-Clifford mission was not unexpected, as the Koreans had already rejected requests made from President Johnson during his state visit to South Korea in November 1966, and from South Vietnam's Premier Nguyen Kao Ky when he visited Seoul in January 1967.

This change in Korea's policy position toward sending aid to South Vietnam could not have been more abrupt, or, as far as the U.S. State Department was concerned, more unwelcome. From 1964 through 1966, the Korean government, given that the United States would provide copious amounts of money, had not refused a single American request for Korean military personnel to serve in South Vietnam. Then, after 1966, the Koreans honored no request for more troops. Although State Department officials did not particularly like this new direction in Korean foreign policy, they nevertheless had to accept the fact that their own actions were responsible to a great extent for determining the Korean government's new course of action. The impact on South Korea's government, politics, and society of America's insistence that Seoul commit two of its best divisions to South Vietnam could not be ignored or discounted.

Perhaps the most significant effect of South Korea's 1964–1966 concurrence with U.S. troop requests lay in the fears of many Korean government leaders. To these leaders, most but not all allied against Park in the National Assembly, the benefits accruing to Korea for its two division troop commitment to South Vietnam did not serve to offset the degradation of Korea's own defensive posture toward North Korea. Several of these leaders had, in fact, expressed this fear even before the deployment of the Dove Unit.[71] Of particular concern to these leaders, and indicative of the validity of their fears, was the increase in North Korean armed provocations across the Demilitarized Zone (DMZ) from 88 incidents in 1965 to 784 in 1967.[72] Given South Korea's traditional problems with its belligerent neighbor to the north, President Park could not ignore the domestic crisis developing as a result of the increased DMZ raids.

Further, it did not help that the cause of these raids was being directly attributed to the Park government's deployment of two combat divisions to South Vietnam.

While Johnson Administration officials were fully aware of Park's political difficulties, both inside South Korea and with North Korea, they were unwilling to allow these difficulties to do more than force a temporary delay in requesting even more ROK troops for South Vietnam. Throughout 1967, State Department officials worked to maintain a constant state of readiness so as to be able to move at the first sign of an easing in Park's troubles: "Recent developments indicate ROK domestic political situation may soon be restored to something appraoching [sic] normalcy. This raises question of when and how we approach Pak [the Korean spelling of Park] on additional troop dispatch for Viet-Nam."[73] Washington wanted to make sure that they were in position to move immediately with another troop request just as soon as Park's domestic problems decreased.

In line with Washington's desires to be ready to request more troops at the earliest opportune moment, the newly appointed U.S. Ambassador to Korea William J. Porter met with President Park and three of his cabinet members on 6 December 1967. While these men met ostensibly to discuss only the political atmosphere then existent in Korean politics, the meeting produced an unforeseen result that was not immediately evident. Because of the subjects discussed, this meeting succeeded in forming the basis for all future U.S.-Korean discussions on sending more ROK troops to Vietnam.[74]

In the course of the 6 December discussions, the officials from the two countries unknowingly established three negotiating conditions that would become points of consideration in all future discussions of Korean troop deployment to Vietnam. In the first case, South Korean justifications for sending their troops to Vietnam underwent a significant change. While, in all former U.S.-Korean negotiations, there had been some concern expressed over how the South Korean troop deployments would affect Korean national security, American economic largess and a continuing U.S. military presence in South Korea effectively prevented these concerns from assuming a dominant role in the discussions. After the 6 December meeting, however, Korean security would become the primary item of consideration in all Korean-American negotiations.

The changed political climate in South Korean politics constituted the second consideration to come out of the December meeting. Though President Park himself continued his personal support of all American requests for more ROK troops for South Vietnam, his support alone no longer guaranteed Korean National Assembly support. In the December meeting, Park admitted that with the current strength of his political opposition in the National Assembly, there was little chance he could now muster the support to deploy further ROK troops to Vietnam.

The final condition on future Korean troop deployments to Vietnam resulted from the meeting participants' acknowledgment that events now made it very difficult, if not impossible, for the United States to obtain any new ROK troop commitments to Vietnam. If, however, it was not now possible to deploy a new contingent of South Korean *military* personnel, Porter, Park, and the ministers reasoned that an alternative still existed that could still send more Koreans to South Vietnam. To these men, it was distinctly possible for the United States to hire, either directly or indirectly, Korean *civilians* and send them to Vietnam as replacements for ROK soldiers working in non–combat related fields. Through the use of this expedient, it was envisioned that enough Korean soldiers could be replaced so as to effectively put an additional "reinforced regimental combat team"[75] in the field without having to send more troops from South Korea.

Ambassador Porter's intimation that Korean civilians might be used in South Vietnam in lieu of ROK troops did achieve one immediate result. Porter's comment, especially when supported by a Seoul request received just two weeks later—"Seoul is also seeking US approval for a Korean logistical service corps made up of Korean veterans to furnish logistical support"[76]—did generate a brief period of excitement in Washington. The sticking point for this idea, however, as was the case for all Korean aid, was how much would the United States have to pay for such a force: "The key issue is the rate of compensation which appears [from the Korean demands] exorbitant."[77]

The Korean government's compensation demands for a civilian task force ultimately served as Washington's excuse for rejecting the idea: "A hastily negotiated and precedent setting wage scale would have an adverse impact on US/GVN and US/Third Country relations."[78] This rationale does not, however, hold true to form with all previous U.S.-Korean arrangements on getting Korean personnel sent to Vietnam. In all previous negotiations for ROK troops, the United States had concluded that no Korean financial demand was too exorbitant, so why should costs alone now cause the United States to reject a Korean offer? A possible answer to this seeming anomaly lies in the composition of the offer—civilians would make up the personnel of the task force, not military troops. By late 1967 and early 1968, the Johnson Administration only sought free world military units to be sent to Vietnam, as these offered the best device to publicize an ally's demonstration of support for the American position in Vietnam.

In his report to Washington on the results of the 6 December meeting, Ambassador Porter painted an optimistic picture of his supposed achievements, but in reality the meeting provided few tangible results. Despite Ambassador Porter's continuing best efforts, and in spite of an almost constant flow of Johnson Administration petitions to President Park and the South Korean government for additional troops for Vietnam,[79] events which neither Washington nor Seoul could control would soon occur that guaranteed that Seoul would send no further troops to aid the Saigon government. Two events of January 1968—President Park's narrow avoidance of assassination by a North Korean death squad and the North Korean capture of the U.S. spy ship *Pueblo*—successfully cast the new South Korean policy in stone. Playing up the idea that the "deployment of both U.S. and South Korean resources to Viet Nam might have helped to provoke the incidents,"[80] President Park's opposition now managed to garner enough votes in the National Assembly to prevent any further ROK involvement in Vietnam. And no amount of American assurances could convince them to change their minds.*[81] After January 1968, the Korean National Assembly considered no Washington plea for more Korean troops.

Despite the Korean National Assembly's refusal to consider further American requests, President Park still wanted to broker Korean troops for additional U.S. economic assistance. In April

*Even during Korea's early involvement in Vietnam, Washington officials had had to constantly reassure the Koreans that the United States would not slight its military obligations to them.

1968, Park made one final, futile offer, knowing full well that his proposal had no support from the National Assembly:

> [South Korea will] discuss sending additional troops, if US promises following: (1) send 10,000-man ROK Supply Service Corps to Viet-Nam; (2) activate one new army division to replace outgoing division; (3) raise allowances of ROK soldiers in Viet-Nam; (4) supply addtional [sic] Phantom jet fighters (in addition to those agreed upon); (5) replace old communications equipment and weapons; (6) supply arms to Homeland Reserve Force; (7) provide modern sophisticated weapons for ROK armed forces.[82]

Perhaps President Park thought that if the United States threw enough money at the members of the National Assembly, they would change their minds. Be that as it may, by this time the State Department realized that Park had no way of fulfilling his end of the bargain and no formal discussions on the overture were ever held.

Even if Korean security had not become the National Assembly's uppermost concern by 1968, the situation was such by then that the United States could no longer reasonably expect to obtain further Korean troops, no matter how generously they paid them. The fact was that by 1968, the principal factor militating against the United States', obtaining more troops was not the threat posed by North Korea, but the vast amount of American economic aid the Koreans were already receiving for the ROK troops then in South Vietnam. Simply stated, because of the large amounts of American aid already flowing into South Korea, the national economy was saturated and thus could not appreciably benefit from an infusion of more aid. Consequently, many Korean officials thus believed that further ROK troop deployments to Vietnam were not only economically unnecessary but potentially detrimental to the economic well-being of Korea.[83] That this may very well have been a valid concern is suggested by an examination of the total package of all U.S. financial aid concessions made to South Korea between 1965 and 1973.

As has already been mentioned, no organization or individual has attempted to determine the total economic benefits Korea realized from its military commitments to Vietnam. Further, the research that has been done, incomplete as it is, is scattered throughout the literature and only intimates at a final total. Nevertheless, what the known records, inadequate as they may be, do reveal, are financial benefits of startling dimensions accruing to the South Korean military, society, and government. For example, official government figures, which only account for the 1965-1970 period, show that it cost the United States over $927 million just to maintain the ROK troops (equipment, pay and allowances, supplies, transportation, housing, etc.) inside South Vietnam during these years.[84] Even this rather substantial total pales by comparison to a conservative estimate of the total costs for the whole period of Korean involvement in Vietnam. Using a reasonable extrapolation of known government figures, for example, it is estimated that the United States paid the Koreans over $1 billion just in pay and allowances during the 1965-1973 period.[*85] One billion or more dollars were spent only to cover the personnel pay, allowances, and benefits of the Koreans actually serving in South Vietnam — and this figure does not even attempt to include all the other expenses occasioned by the ROK presence in Vietnam.

Inadequate and understated estimates are further evident in the few attempts that have been made to determine how much money the United States pumped directly into the South Korean economy. Because the available official data used to estimate these U.S. costs also only include figures from the 1965-1970 period, statements based only on these numbers must be viewed skeptically: "[the ROK economy gained] $150 million in development loans and perhaps $600 million in profits from military procurement, contracts for services, and construction projects."[86]

Clearly, the United States paid very substantial sums to the Republic of Korea for the use of their military forces in South Vietnam, a largess which also directly benefited the individual Korean soldier. From the moment that a Korean soldier set foot on Vietnamese soil, even as a member of the Dove Unit, he started to draw pay substantially higher than he would have had he not elected to serve there. A Korean private, earning a base salary of $1.60 a month, could earn almost that much, from $1 to $1.25, with one

---

*This figure is arrived at thusly: The combined earnings of all Korean civilian and military personnel in Vietnam in 1967 was $135 million, and in 1968 it was $180 million. Using the $180 million figure as the U.S. costs for each of the years between 1968 and 1971, the years of full ROK troop strength in Vietnam, and using a percentage decrease for the years 1972 and 1973, the resulting figure easily exceeds $1 billion.

day's service in Vietnam. Nevertheless, even though the individual Korean soldier received a financial bonanza for his service, the cost of his service to the United States still constituted a bargain. By buying the services of an ROK soldier, the United States only had to pay out about between $5,000 and $7,800 a year, while it cost the U.S. government about $13,000 a year to support an American soldier in Vietnam.[87]

An examination of the facts thus presents an overwhelming case for economic profit being the principal, if not the only, reason the South Korean government sent its troops to fight in Vietnam. For this reason then, the Korean troops serving in Vietnam should be considered an American mercenary force. But the accusation that the Koreans were mercenaries does not now, and did not then, come only from outside sources. Even some in the South Korean citizenry believed their government's actions constituted a Korean supply of mercenary troops to the United States:

> In 1966 and again in 1967, Yun [Korean opposition leader Yun Po-Sun] . . . [charged] that the Korean government . . . was fighting essentially a mercenary operation at the cost of Korean blood. This comment almost led to his arrest.[88]

In retrospect, one cannot help but wonder what might have happened if Seoul had accepted Washington's original offer to only defray Korea's out-of-pocket expenses for deploying their troops. If such a direction had been taken, then the Korean government could have fulfilled all the diplomatic and moral obligations they publicly touted for sending their troops without expending one dollar more than if their troops had stayed home. For whatever reasons, however, they chose not to take this route, electing instead to allow their troops to become mercenaries. Despite this, Korea should not be faulted for their actions. After all, to make a mercenary, one has to have both a buyer and a seller. Thus, the Korean government could not have succeeded in selling the services of their troops if the U.S. government had not been there to buy those services. United States Senator J.W. Fulbright, in his 1970 investigation into the U.S.-Korean negotiations, acknowledged this American culpability when he observed that never before in American history had the U.S. agreed to give such economic perquisites to any ally for their help in fighting a war.[89]

No Johnson Administration official is on record expressly stating that the United States government hired mercenaries in Southeast Asia. Nevertheless, a close reading of the government documents suggests strongly that several high ranking American officials did consider the Korean troops as such. In fact, Johnson Administration officials, while denying the use of mercenaries on the one hand, were drafting official documents that addressed the question of what could be done and said to avoid insinuations of mercenary operations by the press.[90] In yet another example, proof that Korean and other third world country troops were perceived as mercenaries can be found in White House references to those troops being "on our payrolls."[91] The record even indicates that President Johnson himself viewed these troops as being bought and paid for as he, on at least one occasion, referred to the allied troops fighting in Vietnam as being "U.S.-financed personnel."[92]

Senator Stephen R. Young of Ohio, in a 1967 address on the Senate floor, presented a convincing argument for the fact that, despite the repeated denials of Johnson Administration functionaries, the United States was indeed using Korean troops as American mercenaries in South Vietnam:

> In our Revolutionary War, when our patriots were fighting for liberation from England, early in 1776 Lord North of Great Britain for King George III paid thousands of pounds sterling to the Duke of Hesse-Cassel to purchase 10,000 or more Hessian soldiers, who were transported on English ships to America, where they fought beside the Redcoats to crush American rebels. Of course, the British fed and paid these mercenaries. . . . In our involvement in the war in Viet-Nam, we Americans have secured and transported on our ships more than 50,000 Korean soldiers. . . . The facts are that in addition to paying these soldiers, we Americans clothe, feed, arm, and equip them. It is denied that these soldiers are mercenaries. Just what the distinction and difference is between them and the Hessians . . . is beyond me.[93]

Senator Young, using only the small amount of information then available about the United States–Korean arrangements, had come to the conclusion that America was employing Korean mercenaries in South Vietnam. Information since made available has served only to confirm his conclusions.

Chapter 4

The Philippines
PHILCAG Contingent

Although Secretary of State Dean Rusk did not include the Philippines in his initial More Flags listing of allied nations supplying aid to South Vietnam (see Table 1), this omission did not mean the Philippines was not sending aid to South Vietnam. The government of the Republic of the Philippines had, in fact, been sending aid to the South Vietnamese government through two separate programs since 1954, even before South Vietnam declared itself an independent country on 23 October 1955.

Only the first of these two Filipino aid projects, however, OPERATION BROTHERHOOD, because of its humanitarian mission, received any form of public acknowledgment.*[1] Such was not the case for the second project, the FREEDOM COMPANY OF THE PHILIPPINES. Organized in 1955, and administered under the auspices of the U.S. Central Intelligence Agency (CIA), the FREEDOM COMPANY was composed of former World War II Filipino guerrillas hired to perform secret operations throughout the territories of the former French Indochina.†[2]

---

*Operation Brotherhood *was organized in 1954 soon after the Geneva Accords divided Vietnam into northern and southern zones. Its mission was to send teams of Filipino doctors and nurses to work in the rural areas of South Vietnam and it received most of its financial support from various nongovernmental Philippine organizations.*

†*The* Freedom Company *performed many different tasks for the [continued]*

Although both Philippine aid projects continued operations in South Vietnam into the 1960s, Secretary Rusk could not include either one in his first 1964 More Flags list, but for different reasons. While the type of assistance furnished by OPERATION BROTHERHOOD was exactly the type of aid Secretary Rusk desired for the More Flags program, he still had to exclude it from his 1964 list because the operation had ceased working in Vietnam in the early 1960s. As for the FREEDOM COMPANY, the very nature of its clandestine mission precluded its being included despite its continued operations in South Vietnam until the late 1960s.* The very existence of the two Filipino assistance programs, however, did make a direct contribution to the More Flags program. In Secretary Rusk's mind, the two aid programs signified that the Philippines had a "direct interest in [the] struggle"[3] in South Vietnam. He consequently moved quickly to take advantage of this supposed interest by including the Philippines on his first list of five free world countries†[4] specifically targeted as possible sources of South Vietnamese aid under the newly inaugurated More Flags program.[5]

Secretary Rusk's expectations of Philippine support for the More Flags program proved valid when, in the first few days after his 1 May telegram, the Philippines agreed to begin talks on what aid they might send to Vietnam. As a matter of fact, when State Department officials first approached their Filipino counterparts about a More Flags commitment, little time was spent on determining whether or if the Philippines would send aid. Most of the time the discussion centered on what would be the composition of a Philippine aid package to Saigon. The discussions, however, were not free of dispute. From the first day of U.S.-Philippines negotiations, serious differences of opinion existed between what aid the Filipinos thought they could send, and what aid the Americans wanted sent.

U.S. and South Vietnamese governments, including guerrilla warfare activities in North Vietnam. Some members even assisted in the writing of South Vietnam's national constitution. As a general rule, though, the purpose of the Freedom Company was to perform those tasks which neither American nor South Vietnamese government personnel could be openly identified with.

*When the CIA withdrew much of its support for the Freedom Company in the early 1960s, the company was renamed the Eastern Construction Company.

†The others being Australia, New Zealand, Thailand, and Great Britain.

The original Philippine government offer of aid to Vietnam centered on a civic-action unit composed of civilian medical and engineering teams. This was not, however, exactly the type of aid Washington most desired. While the State Department did want Philippine medical and engineering units for Vietnam, it did not want these units manned by civilian personnel. In keeping with the high public visibility sought for the More Flags program, the Johnson Administration thought that a military unit, or units, performing civic action duties, presented the better demonstration of Philippine support for America's policy position in South Vietnam.

Other differences of opinion also existed between the two nations' negotiators over and above the disputes about the civic action unit personnel. In these first discussions—they were not yet considered formal negotiations—the Americans advanced the idea that the Philippines also had the capabilities to commit several guerrilla-warfare training teams to Vietnam.[6] Although Washington did not consider these teams, similar to the U.S. Army's Special Forces A-Teams, as combat units, to the Filipinos these troops were too closely identified with combat personnel and they thus resisted making a commitment of these troops.

On 5 May 1964, four days after the More Flags program began, the American embassy in Manila reported on the results of their early talks with the Filipinos. In this message the Manila mission not only detailed what they thought the ideal Philippine aid package should be (see Table 7), but they also questioned for the first time who, and how, the financing for the package would be accomplished:

> Inevitable question which US would have to face in raising question with GOP [Government of the Philippines] is whether US would be willing to finance all or part of such effort. GOP has capacity to finance the effort. Believe we should initially indicate that we expect them to do so. Further insistence on this point would depend upon degree of importance US attaches to Phil presence in South Vietnam.[7]

With More Flags less than a week old, it is understandable that America's overseas embassy personnel might question the level of emphasis they should attach to the program. For the Philippine embassy staff, however, Washington's instructions sent in regards to the first Filipino aid package to Vietnam were sufficiently clear to remove any possible doubts as to the program's priority status with the Johnson Administration.

Table 7

Composition of Initial American "More Flags" Aid Request from the Philippines

According to the American embassy in Manila, the Philippines had the following military units available for deployment to South Vietnam in May 1965:

1. Five medical and engineering teams patterned after United States Special Forces Teams, each to consist of
     1 officer–team leader
     2 operations and intelligence noncommissioned officers
     2 medical specialists
     2 demolition specialists
     2 communication specialists
     4 weapons specialists

2. Two Philippine Pioneer Platoons, each consisting of
     1 officer with engineer construction experience
     20–25 enlisted men capable of minor engineer construction requiring no heavy equipment

3. An unspecified number of field dispensary [medical] units

Source: Message, AmEmbassy Manila to SecState, 5/5/64, "Vietnam Memos, Vol. VIII, 5/64," Item No. 107. NSF Country File-VN, Box 4, pp. 2–3. L.B.J. Library.

Because of the worsening military conditions inside Vietnam during mid–1965, the State Department informed its embassy in Manila to delay opening formal negotiations for the entire Philippine aid package. The Manila embassy was ordered instead, because of the high number of casualties suffered by the South Vietnamese Army during this period, to concentrate only on getting the Philippine field dispensary, or medical, units committed to South Vietnam as quickly as possible.[8] While the State Department message did not expressly state that the U.S. negotiators in Manila should grant economic concessions to the Philippines for the dispatch of their medical units, by instructing its Manila personnel thus: "In order to enhance possibility of maximum Philippine contributions ... [you are to] be prepared to add supplemental inducements,"[9] its meaning became perfectly clear to embassy officials. With the order to "add supplemental inducements," the State Department was informing Manila that More Flags aid was so important that, if it became necessary, it would be bought. Manila embassy personnel now knew how very important Washington viewed free world aid under the More Flags program.

American financial concessions then, almost from the first day of the negotiations, played a central role in the first U.S. discussions with the Filipinos for aid to Vietnam. Further, this initial aid package also provided Washington with an idea of what the future held in store, as through it the Philippine government served notice to Washington that it viewed the economic benefits derived from sending their aid to Vietnam to be the determining factor in all negotiations. How much the Filipino aid would cost the United States became the abiding question in all U.S.-Filipino negotiations.

Secretary Rusk did have one very important ally in his quest of a More Flags commitment from the Philippines: President Diosdado Macapagal. In fact, soon after the United States made its first More Flags overtures to the Philippines, Macapagal went on record with his support by stating that the Philippines could be counted on to extend "meaningful help"[10] to the Saigon government. Despite Macapagal's assurances of support, his word alone could not, however, guarantee that Vietnam would receive an aid package from the Philippines. Any Philippine foreign aid action would also require support from the Philippine Congress, and it was this third player in the early More Flags negotiations that presented the State Department with its biggest challenge. Whatever may have been Secretary Rusk's expectations about what the United States would have to concede to get a More Flags commitment from Macapagal, he knew definitely what the Philippine Congress expected to obtain. Rusk knew that no matter how much Philippine executive office support the More Flags program might have, any actual aid authorization still hinged "primarily on [the] extent of U.S. financing"[11] that the Philippine Congress could wrest from the Johnson Administration.

There are no currently available documents citing exactly what economic concessions the United States had ultimately to make to get the first Philippine aid package sent to Vietnam. With American-Filipino negotiations for a much larger aid contribution to South Vietnam soon to start, the particulars for this first, small arrangement became lost in the shuffle. Nevertheless, the record does show that the Philippine Congress authorized deployment of the first Philippine Contingent (PHILCON I)[12] to South Vietnam by passing a one million peso (approximately $250,000 in American dollars) appropriations bill on 7 July 1964, "with minimal opposition and debate."*[13] Even with only about 40 people, logic alone would indicate that one million pesos would be insufficient to cover all the unit's expenses for a one year period. Yet this amount was all the Philippine legislators deemed necessary. It thus becomes a reasonable assumption that, with the U.S. desire to get a Philippine More Flags commitment into Vietnam, the Philippines obtained sufficient U.S. economic guarantees that the legislators could vote any level of support for PHILCON I and still see it deployed.

Although the PHILCON I authorization bill passed through the Philippine Congress with little debate, the bill still received some resistance from Macapagal's political opposition in the Congress. While this opposition, headed by House Minority Leader Jose Laurel, Jr., and Senate Majority Leader Ferdinand Marcos, was not strong enough to defeat the PHILCON I package, they could still muster enough support to force Macapagal into justifying a Filipino involvement with the United States in Vietnam. Not surprisingly, Macapagal's justifications were predictably self-serving, presenting only the most beneficent motives for his administration's actions. To Macapagal, the Philippine nation, government, and people were

---

*Philcon I *consisted of two military surgical teams and a psychological warfare detachment, about 40 men and women. Periodically augmented by other surgical teams, it would eventually expand to a maximum of about 70 people.*

sending aid to Vietnam only because of their deep commitment to democracy and freedom. And if th' alone proved insufficient, Macapagal cited the Philippine ment's obligations as a member of the Southeast Asia Treaty Organization (SEATO) as an added reason for their sending aid to Vietnam. This latter rationale was, however, not original with Macapagal, as he borrowed it from the United States. According to American reasoning, and the Philippines mimicked the position, the United States was obligated to aid Vietnam because of its SEATO treaty obligations.[14] The use of this argument was especially appealing to the political leaders of the two countries because with it their actions gained some semblance of international validation.

The use by either the United States or the Philippines of SEATO obligations to justify their actions in South Vietnam, however, was spurious. Although the two countries were SEATO members, South Vietnam was not. Therefore, there existed no *pro forma* obligation for any SEATO member to act in defense of any threat to Vietnamese national sovereignty. Even futher, SEATO, as an organizational unit, never adopted an official policy position for or against its members becoming involved in Vietnamese affairs. A major reason why SEATO chose not to get officially involved was the opposition by two SEATO members, France and Pakistan, to any SEATO action in Vietnam. As a direct consequence of French and Pakistani antipathy, the United States actively worked to prevent any question of South Vietnamese aid from being addressed in any formal SEATO organizational meeting. The United States, however, and by extension, the Philippines, never permitted the true state of affairs to interfere with their continuing to use SEATO obligations to justify their actions in South Vietnam during the remainder of their involvements in the Vietnam War.

In a move that mirrored the situation with the South Korean More Flags aid commitments, the South Vietnamese government was not allowed to play a direct role in the early U.S.-Philippine aid discussions. Just as with the Korean aid packages, Saigon got involved only after the American and Filipino negotiators first determined among themselves what aid the Philippines would commit to Vietnam. Consequently, Saigon did not submit a formal request to the Philippines for aid until 10 June 1964, some weeks after the start of the U.S.-Filipino negotiations.[15] If the dutiful obsequiousness of the Saigon government toward Washington had not become the established pattern during the Korean negotiations, it would have with the Philippine aid commitments.

On 25 July 1964, even before the first elements of PHILCON I began arriving in Vietnam,* the South Vietnamese government, again as directed by the United States, submitted yet another request to the Philippine government for more aid. A Philippine consideration of this new request had to be delayed, however, as the Philippine Congress was then in its end-of-term recess until January 1965.[16] Nevertheless, the State Department did not allow this delay to impede its pursuit of more Philippine contributions to the More Flags program. With President Macapagal scheduled to visit Washington in October 1964, the State Department used the time interval to develop a comprehensive package of desired Philippine assistance to Vietnam. It was expected that, on Macapagal's arrival in Washington, the completed package would become an integral part of the discussions held between the two presidents. State Department officials received further encouragement in their aid package preparation when Filipino officials, in Washington to arrange the details of Macapagal's visit, confided to some White House officials that the Philippine government would be willing to play a greater military role in South Vietnam, if "certain conditions" were met.[17]

Macapagal's visit to Washington on 5-6 October 1964 resulted in the first official acknowledgment that the two countries had begun discussions about committing a 2,000-man Philippine troop detachment to South Vietnam. Evidence does not reveal, however, which leader first suggested the troop deployment. Although the joint communique issued after the meetings does not mention which side first brought up the subject,[18] both Macapagal and Johnson are on record as saying that it was the other who first brought up the subject. According to Macapagal's recollections, the pressures exerted on him from Johnson and members of his cabinet forced him into agreeing to the troop request:

> President Johnson personally and through top advisors like the
> Secretary of State, . . . [Secretary of] Defense and the American am-
> bassador . . . undertook steady persuasions as tactfully as they could

*See Appendix C for a chronological listing of the Philippine troop commitments to South Vietnam.

to *make* [emphasis added] my administration send a 2,000 man engineer contingent to Viet-Nam.[19]

Support for the American assertion that it was Macapagal who made the original suggestion is found in a State Department message from William Blair, Jr., the U.S. Ambassador to the Philippines. In reporting on a conversation he held with Macapagal after the Filipino's Washington visit, Blair wrote Secretary Rusk that President Macapagal "spoke of sending health, medical, engineering personnel and military special forces ... which president [Macapagal] had offered during state visit."[20] Despite the seeming desire of both parties to attribute the troop offer to the other's efforts, the facts suggest a mutually agreed on decision. When one couples the State Department's advance work on developing a desired Philippine aid package with Macapagal's known predisposition towards a deployment of Philippine troops to Vietnam, the offer most likely came about through the process of Macapagal's readily agreeing to a Johnson request.

Almost six months elapsed between the time the State Department first determined what should be the ideal More Flags aid package from the Philippines and the beginning of the Johnson-Macapagal meetings. During this period, with the exception of the hurried negotiations for and commitment of the PHILCON I detachment, no official negotiations took place to determine whether the rest of the Philippine aid desired by the Americans was aid that the Filipinos wanted to send. With the long delay in negotiations, it is perhaps understandable why, when the two sides did finally begin discussions in late October 1964, the resultant Philippine commitment to South Vietnam bore little resemblance to Washington's earlier request.

Since the October 1964 discussions on a new Philippine More Flags commitment were held between military representatives from the two countries, it was not surprising that the composition of the new aid package addressed mostly military concerns. Even so, although the negotiators determined that the next Philippine aid commitment to Vietnam should consist of a

Task Force of approximately 1800 personnel ... composed of an engineer construction battalion, civic action specialists and medical specialists, a C-47 squadron, an LST, and civilian district teams.[21]

they understood that their decisions were subject to amendment when nonmilitary negotiators became involved. The military officials' expectations proved correct as, during the early months of civilian government negotiations, the actual contents of the package underwent a series of revisions. Of particular concern to the civilians was the total number of military personnel the package would contain with the numbers fluctuating almost day-to-day between a high of 2500 and a low of 1500. In the end, though, the formal agreements over the specific details of the aid package, entitled the Philippine Civic Action Group (PHILCAG), and its mission objectives, were determined by the civilian negotiators from within the Johnson and Macapagal administrations.

Although discussions between the military negotiators took place in late 1964, both administrations understood that formal discussions on PHILCAG could not begin until after the Philippine Congress reconvened in January 1965. Both the State Department and Macapagal fully recognized the necessity of a congressional contribution if the negotiations were to succeed in getting PHILCAG sent to Vietnam. The informal talks conducted during the delay, however, did not give particular encouragement to the Americans. Despite the Filipino negotiators' "protestations of support and promises,"[22] State Department officials perceived that their Filipino counterparts demonstrated very little real enthusiasm for a commitment of Philippine aid.

The delay furnished Washington with yet another opportunity that they hastened to take advantage of. While waiting for the Filipino Congress to reconvene, Johnson Administration officials determined, as best they could, what would be their negotiating position on the funding of the PHILCAG detachment when the formal talks began. The official U.S. position on this subject was outlined for the Manila embassy in a message from the Chairman of the Joint Chiefs of Staff, General Earle G. Wheeler, acting as the spokesman for the Johnson Administration:

> Recommend you let Macapagal raise question of funding. Standard guidance still applies: in order preserve US MAP and AID funds, but more particularly to preserve genuine character of "more flags" donation, we prefer donor countries support costs of contributions to greatest extent possible. Nevertheless, if necessary in order to

secure meaningful and substantial third country aid to Viet Nam, we are prepared to pay entire bill.[23]

From the record then, it becomes obvious that the Johnson Administration, from the outset of formal negotiations, did not perceive the early differences of opinion on specific military units and total personnel numbers to be an insurmountable source of disagreement between the two countries. These officials did worry, however, that funding disputes would become a major point of contention, and they were right. During the entire period of the U.S.-Philippine PHILCAG negotiations, only one major point of contention ever developed between the two nations' officials: how much the United States would have to pay for the Philippines' deployment of PHILCAG to South Vietnam. The State Department, for its part in the negotiations, entered the discussions with a plan that would insure that the government of the Republic of the Philippines could send their PHILCAG detachment to South Vietnam at absolutely no cost to their national budget. Nevertheless, Washington still feared this plan would be insufficient to appease the Filipinos, which eventually proved to be the case. The Johnson Administration soon learned that if the United States were to obtain a further Philippine More Flags commitment, it would indeed have "to pay entire bill."

Official negotiations for the PHILCAG detachment began with the Filipinos submitting a substantial list of concessions they expected the United States to make (see Table 8). Because of their earlier planning and expectations that the Filipino demands would be "of [a] questionable or debatable nature,"[24] the State Department diplomats viewed all but one item on the Filipino list as negotiable. With the Wheeler message of 4 November serving as their negotiating guideline, the American negotiators disputed only the amounts of the overseas per diems and allowances the Filipinos wanted the U.S. to pay their troops:

> Phil negotiators . . . have told US [that Phil legislation provides for per diem rates of 15 dollars for field grade officers, 12 dollars for company grade officers and eight dollars for enlisted personnel for military service outside Philippines. These allowances, from our point of view, are excessive. It would be much preferable to have

Table 8

Financial Incentives Demanded by Filipinos for Commitment of the PHILCAG Detachment

1. Complete equipment and logistic support of PHILCAG while in South Vietnam
2. Overseas allowances
3. Costs for a replacement unit in the Philippines
4. Two swiftcraft (river patrol boats) in addition to two already promised
5. Accelerated funding for three already funded engineer construction battalions
6. M-14 rifles and M-60 machine guns for a Filipino battalion combat team to be stationed in the Philippines

Source: U.S. Congress. Senate. Committee on Foreign Relations. *The Republic of the Philippines: Hearings Before the Subcommittee on United States Security Agreements and Commitments Abroad*, Part 1, 91st Cong., 1st sess., 1969: 255.

> . . . a flat monthly allowance for service in combat area. For example, 50 dollars per man per month.[25]

Despite the Americans' belief that the rates demanded by the Filipinos were "completely out of line,"[26] Philippine negotiators refused to yield on the subject. Even Washington's repeated assurances to the Filipino negotiators that the United States was willing to pay all of the Philippines' extra, out-of-pocket, expenses for their deployment of PHILCAG, carried no weight with the Filipino officials. Until the Americans agreed to pay these allowances in full, there would be no consideration given to the deployment of the PHILCAG detachment.

The Filipino negotiators' unbending position over the per diem amounts almost succeeded in bringing the negotiations to an abrupt halt with neither side willing to move from their stated positions. Ambassador Blair, thinking that perhaps Macapagal's direct intercession into the talks would get them moving again, arranged a meeting with the Philippine president in early January 1965. In this meeting, Blair pointedly reminded Macapagal of his administration's need to maintain an atmosphere of good relations with the United States by pointing out the "political damage"[27] that would accrue to Macapagal's government if the Filipinos forced the Americans into agreeing to the inflated per diem scale. As support for this observation, Blair noted that the demanded per diem schedule greatly exceeded the amounts the United States was then paying all other soldiers, including its own, then serving in Vietnam. Thus, if the United States acquiesced to the Filipino demands it would only succeed in "creat[ing] morale problems among other personnel serving in Vietnam."[28] Despite President Macapagal's attentiveness to Blair's presentation, the ambassador received little encouragement from the meeting. Macapagal's only comment at the meeting's conclusion was a vague promise to study the situation.

While the State Department experienced some frustration over this early deadlock in the PHILCAG discussions, the per diem dispute also served to discomfit them in another area. Because of the per diem dispute, Johnson Administration officials had to delay their plans to obtain a Filipino combat unit for service in Vietnam. As early as 6 November 1964, Washington officials had noted the Philippine capability of sending a ground combat team to South Vietnam in addition to the engineering group then under discussion.[29] Then, when President Johnson issued his December 1964 decision "to seek the military and political cooperation of the governments of Thailand, the Philippines, Australia, New Zealand, and the United Kingdom,"[30] the possibility that Filipino combat troops would soon join the Koreans in South Vietnam became the subject of vigorous debate inside the State Department.[31] The discussions within the State Department eventually progressed to the point that contingency plans were drawn up that would have the United States "ask Philippines, Australia, and New Zealand . . . for a contribution of combat units to accompany U.S. combat units when and if it should become necessary."[32] The Filipino obduracy on the PHILCAG per diem issue however, ended all these speculations. There are many State Department messages dating from 1965 through 1968 that address the desirability of the United States' obtaining a Filipino combat unit for service in Vietnam, but there is no evidence the two countries ever began formal negotiations over the deployment of such a unit.

Even though the per diem allowance issue was temporarily stalling the formal negotiations, State Department planning and preparation for PHILCAG's ultimate deployment to South Vietnam continued unabated. In a 15 January 1965 message to all U.S. embassies, the Office of Strategic Development (OSD) ostensibly sought to detail the general "mechanics and policy involved"[33] in the American funding of all free world aid to South Vietnam. This message contains, however, a significant reference to the Philippines per diem question that reveals the continuing American thought being given to the problem. A "For Your Information" instruction in the message implies that the State Department was not only thinking about the per diem dispute with the Philippines, but was considering the possibility of bowing to the Philippine demands: "FYI if country to country exceptions are required, as appears may be the case for the Philippines, these should be on a bilateral footing with the country concerned."[34] Despite such suggestions of possible courses of action, however, several weeks would elapse after the Blair-Macapagal meeting before Johnson Administration officials would determine what would be the official Washington position in the PHILCAG negotiations.

After months of intense discussion between officials from both countries, Secretary of State Rusk decided the negotiations had gone on long enough and brought them to an end. On 19 February 1965, Secretary Rusk notified the embassy in Manila to inform the Philippine government that the United States would agree to their deploying a 2,300-man engineering task force to South Vietnam at a funding level of $9.13 million a year.*[35] While Secretary Rusk's acceptance of the $9.13 million figure indicated his tacit acceptance of many, but not all, of the Filipinos' demands, the message also made it clear that Secretary Rusk had not made these concessions with equanimity. In a forceful caution to the American negotiators in Manila, Secretary Rusk emphasized that they make absolutely sure the Filipinos fully understood that the American financial concessions, if accepted, did not constitute "an open-ended commitment"[36] of American aid to the Philippines.

---

*While the authorization message cited a mixture of MAP and AID accounts as the funding sources for the task force, in actuality the primary source would be AID's PL-480 program.

While Rusk's 19 February message did not mention the per diem issue at all, because of the unyielding nature of its wording and emphasis, it still succeeded in finally ending the per diem stalemate. Realizing that the United States would not be pushed further on the per diem and allowance dispute, Filipino officials agreed in early March to accept a compromise solution advocated by Secretary Rusk.[37] The Filipinos, nevertheless, still obtained most of the monies they wanted. Even though they agreed to the American-demanded $1 a day overseas allowance (see Table 9), the Americans agreed to fund almost all of the per diem amounts the Filipinos

Table 9

Per Diem and Overseas Allowances for PHILCAG

	Per diem / per day	*Overseas allowance / day*
Brigadier General	$6.00	$1.00
Colonel	5.50	1.00
Lieutenant Colonel	5.00	1.00
Major	4.50	1.00
Captain	4.00	1.00
1st Lieutenant	3.50	1.00
2nd Lieutenant	3.00	1.00
Master Sergeant	1.50	1.00
Sergeant 1st Class	1.00	1.00
Sergeant	.50	1.00
Corporal	.20	1.00
Private First Class / Private	.10	1.00

Source: U.S. Congress. Senate. Committee on Foreign Relations. *The Republic of the Philippines: Hearings on United States Security Agreements and Commitments Abroad,* 91st Cong., 1st sess., Part 1, 1969: 275.

fought for. With the compromise schedule, all PHILCAG and PHILCON I personnel would receive, in addition to their regular monthly salaries and the $1 a day overseas allowance, a daily per diem ranging from 10 cents to $6 for each day spent in South Vietnam, depending on the individual soldier's rank. Agreement on the U.S. funding levels for PHILCAG did not result, however, in the unit's being immediately deployed to South Vietnam. Before this could occur, Johnson Administration officials would have to endure months of internal Philippine political infighting as little more than interested bystanders.

All the State Department really accomplished with all the negotiations conducted up through mid–March 1965, was essentially nothing more than an agreement with the Macapagal Administration. The PHILCAG deployment to Vietnam still could not take place without a Philippine Congress authorization, and getting this authorization in 1965, a Philippine presidential and legislative election year, remained problematic at best. State Department officials, in their desire to get the Macapagal-negotiated agreements implemented, viewed it as America's best interest to support Macapagal in his 1965 presidential campaign against a forceful challenge by Ferdinand Marcos, the Majority Leader of the Philippine Senate. To this end, the Johnson Administration implemented a number of U.S. actions directly designed to benefit the Philippine national economy which would, in turn, increase Macapagal's popularity with the general Philippine population:

> a. Early resolution of outstanding PL-480 negotiations . . . on terms favorable to GOP [Government of the Philippines]; . . . b. Resolution of sources of friction that derive from our military bases; . . . c. U.S. agreement to underwrite costs of improving Philippine defenses in the southern islands. d. Increased military assistance of a type specifically desired by GOP.[38]

Washington obviously felt it could not simply sit back and await the election returns.

Even as Washington was doing its best to improve Macapagal's election chances, and though they acknowledged his difficulties in pushing a PHILCAG authorization through the legislature in 1965,[39] State Department officials still continued to pressure the Philippine president into trying to get the authorization bill passed. Macapagal, however, would not be pushed, and he delayed doing so, generating some real annoyance inside State Department circles:

> Attempts by Phils to rationalize their inaction on basis domestic political maneuvering and assurances regarding reconsideration following elections would not . . . mitigate damaging effect here.
> . . . Bill has taken on international and bilateral importance transcending domestic politics and Macapagal should be left in no doubt on that score.[40]

Nevertheless, Macapagal, "conlud[ing] that it [was] not possible to obtain passage of Vietnam aid bill"[41] before the elections, decided that he would bide his time in pushing the Congress for a PHILCAG authorization bill. Macapagal's attitude and reticence did little to encourage the State Department and even prompted some to question his true commitment to PHILCAG's deployment as they perceived him as being "lukewarm"[42] at best to the idea. Still, there was little more Washington could do but wait until after the Philippine elections and then begin to work with a new government to get PHILCAG passed through the Philippine Congress. Moreover, State Department officials, because of the agreements already negotiated and in spite of the cooled relations between the two governments, even hoped that this new government would again be headed by President Macapagal.

The November 1965 Philippine elections did not turn out as either Macapagal or the State Department hoped. Unexpectedly, the Filipino voters elected Ferdinand Marcos, who had a long history of opposition to sending Filipino military aid to South Vietnam,[43] as their new president. Washington officials did not, however, permit this detail to impede their pursuit of the PHILCAG detachment. Filipino officials had hardly completed tallying the November ballots when Washington acted. Between December 1965 and January 1966, in addition to almost constant local pressure applied by Ambassador Blair,[44] Lyndon Johnson sent five diplomatic missions, headed by Vice President Hubert Humphrey, Secretary of State Dean Rusk, Senator Mike Mansfield, Ambassador W. Averell Harriman, and General Ed Lansdale, to the Philippines to pressure Marcos into changing his mind about sending Philippine troops to South Vietnam.[45] These American pressure tactics were successful only to a degree. They did manage to persuade Marcos to reverse his position on sending a detachment of Philippine troops to South Vietnam, but Marcos' acquiescence was not total.

Marcos felt that, because PHILCAG was only an engineering and civic action detachment, and not a combat unit, he could agree to their deployment without compromising his beliefs and promises made to the Philippine people. Much to Washington's dismay, however, Marcos remained adamant about not sending a Philippine combat unit to Vietnam.

Once Marcos made the decision that sending PHILCAG to South Vietnam would be in the best interests of the Philippines, it became necessary to explain his decision to the Filipinos who had elected him, many of whom had voted against Macapagal because of their objections to any such action. Marcos justified the deployment of PHILCAG by employing essentially the same arguments used by the Macapagal administration,[46] but with one major omission. One of the primary reasons behind his decision, the economic incentives offered by the United States, was not made public. Fearing that he would be accused of being bought by the United States, Marcos deemed it an absolute necessity that the economic benefits the Philippines would derive from sending PHILCAG to South Vietnam be hidden from the Philippine citizenry. Further, he did not want the Filipino general population to know that the U.S. concessions would also be used to strengthen and extend his power base in the Philippines:

> From the first he had worked on a plan that would modernize the
> military and extend its influence in the countryside, thus giving the
> administration a greater capability for governance. There was no
> way of raising the funds required for this plan internally. Support
> had to come from the United States . . . and no such support could
> possibly be forthcoming to the Philippines unless she helped the
> United States by a show of support in Viet-Nam.[47]

While the Johnson Administration's relations with the new Philippine government did receive a boost from Marcos' decision to send the PHILCAG detachment to South Vietnam, U.S. officials were still faced with a renegotiation of the exact terms and particulars for PHILCAG's deployment. At the start of their negotiations with the Marcos representatives to decide these issues, Washington officials expected that they would be able to "get the contingent to SVN on the original Macapagal terms."[48] As things worked out, the original agreements made with the Macapagal Administration did serve as a base for the Marcos negotiations, but with two major modifications. First, Marcos rejected out-of-hand the agreement wherein the United States was to pay the full costs of forming new units in the Philippines to replace those sent to South Vietnam. As Marcos saw it, if his government permitted the United States to do this, then Filipino troops would be perceived as only serving as "cannon fodder" for the Americans, leaving the Philippines with "little room left for honor."[49]

The second major modification Marcos insisted on making in the Macapagal agreements centered on the American concession to fully fund the equipment needed for three engineering battalions that would remain in the Philippines. Instead of furnishing the funding necessary to equip three battalions, which Washington had already agreed to, Marcos now insisted on adding seven additional battalions to the list, bringing to ten the number of battalions the United States was expected to outfit. After some discussion, State Department officials finally agreed to fund an additional two battalions, for a total of five, but they refused to fund the remaining five.

While the negotiations were still going on, and although he did not yet have a firm U.S. commitment on every detail of the terms for deploying PHILCAG, Marcos felt that there was sufficient progress to allow him to bring the PHILCAG authorization bill before the Philippine Congress. On 3 June 1966, after overcoming heavy opposition to the deployment, Marcos succeeded in getting the Philippine Congress to authorize an expenditure of 35 million pesos (about $9 million U.S. dollars) to fund PHILCAG for one year. After more than two years of work, Lyndon Johnson finally had an official Republic of the Philippines agreement to send a military unit to South Vietnam. On 14 September 1966, three months after the congressional vote, PHILCAG began arriving in Vietnam.

No attempt was made in the PHILCAG negotiations to address a number of longtime economic disputes between the United States and the Philippines. Negotiators from both countries purposely restricted the PHILCAG discussions to only such issues as concerned PHILCAG directly. Because of a scheduled Marcos state visit to Washington in September 1966, however, these disputes would play a significant role in getting PHILCAG sent to Vietnam.

The list of unresolved problems between the United States and

the Philippines assumed top of agenda status when officials from
both countries, in July 1966, began preparations for the Marcos
visit. From these officials' viewpoints, the problems scheduled for
discussion between the two national leaders fell basically into two
broad categories: new points of dispute like PHILCAG's ten engineer
battalions, the employment of Filipino civilians in South Vietnam,
general economic and military aid, and Vietnamese offshore procurements; and issues of long standing disagreement such as the
claims and benefits for Filipino World War II veterans and the extension of the Laurel-Langley Trade Agreement.*

Normally, when a U.S. president meets with the leader of
another country to discuss mutual problems, the State Department
furnishes him with a list of suggestions outlining potential U.S.
positions on these problems. As the time neared for the Marcos-
Johnson meeting, however, State Department officials still had no
definitive suggestions they could make to President Johnson on how
to handle the various Philippine problems:

> Equipment for 3 battalions will be funded by Defense as "Viet-
> Nam related." Two more with be funded from FY'67 MAP. . . .
> Problem: The other 5. Defense has refused to fund on grounds of
> unavailability of '67 MAP funds. AID is unwilling to complete an
> essentially military assistance program. . . . State underlines that
> this item is "the single most important item in the package we are
> trying to arrange for Marcos." . . . On benefits, . . . estimated cost
> of the benefits package: about $17 Million a year. On claims, . . .
> estimated cost of the two claims: about $42 Million. Economic Aid.
> The Filipinos has [sic] given us a number of very large and am-
> biguous requests for military and economic aid. They have not
> defined priorities sharply, nor have they justified projects for
> workable loan proposals.[50]

Nevertheless, by the time Marcos actually arrived in Washington,
officials from the State Department and the Department of Defense
were able to present President Johnson with a list of suggested U.S.

---

*Laurel-Langley was a U.S.-Philippines trade agreement signed in 1955 which
gave Filipino companies preferential treatment in their imports export trade
with the United States. The State Department did not want to extend the
agreement past its 1974 expiration date, while the Philippine government did.*

positions on these thorny questions. President Johnson made it known, however, on receiving these suggestions, that he would make no final decision on any issue until after he had a chance to meet personally with Marcos.[51]

Even with the current availability of previously restricted materials, it still remains impossible to directly link the PHILCAG negotiations with the Johnson-Marcos discussions. At no time during or prior to the Marcos visit did any American or Filipino official ever explicitly mention PHILCAG in relation to the visit. Even the official joint communique issued after the Johnson-Marcos meeting did not link the PHILCAG negotiations to the economic particulars contained therein, although it did mention the PHILCAG deployment in passing. Even so, several of the U.S. negotiators at that time later voiced doubts that the disputed issues discussed by Johnson and Marcos would ever have come under consideration had the Philippines not sent PHILCAG to South Vietnam.[52]

There is yet another piece of evidence, however, that would tend to validate the argument that the Marcos-Johnson agreements were directly tied to PHILCAG's negotiations — Lyndon Johnson's propensity for making large U.S. concessions to obtain free world troop support for Vietnam. It is hard not to imagine, when one reads the long list of U.S. concessions contained in the joint communique, that they did not pertain directly to the PHILCAG negotiations. In the communique, Johnson granted concessions to Marcos that included something for almost every segment of the Philippine economy including, for example, such items as malarial mosquito control programs and cadastral survey assistance. The United States even allowed for a funding of projects that might conceivably come up in the future by granting an almost unlimited line of credit for "other new projects" as yet undetermined. Even more, Johnson all but guaranteed Marcos all ten of the disputed engineer battalions: "President Johnson was pleased to inform him that the United States would within this fiscal year provide equipment for five engineer construction battalions . . . and would consider furnishing equipment for five more such battalions in the next fiscal year." Such a large number of American concessions thus begins to make perfect sense if one views them as being an extension of the PHILCAG negotiations.[53]

President Johnson's largess to President Marcos even went further than all the loans, grants, and concessions mentioned in the communique. Just in case these did not serve as enough incentive for Marcos to send PHILCAG to Vietnam, President Johnson also surreptitiously presented Marcos with an additional $45 million cash grant to take back with him to the Philippines.[54] As had the South Koreans before them, the Filipinos discovered that Lyndon Johnson could be exceedingly generous in paying for what he wanted, and he very much wanted PHILCAG sent to Vietnam.

Despite the large amount of financial aid the United States sent to the Philippines as payment for the PHILCAG deployment, the official record still shows the Philippine government as paying almost all of PHILCAG's expenses in Vietnam. This state of affairs did not, however, occur by happenstance. Because of the Johnson Administration's need to maintain the public image of PHILCAG's being solely a Philippine financed contribution to the More Flags program, the State Department worked diligently to hide almost all American aid arrangements with the Philippines. Washington made sure that the American people would not find out that U.S. funds were being funneled into the Philippine budget to cover PHILCAG's expenses. As a result of these covert arrangements, the public record only shows the U.S. providing a very small amount of the expenses PHILCAG incurred while serving in South Vietnam other than these supplies furnished to all allied troops while they were actually in South Vietnam (such things as transportation, building supplies, arms and ammunition, medical supplies, etc.).

The covert financing of PHILCAG, however, became a two-edged sword for both the Marcos and Johnson administrations. While their obfuscation of the American funding did succeed in maintaining the political facade desired, it also resulted in making the Philippine legislature the middle-man in the funding process. If the image of a Philippines-financed PHILCAG were to be maintained, all funding for the unit would have to come through the Philippine Treasury which in turn relied on authorization votes from the Philippine Congress. The continued presence of PHILCAG in Vietnam, since the original authorization bill of 3 June 1966 only provided for the official support of PHILCAG in one year increments, thus became dependent on the passage of year-by-year authorization bills. The need of the U.S. and Philippine governments to hide PHILCAG's funding thereby afforded Marcos' political opposition a yearly opportunity to pursue their goal of ending, or at least limiting, Philippine involvement in South Vietnam.

In early 1967, with opposition to PHILCAG growing even from within his own party, Marcos realized that he had no guarantees on getting a 1967-1968 funding authorization through Congress. Consequently, as the original 1966 funding began to run out in July 1967, Marcos elected not to even approach the Philippine legislature for additional monies to keep PHILCAG deployed for another year. Marcos instead chose to utilize the fungible power granted him by Philippine law to continue funding the PHILCAG unit's continued service in Vietnam.*⁵⁵ An immediate problem developed, however, with this more personal method of financing — the monies Marcos so generated were not sufficient to fund the entire 2,000-man PHILCAG contingent. Marcos was forced, if the funds were to fit the manpower, to reduce PHILCAG personnel in Vietnam. As a direct result of Marcos' new funding methods, then, PHILCAG personnel numbers in Vietnam began falling, from a high of 2,050 in 1966 and 1967 to approximately 1,500 in 1968.

At about the same moment that Marcos undertook his personal financing of PHILCAG, in July 1967, the United States and the Philippines began discussions over a somewhat related issue. By this time, the United States had accepted the fact, however reluctantly, that the Philippines would send no combat units to Vietnam. It appeared, on the surface at least, that PHILCAG, or a unit similar to it, amounted to the maximum aid the United States could expect from the Philippines. However, there remained yet one other slight possibility for the United States to obtain a further Philippine military commitment for Vietnam. Since prior to World War II, it had been possible for Filipino civilians to enlist in the various military branches. Harking back to this long standing military tradition, Marcos Administration officials advanced the idea for a plan that would have 2,000 or more Filipino citizens enlist in the U.S. Army. Then, after training, these enlistees would serve as an all–Filipino combat unit in Vietnam. By the use of such a stratagem, the Marcos government felt that both Philippine and U.S. goals

---

This law permitted Marcos to shift monies among and between the various executive department budgets. Thus, by taking some funds from each department, Marcos could keep Philcag funded.

could be achieved: The United States would get another combat unit sent to South Vietnam and the Philippines would receive the substantial economic benefits accruing from their citizens' military service. Nevertheless, despite the idea's advantages to both countries' governments, the suggestion never got past the discussion stage. Policy makers in the United States simply felt the American press and public would not stand for the United States supporting a so patently obvious mercenary unit.[56]

Although President Marcos did manage to find the funds to keep PHILCAG in South Vietnam after 1967, his method of paying their way, and the concomitant reduction of the unit's personnel levels there, reflect one of the most contradictory anomalies of the Philippine commitment to the Vietnam War. Over a two year period between 1964 and 1966, two separate Philippine governments had succeeded in negotiating a very lucrative financial deal for deploying their troops to South Vietnam. This arrangement not only guaranteed an income bonanza for the individual Filipino soldier serving in Vietnam — because of the pay and benefits (see Table 10), there would be five volunteers vying for every open position in PHILCAG[57] — but also greatly benefited the entire Filipino economy and society. Further, and on a more personal level, the U.S. aid greatly assisted Marcos in strengthening his own power base within the Philippines. Yet, after working diligently to get these troops deployed to Vietnam in the first place, Marcos then refused to even chance an approach to the Philippine Congress for further support in keeping PHILCAG there. A further contradictory element lay in the fact that not only did Marcos allow the troop levels to fall, but he actively resisted all American entreaties to maintain or increase Filipino troop levels in South Vietnam. He resisted even though he knew that Lyndon Johnson would willingly pay handsome sums for such increases.[58] In one last incongruity, on 14 November 1969, with little advance notice, Marcos ordered the PHILCAG detachment completely withdrawn from Vietnam, leaving only the PHILCON medical units to show the Philippine flag inside Vietnam.[59] By the end of December 1969, despite all Washington could do to prevent it, the PHILCAG detachment had returned to the Philippines.

When viewed in retrospect, several contributing factors appear to have played a role in Marcos' first deciding to limit the size of PHILCAG in Vietnam, then to withdraw it completely. As one

Table 10

Total PHILCAG Allowances (in dollar equivalents)

(Q&A = quarters and allowances; O.A. = overseas allowance)

	Phil. Base Pay	Phil. Q&A	U.S. Per Diem	U.S. O.A.	Phil. Total	U.S. Total
Brig. Gen.	275	30	180	30	305	210
Col.	210	25	165	30	235	195
Lt. Col.	175	20	150	30	195	180
Major	138	15	135	30	153	165
Captain	112	13	120	30	125	150
1st Lt.	92	10	105	30	102	135
2nd Lt.	80	10	90	30	90	120
M/Sgt.	44	9	45	30	53	76
Sgt. 1st	44	9	15	30	53	45
Cpl.	37	6	6	30	43	36
PFC/Pvt.	33	6	3	30	43	33

Source: U.S. Congress. Senate. Committee on Foreign Relations. *The Republic of the Philippines: Hearings Before the Subcommittee on United States Security Agreements and Commitments Abroad,* Part 1, 91st Cong., 1st sess., 1969: 265.

---

scholar suggests, Marcos could have simply come to the conclusion that Vietnam was no longer the "key to peace or security in Southeast Asia,"[60] and acted to extricate the Philippines from a now questionable situation. Or, as yet another scholar notes, since the U.S. aid already sent to the Philippines constituted a "pay off"[61] for Marcos' support of the American position in South Vietnam, and feeling he had fulfilled his end of the bargain, Marcos felt free to withdraw PHILCAG when and if he saw fit. The most likely reason for Marcos' decision to withdraw PHILCAG from Vietnam, however, was that PHILCAG became an "embarrassment"[62] to him. Support for this contention is found when one examines the evidence brought to light by a series of U.S. Senate subcommittee hearings conducted between 30 September and 3 October 1969. It was these hearings, called to investigate the financial dealings underlying the Philippines

More Flags contribution, that most probably served to push Marcos into withdrawing PHILCAG from Vietnam:

> When the Symington hearings ... made public the extent of American financing, a tremendous crisis of confidence, and a self-perceived loss of face ... developed in the Philippines. Consequently, President Marcos withdrew the rest of PHILCAG more suddenly than had been anticipated.[63]

It was not, however, the general Filipino population that experienced a "loss of face," it was Ferdinand Marcos himself. In his desire not to be considered a lackey of the United States, Marcos, from the moment he became president, had insisted that all details of the Filipino-American funding negotiations for PHILCAG be hidden from the Philippine public:

> Marcos takes the position that he does not RPT not want the terms of our delivery with him to be revealed. ... As usual, we have the ambivalent Phil attitude of not wanting to appear to be bought, but at the same time wanting something that they can show their people.[64]

Because of the Senate hearings, most of the PHILCAG negotiations Marcos wanted kept secret became public knowledge, and he now had to move quickly to minimize their damage. On 14 November 1969, just days after the Senate published the hearing results, Marcos notified the U.S. Embassy in Manila that PHILCAG would soon be withdrawn, and, by 15 December, PHILCAG was gone from Vietnam.[65]

President Marcos was not alone, however, in wanting a shroud of secrecy draped over the details of the Philippines' More Flags contribution. The Johnson Administration also wanted very much to hide their actions in the matter from the American people. In fact, the Americans began hiding their involvement in the funding of a Philippine military commitment to South Vietnam in 1965, even before Marcos was elected president:

> It is highly desirable that the U.S. financial support not be apparent, to avoid lending credence to possible accusations that IMAF

personnel are U.S. 'mercenaries.' This will not be a problem with the MAP input, which will come largely as additions to regular programs, but to effectively conceal the U.S. payment of other items of cost the use of unvouchered funds is considered necessary. It is, therefore, proposed that funds be provided as a cash grant to be used in two ways—to pay special overseas allowances and support costs of the contingents in Vietnam and to provide budget support to the Government of the Philippines to enable it to assume the pay and allowances of the replacement troops.[66]

Still, even this early action was not the first time that the State Department conspired to prevent both the American and Philippine citizenry from learning that U.S. tax dollars were buying Filipino soldiers to serve as mercenaries in Vietnam. From at least as early as December 1964, at the very beginnings of the Macapagal negotiations, Washington tried to hide the facts behind their funding of the Philippine aid to South Vietnam: "In order that the Phils can state that they are providing the force and funds for the operation, the use of 'indirect funding' should be considered."[67] Later State Department determinations would result in the most frequent "indirect funding" techniques of "the use of PL-480 rice to generate local currency"[68] for Philippine government use, and the disbursement of "unvouchered funds"[69] from AID.

Whatever may or may not have been his reasons for doing so, the fact remains that Ferdinand Marcos did withdraw the PHILCAG detachment from South Vietnam in December 1969. And in so doing, he ended the Philippines' contribution of mercenary troops to the United States' war effort. There has been some after-the-fact argument that PHILCAG did not constitute a true mercenary force because the Filipino engineers and troops served only in a civic action capacity and did not actively participate in ground combat operations. This is, however, a specious argument. The PHILCAG funding negotiations plainly show that the Philippine government sent a military unit to South Vietnam only after forcing the United States into making substantial and exorbitant financial concessions to both the Filipino soldiers and to their government. While it is true that the United States did agree to these concessions, and thus must accept its share of the responsibility, this does not change what happened. The fact remains that two separate Filippino governments made economic gain the primary reason for sending their troops to South Vietnam.

There is even further evidence available that supports the contention that PHILCAG was indeed a mercenary force. Officials from both countries are on record as admitting that the American funding of PHILCAG created a mercenary relationship between the United States and the Philippines.[70] The Philippines' PHILCAG detachment thus became the second of three allied military forces that Lyndon Johnson hired to serve as America's mercenaries in the Vietnam War.

Chapter 5

The Thai Troop Commitment

Of the five free world nations that sent combat troops to South Vietnam under the auspices of L.B.J.'s More Flags program, only the Kingdom of Thailand physically occupies the Southeast Asian landmass with the countries of the former French Indochina. It can thus be argued that Thailand, of all the free world troop contributing nations, had sound political reasons for becoming militarily involved in the Vietnamese conflict. The validity of this argument, however, rests on a disputed cold war maxim. It can be supported only if one accepts the domino theory and its basic tenet that all of Southeast Asia would likely fall to the communists if South Vietnam fell. For those holding such beliefs then, because of Thailand's singular geographic circumstances, its commitment of combat troops to assist the South Vietnamese was regarded as a justified response to legitimate Thai national interests. An investigation of the documentary record of the motives behind Thailand's sending combat units to Vietnam does not, however, support such an explanation. The Thai military contingent deployed to South Vietnam, as were the Korean and Filipino commitments that preceded it, was a mercenary force bought and paid for by the United States.

Since Thailand's national borders were less than 90 miles from either North or South Vietnam, separated only by the former French colonies of Cambodia and Laos, it is not surprising that geographic proximity would play a significant role in determining Thai military and diplomatic policies during the years of the Vietnam War.

Nevertheless, during the 1960s and early 1970s, neither the Thai government's foreign policy positions, nor the military preparedness measures they took in response to the potential threat presented by the warring nations of Southeast Asia, reflected only Thai national interests. Instead, the "patron-client relationship"[1] which had recently developed between Thailand and the United States served as the dominant determinant of Thailand's diplomatic and military relations with Laos, Cambodia, and North and South Vietnam. During the period in which this relationship existed, essentially from the early 1960s to the mid–1970s, Washington effectively controlled Thailand's affairs with the nations of Southeast Asia, not Bangkok. And it was these decisions which ultimately dragged an unwilling Thai government into America's land war in Vietnam.

The base factors which helped determine the course of Thai government decisions toward the nations of the former colony of French Indochina, did not, however, result only from the events of the 1960s and 1970s. In fact, many, if not most, of the military and political decisions made by Thai government leaders during the Vietnam War years were foreordained by an event that occurred decades earlier—the 1932 military coup overthrowing Thailand's hereditary monarchy. As a direct result of this coup, the Thai governmental system experienced two major changes, and it was these two changes that established the foundation for determining Thailand's political policies and practices in the 1960s.

The first fundamental change the coup made in Thailand's form of government was in its structure and administration. While the leaders of the 1932 coup ostensibly sought to replace the absolute monarchy with a more democratic constitutional monarchy, this was only a facade. The realities of Thai national governance have been an almost unbroken series of governments ruled by military dictate since 1932. In fact, there is only one exception to military leadership in Thailand, the civilian rule between 1945 and 1947, and that came about only because of the military's being discredited for allying Thailand with Japan during World War II. True democratic government in Thailand was shortlived, however, as a coup in 1947 reestablished military rule in Bangkok.

The 1932 coup also succeeded in initiating a basic change in the traditional Thai foreign policy posture. For over a century, in an attempt to keep Thailand from being drawn into the disputes between the British, French, and Dutch colonial empires, the Thai monarchy had worked assiduously to maintain a strict neutrality in the region. Thailand's neutral tradition died, however, with the advent of the fervently anticommunist ideologies of the post–1932 military governments. Bangkok governments now took sides.

As a result of Thailand's newly established governmental organization and political doctrine, Thai governmental leaders after 1932 found themselves facing new diplomatic pressures they had little experience dealing with. Of particular concern to these military men, after they resumed power in 1948, was the seemingly unchecked growth of communist states in the Far East after World War II. Especially disturbing, because of their physical proximity to Thailand, were the 1949 and 1954 communist victories in China and Indochina. Thailand's anxiety toward the developing political realities of Southeast Asia then took another turn for the worse when both Great Britain and France began their slow withdrawal from the Far East during the 1950s. A coupling of the political changes wrought by the 1932 coup with the changing world order of the 1950s now produced a situation in which the Thai government found itself being drawn inexorably into an alliance with the United States, "the only great power with both the strength and the will to assist them."[2]

Thailand's pursuit of an extended diplomatic relationship with the United States during the 1950s came as a new experience for both countries. Because of Thailand's historical reliance on maintaining a neutralist position in the Far East, Washington had, until 1950, almost no diplomatic agreements with Bangkok and only a few commercial ties. (Understandably, even these commercial arrangements became void during the World War II period when Thailand was an ally of Japan.) As a direct result of its growing apprehension over the postwar growth of communism in the region, however, Thailand signed the first of what would eventually be many military aid agreements with the United States in October 1950. The embryonic political and military ties between the two countries received further strengthening when, in September 1954, Thailand joined with the United States and five other nations in the founding of the Southeast Asia Treaty Organization (SEATO).[3] It was not long, however, before Thai government officials began to

feel that even these measures were insufficient to guarantee
Thailand's national sovereignty. As communist power and in-
fluence continued to grow throughout the region, Thailand's
leaders felt it necessary to forge even closer military and political
alliances with the United States.

While the Thai government, during the late 1950s, watched a
growing communist base in Sukarno's Indonesia with apprehension, it was the spreading communist insurgency in South Vietnam
and Laos during the early 1960s that served to push Thailand into
seeking a closer military and political relationship with the United
States. Although a small communist movement had existed in
Thailand since the 1930s, communist inspired incidents within
Thai national borders still remained small and infrequent and thus
did not seriously alarm the Thai government. When the war then
raging in South Vietnam and Laos began to spill over into its own
northeastern states, however, Thai officials began to grow alarmed.
As the incidents attributable to communist actvities increased in
both numbers and level of violence, Thailand felt it necessary to
seek a more concrete demonstration of support and protection from
the United States.

For its part, the Kennedy Administration was delighted to accede to Bangkok's desires for closer military and political alliances
with Washington. Viewing Thailand's national security needs at the
time as being coincident with American foreign policy needs for
Southeast Asia, the United States began the process of irrevocably
linking the Thai government to the American foreign policy positions for the region. In the Rusk-Thanat Treaty of 1962, the first
Kennedy Administration move to achieve this end, the United
States furnished the Thai government with a guarantee afforded few
other American allies, a *unilateral* assurance that America would
come to Thailand's defense in case of invasion.[4] Then, following
almost immediately its negotiations for the Rusk-Thanat Treaty,
the United States demonstrated its support of the Thai government
in a more tangible way by sending a battalion of United States
Marines to assist the Thais in patrolling their northern borders. In
one final move to tie Thailand to American interests in the region,
the Kennedy Administration increased by $50 million the amount
of military aid sent to Thailand.[5]

Although these various actions directly benefited the Thai

government by furnishing Thailand with both the national security protections it desired and the means to improve its military capabilities, the United States also gained substantial benefits from the arrangements. With its new agreements with Bangkok, Washington now firmly established a United States presence in a Southeast Asian nation other than South Vietnam, and it did not take the Kennedy Administration long to begin taking advantage of this fact. The Americans had insisted, as a secret condition to the $50 million in additional aid, that part of this largess would go to finance a joint Thai-U.S. covert military operation in Laos.[6] In their acceptance of the $50 million, and the conditions that came with it, Thailand thus became in mid–1963 when the covert operations began, directly enmeshed in America's war in Vietnam. When Lyndon Johnson became president in November 1963, he found that the Kennedy Administration had already begun the groundwork for converting Thailand into another of America's Southeast Asian client states.

If only the public record is examined then, a valid argument can be made that the Thai government was manipulating the United States during the 1962 and 1963 period:

> the Thai were pursuing foreign policy goals of their own that were not necessarily congruent in every detail with those of the United States. They manipulated their relationship with the United States to pursue their own goals, which in the first place were to establish or maintain friendly, non–Communist, anti–Vietnamese governments in Laos and Cambodia.[7]

Yet, while there unquestionably existed a certain degree of Thai manipulation, the developing relationship between the two nations still furnished the United States with the opportunity to achieve several distinctly American objectives. And it was these objectives which, in time, would prove incalculably important to furthering America's plans for the future of the Southeast Asian region.

The $50 million increase in American financial aid sent to Thailand in 1963 succeeded in achieving the most immediate U.S. objective Washington sought from its increased diplomatic ties with Thailand. American military experts knew the Thais wanted this aid to finance a strengthening of their internal military defense capabilities. In giving the Thais this money, the United States not only ingratiated itself with the Thai military since this would increase Thailand's own national security posture, but the aid's use in this manner would also succeed in the "creation of a 'war infrastructure' in Thailand."[8] Such developments inside Thailand were felt necessary because, even in the Kennedy Administration, the feeling in Washington was that the conflict then being waged in South Vietnam could easily spill over into Thailand. American military planners thus felt, if such an event transpired, that Thailand's basic military infrastructure needed expanding and modernizing so it would be capable of accepting possible future American military missions.

As future events proved, the $50 million in aid also constituted the beginning of the achievement of another American objective which most, if not all, U.S. policymakers at the time probably never imagined. As it turned out, the $50 million in aid actually comprised only a small part of a United States assistance program to Thailand which would exceed $1.5 billion by 1971. Although a moderate amount of U.S. aid was sent to Thailand between 1951 and 1962, the vast majority of the monies involved came during the Johnson and Nixon administrations. It was during these two administrations that Thailand would receive: $650 million in direct economic development aid, $935 million in military assistance, $205 million to construct several military air bases, and $760 million more to run those bases. Further, it is also estimated that American servicemen, either serving in Thailand or visiting there on so-called rest and relaxation (R&R) leaves from the Vietnam War, added another $850 million to the Thai economy between 1962 and 1972.[9] The Thai national economy thus received approximately a $3 billion boost from the American taxpayer. American largess in such large amounts could not help but achieve the Washington goal of obligating the ruling Thai military government to a wholehearted support of U.S. Southeast Asian interests.

When an in-depth examination is made into every aspect of the record, a determination of who was manipulating whom becomes difficult to assert. While Thailand may well have been manipulating the United States in 1962 and 1963, after that date, the roles were reversed. Through the high level of American economic assitance over the succeeding years, Washington assured itself that, after 1964, it would do the manipulating.

Washington's continuing efforts to increase and enhance America's military presence in Thailand partially explains why the State Department did not seek a large More Flags commitment from Thailand when that program began in 1964. Other than making a request for a few "C-47 pilots to fly with [the] Vietnamese Air Force,"[10] which would allow Thailand to show its flag in Vietnam, Washington did not immediately press the Thai military government for a further aid commitment to South Vietnam. When the Thai government quickly fulfilled this request by deploying a small 16-man air force contingent to South Vietnam on 29 September 1964,*[11] the State Department contented itself in making only small requests from the Thais through the end of 1965.†[12] Washington evidently felt that Thailand, by permitting the United States to build military bases on Thai soil and through its covert commitment of several hundred "badly-needed personnel . . . to strengthen the non-communist forces in Laos,"[13] was sufficiently demonstrating its support of American policy positions in Southeast Asia.

Even President Johnson's December 1964 decision to begin a more active pursuit of free world military aid for Vietnam[14] did not change the State Department's More Flags arrangement with Thailand. In fact, President Johnson received pointed advice not to include Thailand in any military aid request he might make from America's other allies: "Since their covert contribution (over 300 fighting men) to our efforts in Laos is of great significance, we have hesitated to press the Thai very hard for more help in Viet-Nam."[15] Even when the United States began a frantic search for allied troop commitments to South Vietnam after the March 6, 1965, deployment of U.S. combat troops to Vietnam, no requests were made of Thailand. State Department officials simply felt that Thailand was doing all it could at that time: "We have not requested additional Thai assistance for Viet-Nam because of heavy Thai commitments to other operations in Southeast Asia."[16]

---

*See Appendix B for year-to-year totals of Thai military personnel in Vietnam, and Appendix C for a chronological listing of Thai troop commitments there.

†In the twelve months after the Thai Air Force detachment arrived in Vietnam, Thailand's aid commitment grew to include a small naval detachment, jet training for South Vietnamese pilots inside Thailand, and a small amount of dry goods.

As is the case for all diplomatic negotiations, officials from both Washington and Bangkok spent much of their time during the early 1961–1963 negotiations simply learning about each other's needs and expectations. Although the negotiations agenda centered on how they could best meet the threat of communist subversion in Southeast Asia, this consideration alone was not the negotiators' only concerns. Each nation's representatives had to also discern their counterparts' particular interests and expectations. In these early meetings then, it soon became evident to the Americans that the driving force behind Thailand's desire to increase its ties with the United States was their perceived vulnerability to a mainland Chinese–directed communist threat. Conversely, the Thai negotiators undoubtedly determined early that a key underlying focus of the State Department negotiators was their desire not to make any move that might disrupt or destroy the perceived political fragility of Thailand's military-dominated government.

Even during the early talks between Kennedy Administration officials and the Thais, the relative order of importance Thai officials attached to the items on their agenda perplexed the American diplomats. To the Americans, it only made sense that the escalating war in Vietnam and Laos should be the source of most concern to the Thai government. The Thai government's position was, however, that while they did consider the events occurring along their borders a problem, these events did not top the list. To the Thais, even though communist-led guerrilla raids on Thailand's northeastern provinces were a constant occurrence,[17] they did not look on these activities as presenting a "major internal threat"[18] to Thailand's national security. To the Thai government officials the major threat to their sovereignty came from another source. Feeling "confident that they [could] contain any threats from Indochina alone," the Thai government felt that a direct confrontation with Communist China presented the only real danger.[19] Thai national security concerns then, as reflected in their negotiations with the United States throughout the 1960s, focused on questions of how Thailand could best defend itself against Red China. To these Thai government officials, because of their abiding fear of a direct confrontation with the Communist Chinese, it became absolutely mandatory for Thailand to maintain a close military and political alliance with the United States, no matter the cost.

The U.S. State Department, for their part in the negotiations, found themselves constantly forced to temper their actions so as not to disturb the tenuous control the Thai military leadership maintained on the Thai central government. After the 1932 coup established military-dominated governments as the norm for Thai governance, Thailand had suffered through a long period in which stable, long-lasting governments were the exception.* The established norm of Thai political life became an almost continual round of coups, countercoups, and threatened coups. As a result, while the government in Bangkok during the 1960s had been able to maintain itself in power longer than most of its predecessors—it had controlled the government since the 1958 Coup of General Sarit Thanarat—its hold on political power remained very tentative throughout the period of the Vietnam War. This Thai state of affairs therefore forced American diplomats into a constant consideration of what effect their actions, activities, or programs might have on the current government's tenure in political power.

As much as they could, then, American diplomats in Bangkok used the uneasy stability of the Thai government to further U.S. interests in the country and the region. The base fact that the Thai government was not democratic, however, never prejudiced the State Department's dealings with the Thai leadership. American officials would not allow the knowledge that U.S. economic and military aid was being used by the Thai government leaders "to maintain and consolidate their military control of Thailand"[20] to interfere with American designs for the region. Still, even though this use of American aid was perfectly acceptable to both Kennedy and Johnson administration policymakers, Thai government exigencies necessitated a very careful crafting of the physical contents of any U.S. aid to Thailand. Such aid had to serve, in effect, two sometimes dichotomous purposes: it first and foremost had to furnish tangible American support for the upper-echelon military leaders who controlled the government, while at the same time furnishing support

---

* *Through much of the 1960s, both Thailand's Prime Minister, Thanom Kittikachorn, and Deputy Prime Minister, Praphat Charusathien, were former generals in the Thai military. Between the two, they held the governmental posts of Supreme Commander of the Army, Minister of Defense, Commander-in-Chief of the Army, and Minister of the Interior.*

for the second-echelon of military officers, the traditional breeding ground for Thai governmental coups. This second requirement for American aid was deemed an absolute necessity for, as American diplomats feared, if U.S. aid did not adequately placate this lower level of the Thai military, these officers might "very well resume their normal concentration on how to overthrow the present regime."*21 It is thus understandable that, with almost all Thai-American relations being focused on bolstering the various levels of Thailand's military establishment, it was military aid, not domestic aid, which became the dominant type of American aid sent to Thailand during this period.22

Various State Department officials, including Secretary of State Dean Rusk, experienced a brief period of excitement in July 1965 when they learned of a comment made by Thai Prime Minister Thanom to the U.S. Ambassador to Thailand, Graham A. Martin. The comment, that Thanom was ready to "back President [Johnson] to [the] limit on any personal request the President might make directly to him,"23 suggested to Secretary Rusk that it might be possible for the More Flags program to get a commitment of combat troops from Thailand. State Department expectations were short-lived, however, as it didn't take long for the realities of Thai domestic politics to quickly reassert themselves.

When apprised of Secretary Rusk's contemplated actions, Ambassador Martin moved quickly to temper the excitement by cabling a strong warning to Washington not to submit a formal request for Thai combat troops.24 Martin pointed out in this message that the comment under discussion was only a Thanom intimation that, if President Johnson wanted them, Thailand might send its troops into the Mekong River corridor of Cambodia and Laos. Ambassador Martin wanted to make sure that Rusk would not continue in his belief that Thanom's comment meant that he was willing to send Thai troops to South Vietnam. As further support for his advice against a U.S. request for troops, Martin also used his cautionary message to remind Rusk of the very tenuous nature of the Thai government. In truly diplomatic terms, Martin pointed out to Rusk

*The military domination of the Thai government existed not only at the top levels of the government. Former military personnel also dominated the Thai Senate, the membership of which consisted of 105 former military officers, 12 former police officers, and only 47 civilian leaders.

that, since the lower echelon Thai military leaders did not support committing Thai troops to South Vietnam, if the United States were to formally make such a request, and Thanom were to comply, it "might very well bring down this regime."[25] To Ambassador Martin, although he expressed sympathy for the problems Secretary Rusk was experiencing in implementing the More Flags program ("I fully appreciate Washington's desire from a political point of view to secure as great a foreign representation as possible in South Vietnam"[26]), he still made it perfectly clear that a formal request for Thai combat troops was ill advised.

In addition to the possible effects a U.S. request for Thai troops might have on the stability of the Thai government, Martin also perceived another very valid reason for Secretary Rusk not to pursue the matter further. Such an American troop request at this time would potentially endanger other, even more militarily critical, Thai-U.S. negotiations then in their earliest stages. These arguments proved convincing, as Secretary Rusk ultimately chose not to take this opportunity to submit a request for a Thai commitment of combat troops. To Rusk, and Secretary of Defense McNamara, the American-Thai negotiations mentioned by Ambassador Martin, involving receiving permission to base American B-52s in Thailand, constituted a more important issue at that particular moment: "The push for a great increase in the Thai troop commitment . . . [had to wait] until after the Americans had gained the right to base B-52s in Thailand."[27]

With Thai and American negotiators engaged in working out the details of basing B-52s at Thai airfields, discussions about increasing Thailand's troop commitments to South Vietnam all but ceased. While Thai military personnel serving in South Vietnam did gradually increase slightly in 1965 and 1966, these additions either constituted only incremental increases in the Thai military missions already there, or were troop increases already promised but not yet deployed. Only when the B-52 negotiations began to show signs of imminent resolution, sometime late in 1966, did government officials from the two nations begin serious discussions on the possibility of Thailand's introducing a ground combat unit into Vietnam.[28]

Until 1966, geographical considerations alone served as the rationale for the Thai government's becoming militarily involved in

America's war in Indochina. Throughout this early period, both the
United States and Thai governments felt that any direct Thai involvement in the conflict should be limited to actions inside the territories of countries contiguous to Thailand, in Cambodia and Laos.
Neither the U.S. nor Thai government thought that a Thai military
role in South Vietnam was either necessary or even particularly
desirable. Thai government officials had, in fact, made it clear to
the United States as early as August 1964, that while they were willing to send their soldiers into Laos, they would not even consider
sending troops to Vietnam.[29] It would appear then, if the official
Thai government position on not sending troops to Vietnam is
coupled with the known antipathy of the Thai junior officer corps
to such a move, that there existed little possibility of the United
States' obtaining a More Flags troop commitment from Thailand.
Yet, such was not the case. In late 1966, United States and Thai
negotiators began discussions on what it would take for the Johnson
Administration to convince the Thai government to send a Thai
combat unit to Vietnam.

There is no currently available documentation that offers an explanation of why the Thai government chose to abandon its long-
standing position on sending combat troops to Vietnam. The record
simply states that, despite his "not really wish[ing] to send troops
to Vietnam,"[30] Thai Prime Minister Thanom announced to the
world through a press conference held on 6 January 1967, that
Thailand would dispatch a "ground force to take an active part in
the fighting in South Vietnam."[31] Washington had received its first
notification that Thailand had agreed to send "a reinforced Thai
Battalion to fight in Viet-Nam" three days earlier, on 3 January
1967.

Since U.S. and Thai negotiators had already begun formal discussions on deploying a Thai combat force to Vietnam in 1966, Thanom's January 1967 announcement did not come as a surprise to U.S.
government insiders. Still, even while some U.S. officials knew ahead
of time that Thanom was leaning toward a deployment of Thai
troops, they also knew that Thanom had one major problem to overcome before he could publicly announce any troop deployment to
South Vietnam. Thanom may have agreed to deploy these troops,
but this did not by itself solve the problem of Thai junior officer
corps opposition. Events of 30 December 1966, however, succeeded

in significantly reducing Thanom's worries that this opposition would occur, or at least led him to believe that if opposition did arise, it would be minimal. On this date, four Bangkok newspapers simultaneously published stories on the possibility of Thailand's deploying an all-volunteer combat force to South Vietnam. The immediate public response to these articles was almost universal support for the idea, and Prime Minister Thanom had the support he needed to overcome any junior officer objections. If there were any grumblings in the ranks after Thanom's 6 January commitment of Thai troops, they quickly dissipated in the flood of public support that followed Thanom's announcement. The idea of sending Thai soldiers to Vietnam became so popular that, by the end of January 1967, more than 5,000 men in Bangkok alone volunteered to serve in any unit deployed there.[32]

With the removal of all impediments to a Thai commitment of combat troops, Thai-U.S. negotiators could now shift the focus of their discussions to a determination of what would be the exact composition of the now firmly committed Thai contribution.* In all probability, Thanom most likely expected that his government would only send a 1,000-man reinforced battalion to Vietnam, since that was the figure he quoted in his 6 January announcement. By the time the discussions began, however, between Thai military leaders and the U.S. representatives from the Military Assistance Command, Vietnam (MACV), the 1,000-man figure was only a starting point. Ultimately, the two nations' negotiators determined that the first Thai combat unit committed to South Vietnam would be a regimental size unit of between 2,000 and 3,000 men.

Supposedly, because of its all-volunteer composition, the deployment of this first Thai combat detachment to Vietnam (which became known as the Queen's Cobras) had to be delayed until the regiment completed an extensive training period. At least this provided the official excuse for why the unit did not begin arriving in Vietnam until late September 1967, almost eight months after its being formally organized as the Royal Thai Army Volunteer Regiment (RTAVR).[33] This explanation for the deployment delay is

---

* *Most of the detailed information on these negotiations, particularly on the financial arrangements for this initial Thai deployment, is still not declassified. What information that is available is incorporated into the material on the negotiations for the later Thai troop commitments.*

not supported by the evidence, however, since 97 percent of the Queen's Cobras personnel were not untrained volunteers but regular Thai Army soldiers.[34] While the regiment did require some specialized training, organizational, logistical, and supply problems were the main reasons for the unit's delay in arriving in Vietnam.

With the Thai government finally agreeing to a commitment of combat troops to South Vietnam, the floodgates for further U.S. troop requests were opened. Johnson Administration officials now felt that no obstacle remained to hamper their pursuit of even more Thai troops for Vietnam, and they moved quickly to take advantage of their freedom of action. The first contingents of the Queen's Cobras had not even begun arriving in South Vietnam when the United States, in the form of a special presidential mission headed by Clark Clifford and Maxwell Taylor, began pressing the Thais for an even larger military commitment.

Officially, the purpose of the Clifford-Taylor 22 July to 5 August 1967 mission was to apprise the leaders of the allied troop-contributing nations of current and future U.S. actions in South Vietnam.* The two presidential envoys had other, furtive, presidential instructions, however. President Johnson also charged Clifford and Taylor with the responsibility of soliciting each allied leader to increase the numbers of their combat troops committed to Vietnam.

Despite the Thai agreement to commit the Queen's Cobras to Vietnam, Ambassador Martin still felt that their actions were fraught with danger, both for Thailand and for the United States. Thus, when Clifford and Taylor arrived in Thailand, Ambassador Martin hoped to convince them of the inadvisability of making a further military request of the Thais. In an embassy briefing arranged to prepare Clifford and Taylor for their discussions with Prime Minister Thanom, Ambassador Martin reiterated his earlier advice to Secretary of State Rusk—that Thailand's major contribution to the Vietnamese War effort lay in continuing its covert activities in Laos, not by sending more troops to South Vietnam. Ambassador

---

*The mission only visited four of the five troop-contributing nations. In an affront to President Johnson, Philippine President Marcos pointedly denied permission for the mission to visit the Philippines.

Martin's advice was not, however, what Clark Clifford wanted to hear:

> Clifford made it briefly and pithily clear that he wanted to hear no more such talk. What the President wanted was more troops in South Vietnam. Because the President had done everything to support Thailand, the President now expected Thailand to support him. The need was in South Vietnam and that was where the President wanted Thai forces.[35]

President Johnson wanted more troops from Thailand, and more troops from Thailand were what he was going to get.

Official negotiations for the deployment of a much larger Thai troop contribution to South Vietnam began soon after the Clifford-Taylor mission left Bangkok, with "the Thai digging in their heels in order to get everything possible."[36] The forceful demands made by the Thai negotiators did not, however, come as a surprise to the Americans. American diplomats knew that the Thai government recognized the base realities behind the U.S. requests for more troops: that the United States needed additional Thai troops for political reasons, and not to meet any perceived needs of the Vietnamese government. Nevertheless, even though the American negotiators knew the Thais recognized the real reasons for the U.S. requests, they also knew that Thailand had been made so obligated to U.S. interests by 1967 — militarily, economically, and politically — that it was no longer possible for them to refuse outright the U.S. demand for more Thai troops.

Thai diplomats, then, entered the 1967 negotiations holding few illusions that Saigon really needed their troops. Although Thailand had already committed more than 2,000 men to fight in South Vietnam, Thai diplomats knew full well that these young men had been sent to fight and die in an American war for American needs. Still, by 1967, these Thai officials also knew that they had few options available but to comply with American demands. While Thai Foreign Minister Thanat Khoman would later lament his country's acquiescence, he still recognized there was not much more he or his country could do at the time:

> The situation worsened when the United States, feeling lonely in Viet-Nam, began to induce other countries ... to get into the

quagmire that she was, to a certain extent, responsible for creating.
. . . Thailand, *at the U.S. insistence* [emphasis added], had to send
a full division of 12,000 men to join the American GI's.[37]

Although State Department officials considered it an all but
foregone conclusion in 1967 that Thailand would send more troops
to Vietnam, questions on how much the United States would have
to pay for these troops still remained undecided. And if Thai
government officials felt that the Americans were forcing them into
backing a U.S. policy position that might not be in Thailand's own
best interests, at least these negotiators knew Thailand could reap
economic rewards for their troops' services. Knowing of the liberal
concessions the State Department had already made to the Koreans
and the Filipinos for their troop commitments,[38] Thai officials
entered the negotiations with the Americans prepared to insist on
as many U.S. concessions as possible.

The U.S.-Thai negotiations differed on one major point,
however, from the U.S. negotiations with the other two troop contributing nations. While the South Korean and Philippine governments received extensive amounts of aid for the civilian sectors of
their economies, American aid designed to meet Thai civilian purposes never became a point of discussion in the U.S.-Thai negotiations. The Thai negotiators, comprised predominately of military
men, and representing a government that was both dominated and
supported by the Thai military, worked to guarantee that only the
Thai military would reap the benefits of the Thai troop commitment to Vietnam.

The United States entered the negotiations with Thailand with
the same expectations they had carried into their previous negotiations with South Korea and the Philippines, that Thailand should
be able to send their troops to Vietnam at no extra cost to their
budget. The Thais, however, as had the Koreans and Filipinos
before them, knowing they could receive much more, rejected this
approach. After the State Department opened the negotiations
with their offer to defray any extra Thai expenses for committing
their troops, Prime Minister Thanom served notice that Thai troops
would not come cheaply when he notified Washington that the
offer was "not yet to our satisfaction,"[39] and the negotiations had
to continue. Just as Washington knew the Thais would eventually

make a larger troop commitment to Vietnam, the Thais knew that if they persevered, the United States would eventually make almost any concession for the Thai troops.

After an obligatory give-and-take at the negotiating table, Thailand agreed to accept a seven point concession package which obligated the United States to:

1. Pay all training costs for the 10,000 man unit sent to South Vietnam;

2. Supply all equipment for the 10,000 men, equipment that the Thai government would keep when the Thai forces withdrew from South Vietnam;

3. Pay all of the costs of overseas allowances over and above their base pay and allowances;

4. Supply all equipment for the rotational troops during their training period, with Thailand retaining this equipment;

5. Provide a HAWK anti-aircraft battery and the training of Thai personnel to man it, for deployment inside Thailand;

6. Increase the Mutual Assistance Program (MAP) contributions for Fiscal Year (FY) '68 from $60 million to $75 million; and

7. Increase the planned MAP contributions for FY '69 from $60 million to $75 million.[40]

In addition to these specific concessions, the United States also agreed to furnish all the in–Vietnam supplies and support the Thai troops would require. This in-country support, however, since it was also supplied to all allied troops serving with the United States in South Vietnam, was not considered part of the concession package to Thailand.

It would appear, when a comparison is made of the list of American concessions obtained by the Thais for their troops with those obtained by the Koreans and the Filipinos, that the Thais received substantially less U.S. aid for their combat forces than did the other two countries. Such was not the case, however. Inherent in the aforementioned list of American concessions, but not readily apparent, were two major and continuing sources of U.S. aid to the Thai military that succeeded in bringing the amount of U.S. aid to Thailand into a rough parity with that going to South Korea and the Philippines.

The first of these additional benefits derived from the aid

agreement components that had the United States supplying all the military equipment for both the Thai troops actually serving in Vietnam and for those troops training inside Thailand for future rotation to Vietnam. The significance of these concessions becomes clear when the total size of Thailand's armed forces is added into the equation. At the height of Thailand's military commitment to South Vietnam, approximately 14 percent of the entire Thai armed forces were serving there. Thus, when the United States agreement to furnish all the equipment to this 14 percent is coupled to its agreement to similarly equip the Thai troops in training, it becomes clear that Thailand was receiving a very large amount of U.S. aid. These two concessions alone amount to, in effect, the United States guaranteeing the Thai military a continuing resupply of new military equipment for almost a third of the entire Thai armed forces.[41] A direct result of this situation would have been, if Thailand had kept their troops in South Vietnam for several years, that the United States would eventually have provided a complete reequipment of the entire Thai armed forces.

A second major benefit accruing to the Thai military lay in the financial incentives the United States supplied, the payment "of the costs of overseas allowances" for every Thai soldier serving in Vietnam. These U.S. funded overseas allowances (see Table 11) succeeded in more than doubling each Thai soldier's salary. The Americans' financial generosity did not however, limit itself to a funding of the overseas allowances. The Thai negotiators also managed to persuade their U.S. counterparts to furnish even more financial rewards than those specifically mentioned in the formal agreement. As part of their overall economic agreements with the Thais, the United States agreed to furnish each Thai soldier:

1. Death and disability benefits ranging from $2,500 to $5,500 depending on rank;
2. Mustering out bonuses of $400 per volunteer;
3. Special monthly educational qualifications pay for the officer corps of $5 to $42.50 a month (based on individual educational background);
4. Flight pay of between $23 and $76.25 a month for officers and $10.25–$60.25 a month for enlisted men;
5. Parachutist pay of $12.50 a month for a private, $17 a month for NCO's, and $37.50 a month for officers;

6. Combat pay amounting to one or two increased salary steps, depending on conditions;
7. Medical and education allowances for dependents; and
8. Various discounts for housing and transportation costs of dependents.[42]

Table 11

Royal Thai Army Pay and Overseas Allowances in South Vietnam (in U.S. dollars)

	Base Pay (Paid by Thailand)	Overseas Allowances (Paid by the United States)	Monthly Total
Lieutenant General	370	450	820
Major General	330	390	720
Special Colonel	240	330	570
Colonel	190	300	490
Lieutenant Colonel	140	240	380
Major	98	180	278
Captain	70	150	220
Lieutenant	50	120	170
Master Sergeant	48	69	117
Sergeant	38	60	98
Corporal	33	50	83
Lance Corporal	30	45	75
Private	26	39	65

Source: U.S. Congress. Senate. Committee on Foreign Relations. *United States Security Agreements and Commitments Abroad: Kingdom of Thailand.* 91st Cong., 1st sess., 1969: 842.

In addition to these direct monetary incentives, any Thai soldier who maintained a satisfactory war record while serving in South Vietnam could continue to draw his combat pay for the rest of his military career. Plus, every day a career soldier spent in Vietnam counted double for retirement purposes. Combat duty in Vietnam also proved especially advantageous to the career advancement of Thailand's upper and second echelon leadership corps. It seems that, to the Thai military high command, their 12,000-man division serving in Vietnam required the leadership of ten generals and 11 full colonels.[43] That this constituted a grossly inflated command structure becomes evident when the Thai division is compared with a U.S. division. For example, the U.S. Marine Corps felt that it needed only three generals and 11 full colonels to command their Third Division in Vietnam, and this Marine division contained over 24,000 men, twice the number in the Thai division.[44] But then, the United States was not doubling the salaries of their U.S.M.C. generals and colonels while they served in Vietnam.

As a result of continuing negotiations between the United States and Thailand, by the time the Queen's Cobras were due to return to Thailand, after serving a one year tour of duty, a much larger Thai military unit was scheduled for deployment to South Vietnam. In late July 1968, the first elements of the Royal Thai Army Expeditionary Division (RTAED), also known as the Black Panthers, began arriving in South Vietnam as the Queen's Cobras' replacements.[45] Although the two units never served together in Vietnam, because of the Thai government's duplication of the American schedule of only having their troops serve a year's tour of duty in Vietnam, many of the Queen's Cobras eventually returned to Vietnam to serve with the Black Panthers.

The deployment of the Black Panthers to Vietnam represented Thailand's final More Flags troop contribution. By the time the final members of the division arrived in Vietnam on 9 January 1969, Lyndon Johnson had only 11 days left in power and thus could not pressure the Thais further for an even larger troop commitment. Still, even though President Johnson soon left office, Thailand elected not to remove their troops. Thai troops continued to serve in South Vietnam until 1972, leaving only a scant few months before the last American troops departed.

The fact that Thailand kept their troops in Vietnam almost to the very end, when coupled with Thailand's having a closely held interest in the outcome of their neighbor's conflict, would seem to cast doubt on any allegation that the Thai troops in Vietnam served as American mercenaries. After all, Thailand, unlike South Korea and the Philippines, did have its national borders directly threatened by the war then raging in Vietnam. One can argue, then, and Thailand's government did so maintain, that in order to avoid having the conflict spread to its own territory, Thailand had to commit its troops to fight in South Vietnam.

This argument constitutes, however, only a simple after-the-fact justification. Records clearly indicate that the Thai government did not perceive the conflict in South Vietnam as a direct threat to their national sovereignty. To the Thais, only a direct confrontation with Red China could do that. The record also presents ample evidence that Thai government leaders did not want to commit their troops to South Vietnam and, indeed, had a long history of resistance to any such suggestion that they do so. It is thus evident that, until 1967, the Thai government felt that sending their troops to fight in South Vietnam was not in the Thai national interest. However, the fact still remains that they did just that.

When all the evidence is examined, it becomes clear that the Thai troop contingent to Vietnam became an American mercenary operation when the Thai government insisted that the United States make very substantial financial concessions for their deployment. Despite all the arguments, excuses, and justifications, the simple fact remains that Thai troops served in South Vietnam only because the United States paid them to go there. They fought as mercenaries in service to America.

Chapter 6

The Australian and New Zealand Contributions

When the More Flags program became official United States policy on 1 May 1964, both Australia and New Zealand already had long running aid programs operating in South Vietnam.* Because of these existing aid programs, the U.S. State Department did not focus particular attention on either nation when it began its pursuit of free world representation and support for the struggle in South Vietnam. The preexisting Australian and New Zealand aid programs, and the motives underlying their commitment, also served to achieve yet another result unforeseen at the onset of the More Flags program. Because of the rationale behind the policy decisions for the commitment of this pre–1964 aid, and a continuation of these reasons to support their later More Flags troop commitments, both countries would avoid the opprobrium accorded the troop commitments from South Korea, the Philippines, and Thailand. Although the governments of both Australia and New Zealand would play significant roles in the prosecution of the Johnson Administration's More Flags foreign policy, and their troops would fight and die in South Vietnam, neither Australia nor New Zealand supplied mercenary troops to the United States.

Although the justification for such a statement is simple and straightforward — Australian and New Zealand troops accepted no

See Table 1 in Chapter 2 for the Australian and New Zealand aid programs committed prior to More Flags.

117

payment from the United States for their service in Vietnam—it is still necessary to examine the reasons why the Australian and New Zealand governments chose to employ an action so contrary to that taken by the other allied troop-contributing nations. To that end, it becomes necessary to briefly examine elements of the western Pacific and Far Eastern diplomatic history of the United States and Australia at the midpoint of the twentieth century.*

Although both U.S. and Australian foreign policy interests during the 1950–1960 period focused primarily on the threat occasioned by an expanding communist movement within the newly independent nations of the western Pacific region, both nations nevertheless approached the problem from different perspectives. To U.S. policymakers, America's cold war policy of containment required the United States to confront communism on a broad and, in the case of the Far East and western Pacific, region-wide scale. Australia's foreign policy, however, although addressing many of the same problems as the United States, had a narrower, more parochial, focus. To Australian government officials, communist threats to the newly independent island-nations of Indonesia and Malaysia, located immediately to the north and northwest of Australia, became their most important foreign policy considerations. Thus, Australian and New Zealand policy interests complemented, but did not necessarily concur with, U.S. foreign policy interests in the same region.

With its area of primary interest being so circumscribed, Australian government officials in the 1950s felt that Australia, since it was not a major world power, could best effect the most forceful national security shield through the development of a two-pronged "forward defense"[1] strategy. As envisioned by Australian policymakers, the development and maintenance of secure military alliances with Great Britain and the United States would comprise the first component of this strategy. Canberra, in acknowledging their own military capability limitations, planned for these alliances to establish a *cordon sanitaire* between Australia and Communist China. Australian national security necessitated such a move—in effect having Great Power confront Great Power—because China,

---

* *Because New Zealand's foreign policy actions so closely paralleled Australia's during the 1950s and 1960s, references to Australia, unless there is a significant difference, will also signify a reference to New Zealand. This is not to imply that New Zealand foreign policy was subordinate to Australia's. It was not.*

in addition to being the recognized major communist threat to the region,[2] was also the one potential adversary in the western Pacific that Australia knew it could not defeat in a military conflict. This aspect of the Australian strategy did require, however, an Australian contribution to the region's overall defense, a role it fulfilled through its participation in various affiliations and defensive alliances with Great Britain and the United States.*

With a direct threat from China thus removed as its most pressing consideration, Australia could then concentrate on the second half of its "forward defense" strategy, keeping any potential military threat distant to their shores. Through this component of the Australian plan, the primary focus of Australian diplomacy would be on meeting any threat, communist or otherwise, directly affecting its island neighbors. By so doing, Canberra sought to keep all possible enemies out of aircraft range of the Australian mainland. (If Canberra's "forward defense" strategy were not successful, it was then envisioned that the only alternative would be the direct defense of the Australian continent itself, a "Fortress Australia" defense.)

While this two-pronged strategy made good military and political sense to Australian government planners, and it appeared to work very well when first implemented, changes in world balance-of-power alignments soon forced some basic changes in the strategy. When Great Britain, toward the end of the 1950s, began the slow process of limiting its military presence in the Far East, withdrawing its power east of Suez, the English-American component of the Australian "forward defense" model required substantial adjustment.†

---

*These included an affiliation with Great Britain in the British Commonwealth, a treaty with the United States in the Australia–New Zealand–United States (ANZUS) Mutual Defense Pact, and an alliance with both Great Britain and the United States (along with other western Pacific countries) in the Southeast Asia Treaty Organization (SEATO).

†The British suppression, in conjunction with Australia and New Zealand, of the Malaysian communist insurgency in the mid–1950s amounted to Great Britain's last major military action in the Far East. Great Britain did continue to maintain a small military presence in Hong Kong and the Federation of Malay, a former colony which became independent in 1957 (the Federation of Malay was renamed the Federation of Malaysia in 1963 when Sabah, Singapore, and Sarawak joined). The commitment of these latter troops was expected to be temporary, however, as they were primarily to offer protection from Indonesian encroachments.

The Australian government soon found itself forced, whether it wanted to or not, into a closer alliance dependency on the United States. Canberra's need for closer ties with the United States in the late 1950s, however, did not revolve around the same reasons that were extant at the start of the decade.

By the time Great Britain started the gradual dismantling of its Far Eastern military presence, the potential threat posed by Communist China to Australia had already been substantially downgraded because of China's lack of a large naval force. The British withdrawal alone then, if all other factors remained the same, would not have created an inordinate security vacuum in the region. China's role as regional troublemaker, however, was soon filled from a different quarter. The actions of Indonesia's President Sukarno, particularly his claims on the Dutch colony of West Irian, of the island of New Guinea constituted a serious challenge to Australia's "forward defense" strategy and threatened the political stability of the entire western Pacific region.

When Indonesia, itself having only achieved independence from the Netherlands in 1949, began military operations against Dutch West Irian in 1958, a region-wide war became a distinct possibility. Only the support afforded the Dutch position by Great Britain, Australia, and New Zealand prevented this war from erupting as it forced Sukarno to limit his military activities to border incursions. Nevertheless, the struggle over West Irian, or the "Confrontation" as it came to be called in Australia, signalled the start of a long period of strained military and diplomatic relations between Indonesia and Australia.

Even without Sukarno's extraterritorial demands on West Irian, just the fact that his government was suspected of being communist influenced required Australian government policymakers to view Indonesia as a direct challenge to their own national security:

> The China threat ... remained distant ... [because] China, with limited seapower, [remained] separated from Australia by a

The island of New Guinea is a part located immediately north of Australia, and under the political control of both the Netherlands and Australia. The Netherlands had acquired the western half of the island in the 1800s and administered it as its West Irian colony. Australia gained control over the eastern half during the early years of the twentieth century and administered it as the Territory of Papua and New Guinea.

considerable water-gap. This situation could be dramatically altered, however, if a Communist-dominated Indonesia became hostile to Australia or allied with China.[3]

Thus, Australian foreign policy at the start of the decade of the 1960s faced two major problems: how to counter Sukarno's ongoing belligerency towards West Irian while avoiding a war, and how to meet the challenge of Great Britain's declining military presence in the Far East.

The Australian position in the confrontation over Western New Guinea took an unexpected turn for the better, however, with the election of John F. Kennedy to the U.S. presidency in 1961. Kennedy's assumption of the presidency did not, however, have an immediate impact on the strained relations between Indonesia and Australia. The simple fact of the matter was that, although the Kennedy Administration viewed Australia's conflict with concern, the area of the Far East that dominated Washington officials' thoughts was Southeast Asia, particularly South Vietnam. Thus, when the Australian government received, on 17 November 1961, a Kennedy Administration request for aid to South Vietnam as "an indication of Australia's willingness to assist in the struggle [there],"[4] Australian officials quickly realized the request's potential to get the United States more actively involved in their dispute on their side. Canberra did not immediately respond to Washington's request, however, as an Australian involvement in South Vietnam required close consideration of both the benefits and hazards involved. Consequently, the Australian government still had not responded to the American request by 8 May 1962 when Secretary of State Dean Rusk called for a formal meeting of the ANZUS Council.

Ostensibly, Secretary Rusk called for the meeting, the first ANZUS meeting convened for many years, to discuss the generalized problems facing ANZUS due to the increasing number of communist encroachments in the Far East and western Pacific. The meeting's true focus, however, was unquestionably Sukarno's Indonesia. In fact, it is doubtful that Secretary Rusk would have called for a formal ANZUS Council meeting had not Sukarno rebuffed an American attempt in February 1962 to mediate the developing West Irian crisis. Nevertheless, the fact that Secretary Rusk did call for an ANZUS meeting, whatever may have been his motives for doing so, constituted a pleasant surprise for the Australian government.

The ANZUS Council meeting afforded the perfect opportunity for Australian Prime Minister Robert G. Menzies to finally reply to the November 1961 American request for an aid commitment to South Vietnam. Prime Minister Menzies, in a calculated maneuver designed expressly "to ingratiate himself with the Kennedy Administration,"[5] and thus to further "strengthen Australian-American security links,"[6] offered to send a contingent of thirty Australian combat advisors to South Vietnam. And Menzies was not wrong in his expectations that an Australian offer of assistance to South Vietnam would reap benefits for the Australian position vis-a-vis Indonesia. Secretary of State Rusk, on the second day of the ANZUS meeting,

> found it convenient to "clarify" Article V of the ANZUS treaty . . . [so that it] applied in the event of armed attack not only upon the metropolitan territory of any of the parties but also upon any island territories in the Pacific under the jurisdiction of the three governments.[7]

With Rusk's clarification of ANZUS Article V, the United States served strong notice to Sukarno that the Australian government now had the full diplomatic and military support of the United States in their Western New Guinea dispute.

The United States also took the opportunity provided by the ANZUS meeting to submit a formal request to the New Zealanders for South Vietnamese aid. Though New Zealand's Prime Minister K.J. Holyoake personally thought New Zealand should avoid becoming involved in the South Vietnamese conflict, believing that the conflict was "essentially one involving different local political elements,"[8] he reluctantly conceded that New Zealand had an ANZUS treaty obligation to make a token aid contribution. Feeling as he did about the reasons for the conflict in South Vietnam, however, Holyoake did manage to avoid having New Zealand's aid commitment, a small military medical detachment deployed in 1963, sent to Vietnam. To Holyoake's thinking, if New Zealand had to send aid to the Southeast Asian region, its best use would be in Thailand to "assist in the establishment of the neutral regime in Laos,"[9] and not to support the conflict in South Vietnam.

Almost immediately after the ANZUS meeting ended on 9 May 1962, both the Australian and United States governments began actions confirming the newly made commitments to each other. On 24 May 1962, Prime Minister Menzies announced to the public that Australia would send 30 Australian Army military instructors to South Vietnam to assist in the struggle there,* with the first of these advisors arriving in South Vietnam on 31 July 1962.

As for the Americans, "Washington began to put the screws on Jakarta,"[10] in their efforts to force Sukarno to the negotiating table. For his part, once Sukarno realized that the Australian government now had the full support of the United States, he reluctantly agreed to permit a United Nations negotiation of the dispute. Sukarno's reluctance in agreeing to a U.N. mediation of the West Irian problem remains however, somewhat of a puzzle, for despite all his posturing and sabre-rattling, Sukarno had a valid claim to the territory. After all, the state of Indonesia was formed when the Netherlands granted full independence to its colony of the Dutch East Indies, and West Irian was an integral part of the Dutch East Indies. For some reason, though, the Dutch decided to retain control over West Irian while granting independence to the rest of its Pacific colony. Consequently, when the United Nations looked at all the facts of the matter, it granted Indonesia control of West Irian in May 1963. Still, things did not end with a resolution of the West Irian problem. Just because the U.N. was able to negotiate an end to one Australian-Indonesian dispute, this did not mean that Australia was finished with Sukarno's extraterritorial ambitions. The Australian Confrontation with Sukarno would emerge anew in 1964.

Two events occurred in early May 1964 which served to form the basic framework of Australia's western Pacific relations with the United States for the remainder of the two countries' involvement in the Vietnam War. The first event began on 3 May when Sukarno, buoyed by his recent success in acquiring control over West Irian, started a campaign to control the northwestern third of the island of Borneo, which contained part of the newly formed Malaysian Federation.†

---

*See Appendix D for a chronological listing of all Australian and New Zealand troop commitments to Vietnam.

†Although most of the island of Borneo had been part of the Dutch [continued]

The second event occurred just a day later when Australia received its first More Flags aid request from the Johnson Administration.[11] Because of these two events, the bilateral *quid pro quo* agreements developed between Australia and the United States during the 1962 ANZUS meeting became all but cast in concrete. While it can be argued that, prior to 1964, the tit-for-tat arrangement between the two allies constituted only a casual agreement, after May 1964, it became accepted U.S. policy for Washington to trade its support for Canberra's position in the conflict with Indonesia for Australian support of America's position in South Vietnam.

There was little doubt in Canberra or Washington, with all the economic, diplomatic, and cultural ties between the United States and Australia, that the U.S. would continue its support for Australia's position in this new confrontation with Sukarno. Despite this, Prime Minister Menzies felt that it would greatly behoove Australia to maintain as close a relationship with the Johnson Administration as possible. He therefore saw the More Flags request as a means by which U.S. support for Australia's Indonesian situation could be strengthened even further. With these thoughts in mind, when Menzies received the 4 May 1964 More Flags request, it took him "no more than five minutes"[12] to agree to increase Australia's military presence in Vietnam.

After just a few weeks of friendly negotiations, both countries agreed that the increased Australian commitment would consist of sending six caribou aircraft with flight crews to South Vietnam and a doubling, from 30 to 60 men, of its combat advisor force there.[13]

As for the United States, even though Washington officials never openly discussed the matter, they fully recognized that a *quid pro quo* arrangement now existed between Australia and the United States, that the Johnson Administration "was trading support for [Australia's] problems in return for their support for our problems

East Indies, and thus became part of a newly independent Indonesia, the northwestern one-third of the island had been controlled by the British. It contained the three small British colonies of Sarawak, Sabah, and Brunei. During the independence movement of the 1950s and 1960s, Brunei opted to remain under British protection as a sultanate, but Sabah and Sarawak joined with several other former British colonies to form the Malaysian Federation.

in Vietnam."[14] Accordingly, as direct payment for Australia's aid commitment to Vietnam, the State Department began an active campaign to pressure Sukarno into calling an end to his aggressive provocations against Malaysia:

> There was a real element of reciprocity here. Effective Australian support for Malaysia would enable the United States to remain in the wings without having to take center stage, at a time when Washington was attempting to concentrate on Vietnam. By the same token, American pressure on Sukarno would reduce the need for Australian involvement in Malaysia, leaving Canberra freer to show the flag in Vietnam. Assistant Secretary of State for Far Eastern Affairs William P. Bundy accordingly warned Sukarno bluntly that the United States might have to cut off all remaining aid programs to Indonesia if confrontation was escalated.[15]

A close reading of the record thus reveals clearly that Australia did not send its aid to South Vietnam, at least as of May 1964, because of any deeply held Australian concerns for the Saigon government's problems: "The fact of the matter was that the Australian government was not primarily concerned with providing aid to Vietnam. To the Australian officials in Canberra, the primary concern was with establishing a sense of 'mutual alliance with the United States,'"[16] and to provide an investment in "future Australian protection."[17] Prime Minister Menzies succeeded in buying, by the deployment of fewer than 200 Australian military personnel to Vietnam, "the best insurance policy possible for his country."[18]

Given the underlying reasons behind Prime Minister Menzies' agreement to America's initial More Flags request, it is not surprising that Australia's commitment of additional troops to South Vietnam generated almost no debate within the Australian government: "That Australia should provide a contribution was never in doubt."[19] Still, even though the State Department knew that the "Australian government had no thought of refusal,"[20] the prompt nature of the Australian offer, and the rapid deployment of their troops to Vietnam, were particularly satisfying to Washington. Contrasted to the generally indifferent initial worldwide responses to the More Flags program,[21] Australia's almost immediate compliance with the State Department's request resulted in sincere praise:

Request you express USG's [United States Government] sincerest appreciation.... Australian offer is in best tradition US-Australian and general Free World–Australian relations and we are most pleased with what they have offered to do.[22]

American officials were pleased even more when the Australians increased the size and content of their aid package to include several surgical teams and an additional 23 advisors—bringing the number of advisors serving in South Vietnam to 83.

New Zealand also received an additional More Flags request in May 1964, and, like Australia, almost immediately agreed to commit more aid to South Vietnam. However, because of its much smaller size as compared to Australia, New Zealand committed a correspondingly smaller aid package to Vietnam. With the majority of its best troops already serving in Malaysia as New Zealand's contribution to the Confrontation, Wellington found it impossible to effect a substantial increase in the size of its aid package to Vietnam. Further, as long as the tense situation there continued, New Zealand government officials felt that this had to remain its first military priority. Wellington thus decided that deploying an additional 25-man army engineer unit to South Vietnam constituted the largest possible aid increase New Zealand could make.

Although the Australian government continued to "support U.S. policies and actions [in South Vietnam] ... not only to encourage the Americans and earn their gratitude, but to bind America closer to Australia,"[23] throughout the remainder of 1964, their decisions to do so severely strained the capabilities of the Australian military establishment. It soon became evident to all concerned that, if Australia were to properly meet all its commitments in Malaysia and South Vietnam, both the Australian defense budget and the total size of its military forces had to be increased. Thus, in 1964, the Australian government not only substantially increased the spending levels for the Australian armed forces, they also instituted a program that truly reflected the high level of concern in which they held both the Malaysian and Vietnamese situations. Australia, for the first time in its history, began to conscript troops.[24]

With both the Australian and New Zealand governments now firmly committed to America's war in South Vietnam, Washington felt free to increase its requests for them to commit even more military assistance to Saigon.[25] However, one of the particular measures taken by Australia to meet their military obligations—the increase of their military through the draft—necessitated a temporary delay in Canberra's ability to comply with Washington's additional requests. The problem lay in the particular type of aid most requested by the State Department, an increase in the numbers of Australian combat advisors deployed to South Vietnam. Canberra simply could not immediately comply with Washington's petitions because the requested advisors, the most highly trained of the Australian Army's NCO's were needed to train the large influx of new draftees entering the Australian Army.[26]

It should not be construed, however, that the Australian government used the unavailability of their NCO's as an excuse for not becoming more actively involved in the Vietnamese conflict than they currently were. The size and amount of Australia's military commitment to South Vietnam in 1964, both actual and planned, offered ample evidence that Australian policymakers now regarded South Vietnam to be a significant component of their "forward defense" strategy. In fact, toward the end of 1964, as Canberra began increasing its commitments to the More Flags program, Australia's entire western Pacific foreign policy began experiencing a basic transformation. For the better part of a decade, the primary focus of Australian foreign policy had been its relations with Sukarno. By late 1964, however, government officials in Canberra began considering their aid in support of America's effort in South Vietnam to be just as important toward achieving Australia's foreign policy objectives. As Australia's Minister of External Affairs Paul Hasluck observed when he took office in 1964, "If we could get stability and peace in South Vietnam it would be easier to deal with Indonesian Confrontation and vice versa."[27]

With the emergence of South Vietnam as a major Australian foreign policy concern, government officials in Canberra became more than just bystanders to America's military and political activities there, and the events occurring in Saigon during the latter months of 1964 disturbed them. In Minister Hasluck's opinion, a view shared by Prime Minister Menzies, U.S. efforts taken in response to the political instability of the Saigon government were much too moderate and as a consequence, "[they] threatened . . .

Saigon gov' unstable then rebuilt made

Australian security in southeast Asia."[28] To these Australian government officials, since the basic framework of Australian western Pacific foreign policy now depended on a forceful and substantial U.S. policy commitment to Vietnam, it was absolutely necessary for the United States to vigorously prosecute the war there. The images coming out of Washington and Saigon at that time were not, however, encouraging. Both Hasluck and Menzies felt that the United States should be doing more to stabilize both the political and military situations in South Vietnam. Yet, both leaders knew pragmatically that if they were to ask the United States to do more in South Vietnam, Australia itself would also have to do more.

At the start of 1965, however, Prime Minister Menzies was afforded the opportunity not only to inform the United States of his perceptions on South Vietnamese current events, but also to make an offer of Australian assistance to the resolution of the perilous state of affairs there. This opportunity came when Michael Forrestal, an aide to Lyndon Johnson's National Security Advisor McGeorge Bundy, visited Canberra in January 1965 seeking a larger Australian commitment of advisors for Vietnam. On being asked for the men, Menzies not only agreed to the immediate request—he committed an additional 17 advisors—he also offered to send to South Vietnam, if the U.S. requested them, "a combat battalion and a crack Special Air Service squadron."[29] By making this offer, Menzies in effect told President Johnson that not only did he think that the Vietnam situation required a stronger U.S. military response, but that America could count on Australia's help in such an undertaking. Although the Johnson Administration did not then accept the offer, it is significant that neither was the proposal rejected.

On 8 March 1965, Lyndon Johnson committed the United States to a ground war in South Vietnam by landing American Marines at Da Nang, Republic of Vietnam. To the Australian government, this constituted the strong military commitment they had long thought necessary. At the moment that the United States committed its Marines, however, the Australians appeared to draw back from their offer of combat troops. Sensing what they interpreted as an ambivalent attitude from the United States on requesting Australian troops, Canberra began hedging on its offer. Even when the U.S. State Department declared, during the 1 April

1964 Honolulu Conference on the status of free world aid to South Vietnam, that the United States would welcome Australian combat troops in South Vietnam if offered, the Australian government did not view this as a formal request for Australian troops. For reasons not yet fully understood, Australian officials suddenly appeared less than eager to commit their troops, stating only that Australia would deploy its troops if "the appropriate requests were received from the U.S. and South Vietnam."[30]

Further, a review of American actions immediately prior to and following the American dispatch of combat troops to Vietnam does seem to justify the Australian idea that Washington had not yet firmly committed themselves to formally requesting Australian troops. On 3 March 1964, Secretary Rusk notified U.S. Ambassador to South Vietnam Maxwell Taylor that the possibility of employing an international combat force in the northern provinces of South Vietnam still existed only in the contingency planning stage. Then, after the Honolulu meeting in April, the State Department seemed to go out of its way to emphasize the United States plans to increase the size of the South Vietnamese Army, not the solicitation of allied troops, as their first priority. Nevertheless, even with the confusion of signals coming from the United States, Australian government officials felt they could not back down from their offer. On 12 April 1964, just one month after the Americans landed combat troops in South Vietnam, Canberra formally offered Washington a battalion of Australian troops to serve with the Americans there.[31]

The government in Wellington, always the most pensive of the three ANZAC nations, did not immediately emulate the actions of its two allies. The first contingents of the 1st Battalion, Royal Australian Regiment, were in fact already arriving in South Vietnam before New Zealand government officials decided to commit their country to the ground war there. In a reluctant accession to treaty and alliance obligations, Prime Minister Holyoake, on 27 May 1964, formally requested an authorization from the New Zealand parliament for him to deploy an artillery battery to South Vietnam. Although this request did signify Holyoake's bowing to American pressures for a further commitment of New Zealand troops, Holyoake still managed to let the United States know that there were limits to New Zealand's acquiescence. New Zealand would deign to send an artillery battery to Vietnam, but this artillery unit would not be an add-on to the troops already there. The Australians might keep adding troops, always increasing their military levels, but the New Zealanders would not. In Holyoake's 27 May request to parliament, he purposely included the stipulation that the New Zealand engineers be withdrawn from Vietnam on the deployment of the artillery battery. The New Zealand parliament, after only one day of discussion and debate, voted on 28 May 1964 to commit the requested troops to Vietnam. The vote breakdown, however, of 39 ayes versus 33 nays, indicated that Holyoake's reluctance to expand New Zealand's combat role in Vietnam was also felt by a large percentage of his fellow New Zealanders.[32]

During the remaining years of the Johnson Administration, both Australia and New Zealand periodically augmented, replaced, and increased their troop contingents to Vietnam. Soldiers from both countries would continue to serve and die in Vietnam until 1972. Ultimately, at the height of their commitments, over 8,000 Australians and 550 New Zealanders would serve in South Vietnam. The two countries even continued to increase their troop levels after the original justification for their involvement in South Vietnam became moot—the Confrontation with Sukarno's Indonesia ended when a pro–West coup of Sukarno's government resulted in the termination of all Indonesia-Malaysia border incidents.

It should be noted, however, that irrespective of the level of importance Australian and New Zealand government officials may have attached to the Confrontation, they never publicly presented the conflict with Sukarno as a justification for their two countries' becoming involved in Vietnamese affairs. To Canberra, Australia's commitment of troops to South Vietnam came about because Australia felt obligated

> 1) To help the Government of South Vietnam . . . resist armed aggression from the Communist North. 2) To free the fifteen million people of South Vietnam from the threat of oppression and terror and help establish conditions for democratic government. 3) To leave no doubt that Australia is resolved to honor its treaty commitments and alliances. 4) To check the spread of Communism.[33]

As for the New Zealand government's public rationale for becoming involved in South Vietnam, New Zealand sent aid and troops to Vietnam because:

> [as] the Viet Cong have been able to make significant progress in
> the South . . . because of the extent of assistance available from the
> North . . . it [becomes] imperative that other countries should give
> assistance to the Republic of Vietnam to resist that aggression.[34]

What is not found, however, in either country's list of publicly
professed humanitarian justifications, is the single most important
reason for their continued commitment of troops to South Vietnam. Not mentioned at all is the fact that the primary purpose for
the Australian and New Zealand troop commitments was to act as
a buttress to Lyndon Johnson's resolve in maintaining an American
military commitment to the Saigon government. Only with the
continued high military involvement of the United States in Southeast Asia could the Australian and New Zealand strategic plans for
western Pacific defense be assured of success. As observed by Harold
Holt, who became the Australian Prime Minister after Menzies
retired in 1966, Australia's own security in the region required, as
a mandatory prerequisite, "The effective presence of the United
States as a greater power in the area of Asia and the Pacific."[35]

Whatever may or may not have been the reasons behind the
Australian and New Zealand military commitments to South Viet-
nam, the fact remains that they did send their troops to fight there.
And in so doing, their troops joined with the combat forces from
South Korea, the Philippines, and Thailand in fighting alongside
the Americans. Unlike the troops provided by these three other
countries, however, the combat forces provided by Australia and
New Zealand did not constitute a mercenary force hired out to the
Americans. Such a categorical statement can be made because of the
simple fact that they were not paid to fight there. Of all the allied
nations sending troops to fight in South Vietnam, only Australia
and New Zealand refused to accept United States payment for their
troops' service,[36] and payment for services rendered is the defining
element of the word *mercenary*. Not only did both the Australian
and New Zealand governments accept no United States financial
rewards for their troops' service in South Vietnam, they even insisted on repaying the United States for the in–Vietnam costs incurred in fighting there. Although the United States furnished and
paid for all these supplies for its other allies, both Australia and
New Zealand began, in September 1965, to reimburse the United

States for these costs.[37] Consequently, the economic rewards demanded as the primary condition of employment by the South Korean, Philippine, and Thai governments did not apply to the Australian and New Zealand troop contributions.

In the final analysis, the justifications for any nation's sending its troops to fight in another country, whether the reasons are openly advocated or not, do not constitute the most pertinent factor in determining whether or not those troops make up a mercenary force. A mercenary, or a mercenary force, fights for a country not his own because of the financial rewards received. Thus, the only relevant consideration in the definition of a mercenary is simply whether a person's military service was dependent on the receipt of financial benefits.

Of the five free world nations sending troops to fight with the United States in Vietnam, only Australia and New Zealand did so without demanding and receiving financial rewards for their soldiers' service. Therefore, the Australian and New Zealand troops who served in South Vietnam did not meet the definitional criteria for being mercenaries in service to America during the Vietnam War.

Chapter 7

"More Flags": The Final Years

During the entire history of the More Flags program, Johnson Administration officials never publicly deviated from their assertion that the primary purpose of the program was to effect allied assistance programs for the South Vietnamese fight against communist aggression. In actuality, this goal never amounted to more than a secondary consideration for Washington's actions. From its inception, Lyndon Johnson fully intended for the More Flags program to serve primarily as a vehicle for addressing the political needs of his own personal agenda: "Since main purpose of 'More Flags' effort is political . . . our main concern is with political impact of this aid shipment."[1] More specifically, the principal *raison d'être* for the More Flags program was Lyndon Johnson's almost obsessive desire to obtain an international consensus for America's Vietnam policy. Even when the publicly declared character of the program began to evolve, after 8 March 1965, into a dual pursuit of both nonmilitary aid and combat troops from other free world nations, this underlying motive did not change.

Despite Lyndon Johnson's expectations for the success of the More Flags program, however, the program, from day one of its implementation, simply did not produce the level of international support Johnson so desperately sought. Even after being in full operation for a year, a year in which Johnson would commit almost every resource available to him as president of the most powerful nation in the world, the More Flags program could claim only the most nominal successes. In spite of all his efforts, and even despite his resorting to the purchasing of support for the program, Lyndon Johnson discovered that there were very "few of America's traditional allies who were prepared to support him"[2] in either South Vietnam or Southeast Asia. At the end of its first year, few would dispute the assertion that the More Flags program was a failing American foreign policy.

Nevertheless, despite its lack of tangible results, Lyndon Johnson refused to give up on either the program or the program's goal. Johnson's obstinacy thus forced the members of his administration into taking some extraordinary steps to try to produce a semblance of success where no such success existed. Washington's solicitation of free world aid, a relatively orderly and restrained undertaking during the first few months of the program's operation, began a rapid degeneration into an almost frenetic search for almost any international support.

With America's traditional allies pointedly and actively refusing to participate in any "development of a consensus"[3] on America's South Vietnamese policy positions, the State Department felt it necessary to drastically transform the implementation and accounting procedures for the More Flags program. Since the early results of the More Flags program failed to achieve the program's original criteria for success—convincing a substantial number of allied nations to commit aid to South Vietnam—State Department officials began an even more active pursuit of even token aid. Though the solicitation of aid, in any quantity, and from any source, had been a component of the program almost from its start, after 1965 this aspect of their effort began receiving even greater emphasis. If the United States could not obtain a significant aid contribution from an ally, then the Americans would actively solicit and accept even "small symbolic contributions[s]."[4] To Johnson Administration officials, any aid was acceptable as long as it allowed President Johnson the opportunity to present to the world "the impression of a broadly based international effort"[5] in South Vietnam.

As a direct result of the Johnson Administration's pursuit of quantity rather than quality, as if sheer numbers alone would prove that the program was a success, even some free world nations which sent no aid at all warranted inclusion in Rusk's More Flags lists. The only requirement for their inclusion was for them to make a vague promise to commit aid: "Thirty-eight Free World nations are providing *or have agreed to provide aid* [emphasis added] to Viet-Nam."[6] While some of this promised aid would, in fact, eventually be delivered to South Vietnam, to State Department officials whether they did or not was of little consequence. To the Johnson Administration, by the very fact of its offer to send aid, a country demonstrated its support of America's Vietnam policy.

Even with the State Department reporting promises of aid as signifying a nation's approval of U.S. policy positions toward South Vietnam, the More Flags lists remained far too small to satisfy Lyndon Johnson's needs. If the numbers of participants in the More Flags program were to continue as the determinant of international acceptance, other methods had to be found to increase the sum total. One method adopted by Secretary Rusk in 1965 amounted to little more than mind reading. In an effort to make the More Flags program sound more successful than it really was, it became commonplace for him to include with his tallies of allies currently sending or agreeing to send aid, such statements as, "I would make a rough estimate that between 60 and 70 governments support what we are doing in South Vietnam and wish us well."[7]

By the time Rusk began making such statements, however, they were not even necessary. In its frenetic attempts to pad the lists of supportive allied nations, the State Department adopted a policy whereby a nation could be included without even sending aid, or even promising it. When it became evident that the total number of allied nations contributing aid to South Vietnam, or promising it, was not going to increase to an acceptable level, the State Department in June 1965 instituted a policy allowing personal opinions alone to suffice as tangible demonstrations of support. After June, the only requirement was for a governmental leader of a free world nation to "be inclined privately to be sympathetic to our position,"[8] and that personal endorsement would then be counted as a tangible demonstration of support for the goals set for the More Flags program.

Although Washington officials continued promoting their successful prosecution of the More Flags program to the public, anyone choosing to look behind the rhetoric could easily see the "sorry lack of success"[9] the policy was actually engendering. Even some upper level State Department officials were, by June 1965, privately admitting the program's failure: "We have not persuaded either our friends or allies [to send aid]."[10] Even so, Lyndon Johnson adamantly refused to abandon the program. If anything, Johnson began working even harder to establish some semblance of an international consensus for his Vietnam policy. In addition to paying some nations to participate in the More Flags program — through the previously discussed funding of all the costs, and more, of their involvement in Vietnam — after 1965, Johnson even stooped to buying other nations' verbal support for his Vietnam policy: "Eshkol [Israeli Prime Minister Levi Eshkol] was given permission to buy American Phantom fighter-bombers and Skyhawks if he would praise Johnson's war in Vietnam."[11] Lyndon Johnson's personal insistence on continuing More Flags, even when it became obvious that the program had no chance of succeeding, resulted in administration officials continuing to push for even more allied participation in South Vietnam up to the moment of Johnson's departure from office: "In the future we expect to see our allies . . . providing the economic assistance which will make that world stable and prosperous."[12]

With the More Flags program floundering in its quest to obtain generalized aid from America's allies, one aspect of the program did begin showing definite gains during and after 1965. Lyndon Johnson's pursuit of other nations' troops to fight with the United States in Vietnam began showing definite signs of success after he committed American troops to Vietnam in March 1965. Nevertheless, even though Johnson, after his revision of the More Flags program's objectives, did convince five allied nations to commit almost 80,000 of their troops to South Vietnam, he still remained dissatisfied. Just as in the aid solicitation aspect of the program, Johnson wanted an even larger number of allied nations to commit troops. Five troop-contributing nations simply were not enough. Consequently, for the remainder of his presidency, Lyndon Johnson continued to place a high priority on the obtaining of combat troops from free world nations.

Of all the nations considered by the State Department as potential troop contributors, one, Nationalist China (Taiwan), presented Washington policymakers with a dilemma. Despite Chinese President Chiang Kai-shek's offer to deploy a substantial number of Nationalist Chinese troops to Vietnam even before the official start of the More Flags program, Johnson Administration officials reluctantly felt obliged to turn the offer down. Despite President Johnson's desire to put even more allied troops into Vietnam, three problem areas existed which ultimately prevented the United States from acceding to a commitment of Nationalist Chinese troops. The first of these reasons, the South Vietnamese people's long history of distrust and antipathy toward the Chinese,[13] probably would not have been sufficient in and of itself to cause a rejection of Chinese combat troops. After all, similar feelings were being overlooked in reference to the ROK troop commitments. However, when combined with American fears that using Nationalist Chinese troops in Vietnam might possibly bring about the introduction of troops from the People's Republic of China (Communist China) into the conflict,[14] and added to the U.S. desire not to "introduce into the struggle in Viet-Nam any element of the Chinese Civil War,"[15] the State Department saw no alternative but to refuse Chiang's offers.

When the Johnson Administration first began its pursuit of allied troops for Vietnam, almost every free world ally received attention from the State Department; U.S. officials realized nevertheless that not every nation was in a position to send troops. The State Department acknowledged early in the program that most of the United States' smaller free world allies, even if they publicly supported America's position in Vietnam, had valid reasons for not committing their troops. Such nations as Singapore, Malaysia, Iran, and most of the Latin American and African countries had various reasons: internal political problems, small populations, or severely limited economic bases, to name just a few. State Department officials reluctantly concluded they could apply only limited pressure on these countries to send their troops to South Vietnam.[16]

The State Department's depreciation of the potentialities of some of America's allies did not, however, apply to the North Atlantic Treaty Organization (NATO) countries. Lyndon Johnson fully expected most of these countries, particularly Canada and Great Britain, to side with him in South Vietnam, yet to his dismay, every one of America's closest allies repeatedly rejected all entreaties for dispatching even a token military force to South Vietnam.[17] The refusal of one NATO ally, West Germany, to send troops however, did not generate much discouragement in the Johnson Administration.

Although State Department officials did seriously discuss the possibilities of pressuring Bonn for a commitment of troops, such actions were never taken. Washington officials reluctantly determined that German troops serving in Vietnam would not constitute a feasible course of action: "Any request for German troops in Vietnam should be weighed against the fact that the French Foreign Legion comprised a vast majority of German troops and had a very bad effect on the Vietnamese."[18]

After America's NATO allies made it clear that they were not going to commit their armed forces to Vietnam, and when the 1966 Vice President Humphrey Far Eastern trip and the 1967 Clifford-Taylor mission succeeded in obtaining the last vestiges of troops from South Korea and Thailand, the United States was left with no other conventional source of obtaining further troops for South Vietnam.[19] In their pursuit of foreign combat troops to fight with and in place of American boys, however, Johnson Administration officials did not just restrict their activities to conventional tactics. Encouraged by Lyndon Johnson's continued importuning to get more foreign troops into South Vietnam, his subordinates felt unconstrained by any rules of normal and accepted statecraft. To these men, no potential source of troops, no matter how exotic, would remain unexplored.

The State Department, on at least two occasions during the 1966–1968 period, actively pursued extraordinary sources in their quest to obtain other mercenary forces for service in South Vietnam. The first such case occurred in late October 1966 when the State Department learned of Great Britain's plan to disband its Ghurka units. (The Ghurkas, recruited from the Kingdom of Nepal, had served in the British Army as a mercenary force since 1815. They established a distinguished record of combat and are recognized as some of the finest soldiers in the world.) On learning of this possible action by their English allies, U.S. State Department officials began active negotiations with the British to have the Ghurka units transferred to American military command for mercenary duty in South Vietnam. Nothing developed from these negotiations, however, because the British government ultimately decided not to phase out these units before at least 1969.[20]

When the American efforts to obtain the services of the Ghurka units are coupled with the previously mentioned 1968 talks on recruiting Filipino civilians for combat duty in Vietnam, it becomes evident that the Johnson Administration considered no potential source of foreign troops as being too unreasonable to pursue. Once Lyndon Johnson decided to use the More Flags program to hire mercenaries, he placed few restrictions on where, or how, these troops would be obtained. Only happenstance, and the vagaries of history, prevented Johnson's use of even more mercenary troops in Vietnam.

From May 1964 when the More Flags program began, through January 1969 when Lyndon Johnson left the presidency, the State Department made periodic attempts to demonstrate to the world that More Flags was a successful U.S. foreign policy program. The means by which they did this was through the publication of up-to-date lists of free world aid committed to Vietnam. Though these lists, over time, did include changes in the acknowledged reasons for a nation's tendering of aid—for example, Washington finally admitted in 1966 that some countries' aid was not sent as demonstration of support for American policy positions in South Vietnam—every listing invariably presented More Flags as a successful American foreign policy. A close comparison of the last Johnson Administration list, submitted on 1 January 1969 (see Table 12), with the list of 26 May 1965 (see Table 3), gives a better indication, however, of the More Flags program's real level of success.

Table 12

Free World Assistance to the Republic of Vietnam as of 1 January 1969

Country	Type of Assistance
Argentina	Wheat, 20,000 doses of cholera vaccine.
Australia	Military Aid: Approximately 8,000 combat troops, a guided missile destroyer, Canberra bombers, Caribou transport aircraft, combat advisors. Economic and Technical Aid: civil engineers, three surgical teams, dairy and crop practice experts, a

Country	Type of Assistance
	radio expert, 6 community windmills, 1,500,000 textbooks, 3,300 tons of corrugated roofing materials, 15,750 sets of hand tools, in–Australia training for Vietnamese, 400 radio sets, 16,000 blankets, 2,400 loudspeakers, 14,000 cases of condensed milk.
Belgium	Medicines for flood relief, an ambulance, scholarships for Vietnamese.
Brazil	Medical supplies, 5,000 sacks of coffee.
Canada	Ten 200-bed emergency hospital units, 650,000 doses of polio vaccine, $850,000 worth of food aid, a science building for the University of Hue, in–Canada training for Vietnamese, 460,000 copies of a social sciences textbook, C$425,000 in emergency supplies, 9 Canadian teachers and medical personnel.
Republic of China (Taiwan)	An 80-man agricultural team, a 16-man surgical team, an 18-man psychological warfare team, a 34-man electrical power mission, training of Vietnamese power engineers, in–Taiwan training for Vietnamese, prefabricated warehouses, seeds and fertilizers, agricultural tools, 5,000 tons of rice, medical supplies, an electrical power substation, 600,000 school textbooks, cement.
Denmark	Medical supplies for flood relief.
Ecuador	Medical supplies.
Germany	A 3,000-ton hospital ship, medical supplies and a hospital, loan credits, machine tools, a home for juvenile delinquents, loan credits, 100,000 health textbooks, social center funding, high school and college teachers, 200 technical and medical personnel, in–Germany training for Vietnamese, fertilizers.
Greece	Medical supplies.
Guatemala	15,000 doses of typhoid serum.

Country	Type of Assistance
Honduras	Drugs and clothing for refugees.
Iran	Petroleum products, a 20-man medical team.
Italy	A 10-man surgical team from 1964 through 1966, in–Italy science scholarships for Vietnamese, relief commodities.
Japan	$55 million worth of economic assistance from a World War II reparations agreement, technical experts, 20,000 transistor radios, in–Japan scholarships for Vietnamese, 25 ambulances, medical teams and supplies, a neurological surgical ward and team, electrical transmission lines.
Republic of Korea	Military aid consisting of approximately 50,000 troops, 7 civilian medical teams, $50,000 of relief supplies.
Laos	$1 million kip ($4,167) for flood relief in 1965, a cash donation for refugees in 1966, $5,000 in relief supplies in 1968.
Liberia	$50,000 for the purchase of medical supplies and hospital equipment.
Luxembourg	Plasma and blood transfusion equipment.
Malaysia	In–Malaysia training for Vietnamese military and police officers, armored vehicles, relief supplies and medicines.
Morocco	10,000 cans of sardines worth $2,000.
Netherlands	$186,000 relief projects grant, in–Netherlands scholarships for Vietnamese, three tuberculosis centers, renovation of a hospital, milk powder.
New Zealand	Military Aid: an infantry company and artillery battery (550 men). Economic and technical Aid: 3 medical teams, refugee relief, a science faculty building, in–New Zealand scholarships for Vietnamese.
Philippines	A 1,500-man military engineering unit; a 12-man medical team, clothing, food, medical supplies.

Country	Type of Assistance
South Africa	Medical supplies.
Spain	A 12-man medical team, medicines and medical equipment, blankets.
Thailand	A 6,000-man military mission, in–Thailand jet training for Vietnamese pilots, corrugated iron, cement, and vaccines.
Tunisia	Scholarships for Vietnamese.
Turkey	Medicines, cement, vaccines.
United Kingdom	Seven police advisors, a professor of English, technical experts, medical equipment, an 11-man pediatric team, various equipment for schools and facilities in Vietnam, in–England training for Vietnamese, a typesetting machine.
Uruguay	Relief supplies and medicines.
Venezuela	Two civilian doctors, 500 tons of rice for refugee relief.

Nations sending assistance to South Vietnam whose help does not fall under the Free World Assistance Program include France, Ireland, Israel, Norway, Pakistan, and Switzerland.

Source: Free World Assistance to Viet-Nam, Secretary of State Rusk to All Diplomatic and Consular Posts, 1/7/69, "Vietnam 5D, 3/67–1/69," Item No. 2. NSF Country File-VN, Box 85-91. L.B.J. Library.

The 1965 list, which is a compilation of the program's first year achievements, proclaims that 29 free world nations were sending aid to South Vietnam in response to More Flags entreaties. As has all ready been shown, however, only 25 nations, at the most, should have been on this list since the aid sent from France, Israel, Pakistan, and Switzerland did not result from any More Flags request. By 1969, the number of aid contributing countries had grown to 32.*[21] After a two-and-a-half-year period of intense, unrelenting,

*The official State Department list does include a Costa Rican contribution that this author has chosen to omit: "Costa Rica is contributing an [continued]

diplomatic activities, the State Department only succeeded in recruiting eight additional countries for the program: Argentina, Liberia, Luxembourg, Morocco, South Africa, Tunisia, Uruguay, and Venezuela. Further, the aid sent from these eight countries represented only token support. Given the severely limited numbers of aid-contributing nations then, and the particulars of many of their contributions, the actions of 32 nations cannot be interpreted as fulfilling the More Flags program's primary objective. More Flags did not provide Lyndon Johnson with the international consensus he sought.

Throughout its lifetime, the More Flags program sought to achieve three separate purposes: to obtain free world aid for Vietnam, to prove that the United States had an international consensus for its actions in Vietnam, and to purchase mercenary troops to fight there. In its guise as a project for obtaining free world humanitarian aid for South Vietnam, Lyndon Johnson's More Flags program enjoyed some moderate success. Even when one deducts the aid sent by other countries that the United States paid for, there remains an appreciable amount of aid sent by the free world that might not have been offered had the More Flags program not been in operation. On the other hand, More Flags clearly failed to fulfill its role as a means of eliciting an international consensus for America's Vietnamese policy. It failed for many reasons, but mainly because "Democratic governments elsewhere in the world simply did not regard Vietnam as a test case for the defence of democracy,"[22] and thus chose not to become actively involved in America's operations in Southeast Asia. The More Flags program did succeed very well, however, in achieving its third objective. In the only truly successful aspect of the More Flags program, the United States did manage to purchase the mercenary services of over 60,000 Korean, Filipino, and Thai soldiers.

While a sufficient quantity of available evidence now exists to demonstrate that the Korean, Filipino, and Thai soldiers did con-

ambulance for use by the Ministry of Health." This aid is not included in Table 12 because it was only promised, not sent. This contribution, supposedly from the Costa Rican government but actually from a private organization (the Costa Rican Sugar Growers Association), was, in fact, included in the More Flags lists for over a year prior to this date. It would be mid-1969, however, before the ambulance would actually be delivered.

stitute a mercenary force fighting for the United States in South Vietnam, no evidence yet presented addresses the ethical questions of their use in that capacity. Consequently, as no study of America's use of allied mercenaries would be complete with only a detailing of their employment, it becomes necessary to consider the underlying philosophical and ethical questions raised. The United States hired and used mercenaries, but was their use honorable?

Chapter 8

Conclusions

Five free world nations, in addition to the United States, sent elements of their military forces to fight in South Vietnam during the Second Indochina War. If one applies the strictest dictionary definition of *mercenary* to these troop contributions, then the fighting men of three of these countries, South Korea, Thailand, and the Philippines, clearly qualified as mercenary forces. They fought in South Vietnam only after they, and their governments, received substantial financial remunerations from the United States for their services.

A dictionary definition of *mercenary*, however, with its emphasis on pay, only delineates one justification for why a person would choose to fight for a flag not his own. In fact, the pay received frequently constitutes only one of several possible motivations for mercenary service. Although the receipt of pay or material gain is a conditional prerequisite for all mercenary status, in some instances, the financial reward is regarded as only a secondary consideration to a mercenary's desire to fight for a perceived "just cause." There are, in addition, those men and women who choose to fight not for money or cause, but simply for the sheer adventure of the undertaking.[1] A mercenary then, can be either the Hessian who fights only because King George III pays him to, or he can be the von Steuben, Kościuszko, or Pulaski lending their military skills to a cause they believed in. Moreover, the justifications for mercenary service — pay, cause, or thrill — do not have to be limited to an individual's service. They are also often found as the base inducement for the operations of entire military units. In the Spanish Civil War of the 1930s, for example, Franco's Moroccan battalions fought only for pay, while the opposing members of the Abraham Lincoln Brigade fought for a cause. Both units, however, whatever their particular rationale for fighting, shared the common status of mercenaries.

The establishing of an individual's mercenary status thus becomes an exercise that is concurrently both simple and complex. There would be no difficulty, in even a cursory glance through military history, of compiling a long list of individuals and units — the Lafayette Escadrille, David "Mickey" Marcus, Claire Chennault's Flying Tigers, et al. — which are viewed as shining examples of heroism and honor and duty. Yet, for all the acclaim and respect they might engender in some as freedom-fighters or patriots or noble adventurers, to others the same men and units were little more than criminals or bandits, or mercenaries. It is the fate of any foreign national, fighting in or for another country, that they be labeled both as heroic and as unprincipled, honored on the one hand and reviled on the other.

Such is the dichotomous image of the person who fights for pay in a country not his own. No matter the cause, whether the reasons for that service be honorable or not, if pay is received, that service constitutes mercenary status and thus becomes, by implication, disreputable. The central consideration, then, in any discussion of *mercenary,* has to revolve around the negative image accruing to mercenary service — how, and why, even the word itself has come to be viewed with such intense opprobrium.

It is because the word *mercenary* is so evocative, because it has so many negative connotations attached to it, that a simple determination of mercenary status for the U.S.-financed troops in the Vietnam War cannot end just with that finding. Objectivity dictates that an examination be made of the morality and ethics of their use. Does America's recruitment and use of mercenary services in Vietnam constitute a proper and time-honored function of national and international statecraft, or was their use an unacceptable, or at least debatable, implementation of national policy?

It is very probable that the use of mercenaries in combat has a history every bit as old as the history of combat itself. While we can only guess at its use in prehistoric times, it is not difficult to find references to mercenaries in some of our earliest known written chronicles. Further, there are few, if any, historical periods that did not see the use of professional soldiers hired to fight in other people's wars. As a consequence, the use of mercenary troops in conflicts between nations has earned itself an historically accepted position in the conduct of national and international diplomacy. Despite this patina of legitimacy gained from long and repeated use, there still exist questions and doubts over the probity of mercenary use. There are, after all, other military practices — torture, looting, rape — which can claim as long a history as the use of mercenaries, yet few would accept these activities as justifiable exercises in a nation's conflict with its neighbors. What becomes the core issue, then, in any debate on the use of mercenaries?

Since philosophers throughout history have deliberated over questions of what is "right" and what is "wrong," and since these deliberations have still produced no consensus, it would be folly to attempt a determination in a treatise such as this. Still, an evaluation of America's use of mercenaries in South Vietnam, if it is to be comprehensive, necessitates that at least a basic attempt be made at examining the core questions concerning the rightness or wrongness of their use. Nonetheless, care must still be taken in such an evaluation to avoid venturing too far afield. It thus becomes impractical herein to examine the purely philosophical considerations of whether a particular practice is either "right" or "wrong" in every situation, or whether human decisions result from *a priori* or *a posteriori* reasoning.[2] Of necessity, the discussion on the ethical use of mercenaries in this analysis will proceed from a more basic premise.

As has already been stated, mercenary use in the conduct of international affairs is still considered disreputable in many quarters, despite the historical acceptance gained from their repeated employment over the centuries. This negative reputation of mercenary use is further reflected in the inimical feelings the very word itself produces in general use. It would not be an overstatement, then, to assert that *mercenary,* in all its forms, has almost universally negative connotations. Consequently, with a word and practice so denigrated, the basic ethical premise requiring analysis becomes an examination of the why's behind a government's employment of a mercenary force.

In almost any discussion about the ethics inherent in the use of mercenary troops, a purely philosophical consideration of the question rarely takes center stage. Sooner or later in any such discussion, the basis for determining the "right" or "wrong" of mercenary use is resolved not on philosophical grounds, but is determined by the societal and cultural concepts surrounding it. Thus, in order to evaluate the ethical use of mercenaries, it becomes necessary to examine how society has gradually come to view the morality of a country's use of mercenaries. Once this is done, it will then be possible to understand how, in the particular instance of America's use of mercenaries in Vietnam, some people view their use as nothing more than a conventional policy consideration, while others view the practice as a less than honorable exercise in international statecraft.

Historically, a base principle of the use of mercenaries in a conflict among nations was that mercenary forces were usually employed by the richest country involved in the confrontation. Since, by definition, a mercenary fights only if he or she receives pay for their skills, it should not be surprising that those countries or peoples which traditionally made most use of a mercenary's services were the ones best able to meet the requisite financial expenses involved. It thus follows that, in each era, the use of mercenaries has most often been the province of the richest societies. For the purposes of this book, however, it is not necessary to examine representative cases of the use of mercenaries by all the rich nations through history. The time period from about A.D. 1500 to the mid–twentieth century will suffice to provide pertinent examples.

The establishment of European colonial empires between 1500 and 1900 produced a situation in which a colonizing nation's wealth, power, and prestige were, to a great degree, dictated directly by the extent of its colonial possessions. Thus, any nation able to establish a colonial empire also succeeded in becoming one of the wealthier nations of the world and, in turn, became a nation most financially able to hire the services of mercenary troops.

While the use of mercenary troops became a fairly common practice during this period, other than an occasional reference, ethical and philosophical questions over their use generated little serious debate.* Serious consideration of these questions began to

---

*See, however, Niccolò Machiavelli's disdain of the use of mercenaries in his The Prince.

emerge during the first half of the nineteenth century concomitant with the actions of the two dominant colonial powers of the time, Great Britain and France. Rather than hiring a mercenary force of unknown fighting ability as the need arose, these two great colonial powers greatly simplified the process. With the British recruitment of its Gurkha Brigade in 1815, and the 1831 organization by the French of their Foreign Legion, the two nations made mercenary units a permanent component of their overseas military forces.

As the record shows, the nineteenth century saw both France and Great Britain greatly extending their colonial empires — by the end of the century they would dominate over 100 colonial states between them — after they incorporated the mercenary units into their armed forces. It would be, however, irresponsible to equate this growth as coming about directly because of their use of mercenaries, as many other factors contributed to the expansion of the two nations' power. Nevertheless, France and England did frequently use their respective mercenary units to assist them in acquiring new colonies and to maintain control of those states already in their colonial orbs. As a result of their use in such capacities then, by the end of the century, all mercenaries became indelibly stigmatized as being instruments of colonial oppression, especially to colonial populations.

With the advent of the twentieth century, the continued use of mercenaries in European colonial empires served to further reinforce their image as nothing more than a tool of the "haves" in their quest to dictate to the "have nots" of the world. The practice could no longer be excused as a simple continuation of a long and accepted exercise in international statecraft. In the Belgian Congo, Indochina, Algeria, Rhodesia, Malaysia, Kenya, in countries and regions throughout the world, the use of mercenary troops and units against indigenous colonial populations served only to strengthen the negative images of their employment. By the midpoint of the twentieth century, any nation deciding to use a mercenary force in a conflict with a weaker opponent found that their acceptance of a mercenary's service also required them to accept the condemnation that came with the practice. It behooved such nations, faced as they were with censure from many quarters, to find ways of concealing the fact of their hiring of mercenaries. Consequently, since it proved exceedingly difficult for a nation to keep their use of mercenaries a secret, the most common means by which a mercenary's service could be concealed was by presenting the mercenary troops as being something other than the hired soldiers they actually were.

Such was the situation when the United States began hiring foreign troops to fight in South Vietnam. Lyndon Johnson's use of mercenary troops, however, created a special situation for the Johnson Administration. Because of his need to have America's actions in South Vietnam accepted and condoned by the free world community of nations, Johnson did not want to keep the use of foreign soldiers in Southeast Asia a secret. On the contrary, he went out of his way to insure that the allied troop contributions received as much publicity as possible because their presence served as a vindication for his own actions. Nevertheless, since Johnson and his staff fully understood the furor which would inevitably result if these troops were perceived as mercenaries, it became mandatory that these troops carry a more acceptable label.* As a consequence, Washington maintained, throughout the period of America's use of mercenary troops in Southeast Asia, that those countries that sent their troops to fight in South Vietnam did so of their own volition and for their own purposes, and not as a mercenary force. As Washington repeatedly reported to any who would listen, these free world allies freely chose to make "the commitment of the lives and energies of their men for reasons of their own national interests and security, nothing more, nothing less."[3]

Despite their public assurances that the other free world troop-contributing nations were committing their soldiers for their own reasons and not as paid mercenaries, Johnson Administration officials still realized that these troops would generate a certain amount of criticism. These officials believed, however, that this criticism could be kept to a manageable minimum as long as the specific particulars of America's agreements with Korea, the Philippines, and Thailand remained secret. But the White House knew if this information ever became public knowledge, it would be exceedingly

---

*With generations of American schoolchildren being taught that George III's use of Hessian mercenaries during the Revolutionary War was an evil and unconscionable act of oppression, President Johnson was probably right to assume that few among the American citizenry would view his use of mercenaries as anything but a disreputable exercise.

difficult to defend against charges that the administration was hiring and using mercenaries. The resulting effects of such charges would then be nothing less than a total destruction of the political facade they had so patiently erected of an international consensus of support for Johnson's Vietnam policies.

Johnson Administration officials found it increasingly more difficult, as the number of Korean, Filipino, and Thai troops serving in Vietnam grew steadily, to keep secret the particulars of the U.S. arrangements for these nations' troops. Especially troublesome were the American media's demands for information on these agreements. In a 13 December 1967 memo in which he called President Johnson's attention to this problem, Walt W. Rostow, Johnson's National Security Advisor at the time, cautioned the president about releasing too much information to the press: "The mischievous can obviously use this information to push the line that we are using 'mercenaries' in Vietnam."[4] Ultimately, to President Johnson and his people, hiding the whole affair behind a national defense secrecy screen provided the best means to avoid or minimize public criticism:

> The Department has received requests from the press to release the texts of agreements entered into by the USG for assistance to the countries which have contributed forces in South Vietnam and to provide the items and dollar amounts of this assistance.
>
> The Department has concluded that release at this time of certain of the information of the kind requested would be prejudicial to the defense interests of the United States and that the nondisclosure of this information is sanctioned by Section 552 (b), Title 5 of the United States Code.[5]

Not all members of the Johnson White House staff, however, wholly agreed with this decision. Marshall Wright, an aide to Walt Rostow, pointed out to his boss that a total nondisclosure of America's assistance to its More Flags allies would itself prove troublesome:

> If we simply cite Section 552 (B) ... the press will suspect that we are hiding something awful and write the "mercenary" stories accordingly ... [with the result being] every time we try to get some mileage out of third country contributions in Vietnam the story will be soured by references to the mercenary issue.[6]

Though Wright's advice only advocated more government openness in dealing with the American citizenry—the use of mercenary troops would still be denied—President Johnson chose to ignore the recommendation. For the remainder of his time in office, Lyndon Johnson and the members of his administration continued to cite national security considerations as the excuse for not telling the American people about the U.S. use of mercenaries in South Vietnam.[7]

Despite the shroud of secrecy that Johnson Administration officials hung on the details of their hiring, America's use of mercenary troops in Vietnam was fairly common knowledge to many scholars, journalists, and politicians. The cloak of secrecy did, however, insure that the American people would only receive a bare minimum of information about this policy action of their government.

As a result, Washington denied the citizens of the United States an opportunity to air their opinions on whether or not the hiring of mercenaries constituted acceptable governmental policy. Although it may well have been true that there were "lots of Americans who don't give a damn how much it costs to support a foreign soldier so long as it enables an American boy to stay home,"[8] the simple truth remains that Lyndon Johnson never gave the American public an opportunity to make that determination.

It is very probable that there is no single answer to the question of whether mercenary use is or is not ethical or moral. The subject of the use of mercenaries is simply too complex, too tied up in individualized social and cultural values, to permit any philosophical consideration to stand as a single determining standard. Consequently, current and future hiring of mercenary troops, as has been the case in the past, will continue to be evaluated according to the specific situation of their use.

As for Lyndon Johnson's use of mercenaries in South Vietnam, his own actions insured a negative judgment. Given all his efforts to present the hiring of the Korean, Filipino, and Thai mercenaries as only a component of the More Flags program of free world aid to South Vietnam, President Johnson amply demonstrated his belief that there was something not quite moral in his use of mercenaries. Had Johnson and other administration officials considered the use of mercenary troops to be simply another, acceptable, diplomatic tool, then they would not have felt obliged to hide the facts of their employment. By his own actions then, Lyndon Johnson clearly pronounced judgment on the morality and ethics of using mercenaries in service to America.

Afterword

During the Vietnam War it became popular with a substantial number of American citizens to vent their frustrations with that war on the soldiers returning from Vietnam. What these people did not realize, perhaps, in making these assaults is that while soldiers do *fight* wars, governments and politicians *make* wars. Their anger and frustrations were thus misdirected.

A like situation exists with the Korean, Filipino, and Thai mercenary forces. It is true that the soldiers from these three nations fought as mercenaries in South Vietnam, but their service there came about in the first place because their governments and national politicians sent them. And it was these politicians that made the deals that sold the collective services of their soldiers. Thus, if there is a stigma attached to *mercenary,* then the men who made the policy decisions deserve the brand, not the men who only did the job they were sworn to do.

During almost two years of duty in Vietnam, this author had the good fortune to fight alongside, though never with, some units of the ROK Marines, and was never bothered by what label they wore. For mercenaries or no, these men, and their Filipino and Thai counterparts, shared the same dangers, the same hardships, and the same fears as any American there. These Korean, Filipino, and Thai soldiers were simply brave soldiers serving their country because their country's leaders said they had to, and 5,241 of them died following those orders.

There is no rancor nor reproach felt here toward the honorable services of these brave men.

Appendix A:
U.S. Military Losses
in Southeast Asia

Dates	Battle Deaths*	Wounded†
1959–1964	269	800
1965	1,426	3,300
1966	5,036	16,500
1967	9,461	32,400
1968	14,616	46,800
1969	9,413	32,900
1970	4,228	15,200
1971	1,373	4,800
1972	359	600
1973–1984	1,138	50
Totals	47,319	153,300

Missing

Missing, unaccounted for   662
Captured, unaccounted for   33

*Does not include the 10,449 who died of accidents and disease.

†Only those who required hospital care.

Sources: U.S. Bureau of the Census, *Statistical Abstract of the United States: 1986*, 16th ed. (Washington, D.C.: GPO, 1985), 342; and Shelby L. Stanton, *Vietnam Order of Battle* (New York: Exeter Books, 1987), 346.

Appendix B:
Strengths of Allied Military Forces in South Vietnam

*Troop totals in Vietnam as of
December 31 for each year*

Year	Korea	Thailand	Australia	Philippines	New Zealand
1964	<130	—	<200	17	30
1965	20,620	16	1,557	72	119
1966	44,566	244	4,525	2,061	155
1967	47,829	2,205	6,818	2,020	534
1968	50,003	6,005	7,661	1,576	516
1969	48,869	11,568	7,672	189	552
1970	48,537	11,586	6,763	77	441
1971	45,700	6,000	2,000	50	100
1972	36,790	40	130	50	50

Sources: Shelby L. Stanton, *Vietnam Order of Battle* (New York: Exeter Books, 1987), Appendix A; U.S. Congress. Senate. Committee on Foreign Relations. *Republic of Korea: Hearings on United States Security Agreements and Commitments Abroad*, Part 6, 91st Cong., 2d Sess., 1970: 1544; Stanley R. Larsen and James L. Collins, *Allied Participation in Vietnam* (Washington, D.C.: Department of the Army, 1975), 23.

Appendix C:
Chronology of Republic of Korea, Philippine, and Thailand Troop Commitments to South Vietnam

1964

16 August	Arrive	PHILCON I—The Philippine medical and civic action teams
13 September	Arrive	ROK Mobile Army Surgical Hospital and taekwondo instructors
29 September	Arrive	Royal Thai Air Force contingent

1965

25 February	Arrive	ROK Military Assistance Group, Vietnam (the "Dove Unit")
29 September	Arrive	Headquarters, ROK Capital Division
14 October	Arrive	Cavalry Regiment, ROK Capital Division
19 October	Arrive	2nd ROK Marine Brigade
29 October	Arrive	1st Infantry Regiment, ROK Capital Division

1966

16 April	Arrive	26th Infantry Regiment, ROK Capital Division
5 September	Arrive	Headquarters, ROK 9th Infantry Division
7 September	Arrive	28th Infantry Regiment, ROK 9th Infantry Division
14 September	Arrive	1st Philippine Civic Action Group (PHILCAG)
27 September	Arrive	29th Infantry Regiment, ROK 9th Infantry Division
9 October	Arrive	30th Infantry Regiment, ROK 9th Infantry Division

1967

19 September	Arrive	Royal Thai Army Regiment

1968

   15 August   Depart Royal Thai Army Regiment

1969

   9 January   Arrive 2nd Royal Thai Army Brigade, Royal Thai
                                    Army Expeditionary Division

   13 December Depart 1st Philippine Civic Action Group, Vietnam
                                    (PHILCAG)

1970

   15 January   Depart Rear elements of the PHILCAG

1971

   25 February   Arrive 1st Royal Thai Army Brigade, Royal Thai
                                    Army Expeditionary Division

   5 July   Arrive 3rd Royal Thai Army Brigade, Royal Thai
                                    Army Expeditionary Division

   August   Depart 3rd Royal Thai Army Brigade, Royal Thai
                                    Army Volunteer Force*

   5 August   Depart 1st Royal Thai Army Brigade, Royal Thai
                                    Army Expeditionary Division

   December   Depart 1st Marine Battalion, 2nd ROK Marine Brigade
                                    2nd Marine Battalion, 2nd ROK Marine Brigade

1972

   January   Depart 3rd Marine Battalion, 2nd ROK Marine Brigade

   15 January   Depart 3rd Battalion, 2nd Royal Thai Army Brigade,
                                    Royal Thai Army Volunteer Force*

   25 January   Depart 2nd Battalion, 2nd Royal Thai Army
                                    Brigade, Royal Thai Army Volunteer
                                    Force*

   February   Depart 5th Marine Battalion, 2nd ROK Marine
                                    Brigade

   4 February   Depart 1st Battalion, 2nd Royal Thai Army Brigade,
                                    Royal Thai Army Volunteer Force*

1973

   10 March   Depart All elements of the ROK Capital Division

   16 March   Depart All elements of the ROK 9th Infantry
                                    Division

---

*Elements of the Royal Thai Army Expeditionary Division which assumed this name in August 1970.

Sources: Shelby L. Stanton, *Vietnam Order of Battle* (New York: Exeter Books, 1987), 270–273; Stanley Robert Larsen and James Lawton Collins, Jr., *Allied Participation in Vietnam* (Washington, D.C.: Dept. of the Army, 1975), passim.

Appendix D:
Chronology of Australian and New Zealand Troop Commitments to South Vietnam

1962

31 July	Arrive	First contingents of Australian advisors forming the Australian Army Training Team (AATTV)

1964

7 July	Arrive	A platoon of engineers and a medical team of the Royal New Zealand Army

1965

25 May	Arrive	1st Battalion, Royal Australian Regiment 709th Australian Signal Troop Australian Logistics Support Company
21 July	Arrive	161st Artillery Battery, Royal New Zealand Artillery
14 September	Arrive	1st Australian Armored Personnel Carrier Troop 105th Field Artillery Battery, 4th Australian Field Regiment 3rd Field Troop, 1st Australian Field Squadron 527th Australian Signal Troop

1966

31 March	Depart	1st Australian Armored Personnel Carrier Troop 105th Field Artillery Battery, 4th Australian Field Regiment 3rd Field Troop, 1st Australian Field Squadron Australian Logistics Support Company

1 April	Arrive	5th Battalion, Royal Australian Regiment
		6th Battalion, Royal Australian Regiment
		1st Australian Armored Personnel Carrier Squadron
		1st Australian Field Artillery Regiment
		1st Australian Field Squadron
		3rd Australian Special Air Service Squadron
		21st Engineer Support Troop, 1st ATF
		103rd Signal Squadron, 1st ATF
		506th Australian Signal Troop
		520th Australian Signal Troop
		552nd Australian Signal Troop

1966

1 April	Arrive	581st Australian Signal Troop
		Headquarters, 145th Australian Signal Squadron
		1st Australian Logistics Support Group
		55th Australian Engineer Workshop and Park Squadron
		17th Australian Construction Squadron
		1st Royal Australian Army Service
14 June	Depart	1st Battalion, Royal Australian Regiment

1967

15 January	Depart	1st Australian Armored Personnel Carrier Squadron
16 January	Arrive	A Squadron, 3rd Australian Cavalry Regiment
2 March	Arrive	2nd Battalion, Royal Australian Regiment
		7th Battalion, Royal Australian Regiment
		4th Australian Field Artillery Regiment
2 March	Arrive	1st Australian Special Air Service Squadron
		1st Australian Civil Affairs Unit, AFV
		104th Signal Squadron, 1st ATF
		Headquarters, 110th Signal Squadron, AFV
		503rd Australian Signal Troop
		532nd Australian Signal Troop

		547th Australian Signal Troop
		557th Australian Signal Troop
		561st Australian Signal Troop
		704th Australian Signal Troop
		5th Royal Australian Army Service
*11 May	Arrive	"V" Rifle Company, Royal New Zealand Infantry
1 June	Arrive	176th AD Company
5 July	Depart	5th Battalion, Royal Australian Regiment
		6th Battalion, Royal Australian Regiment
		1st Australian Field Artillery Regiment
		3rd Australian Special Air Service Squadron
		103rd Signal Squadron, 1st ATF
		506th Australian Signal Troop
		520th Australian Signal Troop
		527th Australian Signal Troop
5 July	Depart	552nd Australian Signal Troop
		581st Australian Signal Troop
		Headquarters, 145th Australian Signal Squadron
		1st Royal Australian Army Service
13 November	Arrive	1st Australian Field Hospital
20 November	Depart	503rd Australian Signal Troop
		532nd Australian Signal Troop
		557th Australian Signal Troop
		561st Australian Signal Troop
		704th Australian Signal Troop
		709th Australian Signal Troop
12 December	Arrive	3rd Battalion, Royal Australian Regiment
*17 December	Arrive	"W" Rifle Company, Royal New Zealand Infantry

1968

8 January	Arrive	26th Royal Australian Army Service
19 January	Arrive	Second tour of duty, 1st Battalion, Royal Australian Regiment
29 January	Arrive	4th Battalion, Royal Australian Regiment
		C Squadron, 1st Australian Armored Regiment
		12th Australian Field Artillery Regiment
		2nd Australian Special Air Service Squadron

12 February	Depart	1st Australian Special Air Service Squadron
26 April	Depart	7th Battalion, Royal Australian Regiment
28 May	Depart	4th Australian Field Artillery Regiment
18 June	Depart	2nd Battalion, Royal Australian Regiment
5 November	Arrive	9th Battalion, Royal Australian Regiment
5 December	Depart	3rd Battalion, Royal Australian Regiment

1969

28 January	Arrive	Second tour of duty, 5th Battalion, Royal Australian Regiment
3 February	Arrive	Second tour of duty, 3rd Australian Special Air Service Squadron
10 February	Depart	C Squadron, 1st Australian Armored Regiment
11 February	Arrive	B Squadron, 1st Australian Armored Regiment
25 February	Arrive	Second tour of duty, 1st Australian Field Artillery Regiment
28 February	Depart	1st Battalion, Royal Australian Regiment
4 March	Depart	2nd Australian Special Air Service Squadron
11 March	Depart	12th Australian Field Artillery Regiment
7 May	Arrive	Second tour of duty, 6th Battalion, Royal Australian Regiment
12 May	Depart	A Squadron, 3rd Australian Cavalry Regiment
13 May	Arrive	B Squadron, 3rd Australian Cavalry Regiment
30 May	Depart	4th Battalion, Royal Australian Regiment
18 November	Arrive	8th Battalion, Royal Australian Regiment
5 December	Depart	9th Battalion, Royal Australian Regiment
22 December	Depart	B Squadron, 1st Australian Armored Regiment
23 December	Arrive	A Squadron, 1st Australian Armored Regiment

1970

3 February	Arrive	Second tour of duty, 1st Australian Special Air Service Squadron

10 February	Arrive	Second tour of duty, 7th Battalion, Royal Australian Regiment
20 February	Depart	3rd Australian Special Air Service Squadron
24 February	Arrive	Second tour of duty, 4th Australian Field Artillery Regiment
5 March	Depart	5th Battalion, Royal Australian Regiment
28 April	Arrive	Second tour of duty, 2nd Battalion, Royal Australian Regiment
10 May	Depart	1st Australian Field Artillery Regiment
28 May	Depart	6th Battalion, Royal Australian Regiment
November	Depart	"W" Rifle Company, Royal New Zealand Infantry
12 November	Depart	8th Battalion, Royal Australian Regiment
16 December	Depart	A Squadron, 1st Australian Armored Regiment
17 December	Arrive	C Squadron, 1st Australian Armored Regiment

1971

6 January	Depart	B Squadron, 3rd Australian Cavalry Regiment
7 January	Arrive	Second tour of duty, A Squadron, 3rd Australian Cavalry Regiment
27 January	Arrive	Second tour of duty, 12th Australian Field Artillery Regiment
12 February	Arrive	Second tour of duty, 3rd Battalion, Royal Australian Regiment
18 February	Arrive	Second tour of duty, 2nd Australian Special Air Service Squadron
	Depart	1st Australian Special Air Service Squadron
March	Depart	161st Artillery Battery, Royal New Zealand Artillery
10 March	Depart	7th Battalion, Royal Australian Regiment
18 March	Depart	4th Australian Field Artillery Regiment
1 May	Arrive	Second tour of duty, 4th Battalion, Royal Australian Regiment
5 May	Arrive	104th Australian Field Artillery Battery

4 June	Depart	2nd Battalion, Royal Australian Regiment
30 June	Depart	26th Royal Australian Army Service
30 September	Depart	C Squadron, 1st Australian Armored Regiment
15 October	Depart	2nd Australian Special Air Service Squadron
16 October	Depart	1st Australian Logistics Support Group
19 October	Depart	3rd Battalion, Royal Australian Regiment
18 November	Depart	1st Australian Field Squadron
		176th AD Company
25 November	Depart	1st Australian Civil Affairs Unit, AFV
December	Depart	"V" Rifle Company, Royal New Zealand Infantry
9 December	Depart	21st Engineer Support Troop, 1st ATF
14 December	Depart	1st Australian Field Hospital
15 December	Depart	104th Signal Squadron, 1st ATF
20 December	Depart	104th Australian Field Artillery Battery
		12th Australian Field Artillery Regiment
23 December	Depart	547th Australian Signal Troop

1972

12 February	Depart	17th Australian Construction Squadron
12 March	Depart	4th Battalion, Royal Australian Regiment
		A Squadron, 3rd Australian Cavalry Regiment
		110th Signal Squadron, AFV
		55th Australian Engineer Workshop and Park Squadron
		5th Royal Australian Army Service
18 December	Depart	Australian Army Training Team

*The "V" and "W" Rifle companies were provided on a rotational basis from the New Zealand Battalion of the 28th Commonwealth Brigade serving in Malaysia.

Sources: Shelby L. Stanton, *Vietnam Order of Battle* (New York: Exeter Books, 1987), 267–269; and, Harry G. Summers, Jr., *Vietnam War Almanac* (New York: Facts on File Publications, 1985), 264.

Chapter Notes

Introduction

1. John S. Bowman, ed., *The Vietnam War: An Almanac* (New York: Bison Books, 1985), 358.
2. U.S. Congress, Senate, Senator Stephen R. Young of Ohio, 90th Cong., 1st sess., *Congressional Record* (8 March 1967), Vol. 113, pt. 5, 5870.
3. James Otis, "Seoul's Hired Guns," *Ramparts,* Vol. 11, No. 3 (September 1972), 19.
4. William E. McCarron, "On Machiavelli and Vietnam," in *Military Ethics: Reflections on Principles — The Profession of Arms, Military Leadership, Ethical Practices, War and Morality, Educating the Citizen Soldier,* Malham Wakin, Kenneth Wenker, and James Kempf, eds. (Washington, D.C.: National Defense University Press, 1987), 195.
5. Bowman, *The Vietnam War: An Almanac;* Harry G. Summers, Jr., *Vietnam War Almanac* (New York: Facts on File, 1985); and, James S. Olson, ed., *Dictionary of the Vietnam War* (Westport, Conn.: Greenwood Press, 1987).

Chapter 1. Lyndon Johnson and "More Flags"

1. The books and articles used in the writing of this section, in addition to those receiving specific citation, are: Jack Bell, *The Johnson Treatment* (New York: Harper & Row, 1965); James D. Barber, *The Presidential Character* (Englewood Cliffs, N.J.: Prentice-Hall, 1972); Jack Valenti, *A Very Human President* (New York: W.W. Norton, 1975); Doris Kearns, "Lyndon Johnson's Political Personality," *Political Science Quarterly* 91 (Fall, 1976); Alfred Steinberg, *Sam Johnson's Boy: A Close-Up of the President from Texas* (New York: Macmillan, 1968); and Chester L. Cooper, *The Lost Crusade: America in Viet-Nam* (New York: Dodd, Mead, 1970).
2. Paul K. Conkin, *Big Daddy from the Pedernales: Lyndon Baines Johnson* (Boston: Twayne Publishers, 1986), 64.
3. Rowland Evans and Robert Novak, *Lyndon B. Johnson: The Exercise in Power* (New York: New American Library, 1966).

4. Richard N. Goodwin, *Remembering America: A Voice from the Sixties* (Boston: Little, Brown, 1988), 260.

5. Justice Abe Fortas, as quoted in Bernard J. Firestone and Robert C. Vogt, eds., *Lyndon Baines Johnson and the Uses of Power* (New York: Greenwood Press, 1988), 290.

6. Larry Berman, as quoted in Robert A. Divine, "The Johnson Revival: A Bibliographical Appraisal," in *The Johnson Years, Volume Two: Vietnam, the Environment, and Science,* ed. Robert A. Divine (Lawrence: University Press of Kansas, 1987), 14.

7. Kathleen J. Turner, *Lyndon Johnson's Dual War: Vietnam and the Press* (Chicago: University of Chicago Press, 1985), 53.

8. George C. Herring, *America's Longest War: The United States and Vietnam, 1950–1975,* 2nd ed. (New York: Alfred A. Knopf, 1986), 79.

9. I.M. Destler, Leslie H. Gelb and Anthony Lake, *Our Own Worst Enemy: The Unmaking of American Foreign Policy,* updated and rev. ed. (New York: Simon & Schuster, 1984), 196–7.

10. Robert S. McNamara, "United States Policy in Viet-Nam," *Department of State Bulletin,* Vol. L, No. 1294 (April 13, 1964), 562–70.

11. Memo, Forrestal to President, 3/21/64, "Vietnam Memos, Vol. VI, 3/64," Item No. 79. NSF Country File—VN, Box 3. L.B.J. Library.

12. Dallek, Robert, *Lone Star Rising: Lyndon Johnson and His Times 1908–1960* (New York: Oxford University Press, 1991).

13. Vaughn Davis Bornet, *The Presidency of Lyndon B. Johnson* (Lawrence: University Press of Kansas, 1983), 166.

14. Michael Davies, *LBJ: A Foreign Observer's Viewpoint* (New York: Duell, Sloan and Pearce, 1966), 81.

15. Jim F. Heath, *Decade of Disillusionment* (Bloomington: Indiana University Press, 1975), 10.

16. Larry L. King, "Machismo in the White House: L.B.J. and Vietnam," *American Heritage,* Vol. 27, No. 5 (August 1976), 12.

17. Paul M. Kattenburg, "Viet Nam and U.S. Diplomacy, 1940–1970," *Orbis,* Vol. 15, No. 3 (Fall 1971), 834.

18. *Ibid.* Similar ideas can also be found in, Walter LaFeber, "Consensus and Cooperation: A View of United States Foreign Policy, 1945–1980," in *United States Foreign Policy at the Crossroads,* George Schwab, ed. (Westport, Conn.: Greenwood Press, 1982), 8–9.

19. *The Pentagon Papers as published by The New York Times* (New York: Quadrangle Books, 1971), 7–8.

20. McNamara and Rusk, as quoted in John L.S. Girling, *America and the Third World: Revolution and Intervention* (London: Routledge & Kegan Paul, 1980), 84.

21. *Ibid.*

22. Gary Porter, "Globalism—The Ideology of Total World Involve-

ment," in *The Vietnam Reader,* Marcus G. Raskin and Bernard B. Fall, eds. (New York: Vintage Books, 1965), 326; Hans J. Morgenthau, "Vietnam and the National Interest," in *Viet Nam: History, Documents, and Opinions on a Major World Crisis,* Marvin E. Gettleman, ed. (Greenwich, Conn.: Fawcett Publications, 1965), 366–70; Bernard Brodie, *War and Politics* (New York: Macmillan, 1973), 151; and Ralph K. White, *Nobody Wanted War* (Garden City, N.Y.: Doubleday, 1968), 126–8.

23. Clark M. Clifford, "Viet Nam Reappraisal," *Foreign Affairs,* Vol. 47, No. 4 (July 1969), 612.

Chapter 2. "More Flags": The First Year

1. U.S. President, *Public Papers of the Presidents of the United States* (Washington, D.C.: Office of the *Federal Register,* National Archives and Records Service, 1965), Lyndon B. Johnson, November 22, 1963, to June 30, 1964, 285.

2. Stanley Robert Larsen and James Lawton Collins, Jr., *Allied Participation in Vietnam* (Washington, D.C.: Department of the Army, 1975), 1–2.

3. *The Pentagon Papers,* Gravel Edition, Vol. III (Boston: Beacon Press, 1972), 65.

4. Jack Bell, *The Johnson Treatment: How Lyndon B. Johnson Took Over the Presidency and Made It His Own* (New York: Harper & Row, 1965), 203–4.

5. Message, Rusk to AmEmbassies, 5/1/64, "Vietnam Memos, Vol. VIII, 5/64," Item No. 110, pp. 3–4. NSF Country File—VN, Box 4. L.B.J. Library.

6. *Ibid.,* 4.

7. *Ibid.*

8. Message, Ball to AmEmbassies, 7/10/64, "Vietnam Memos, Vol. XIII, 6/64–7/64," Item No. 31, p. 3. NSF Country File—VN, Box 6. L.B.J. Library.

9. Status Report, 12/20/67, "Vietnam 5D 3/67–1/69," Item No. 35f. NSF Country File—VN, Box 85–91. L.B.J. Library.

10. *Ibid.,* 7.

11. *Ibid.,* 14.

12. Message, AmEmbassy Saigon to SecState, 5/11/64, "Vietnam Memos, Vol. VIII, 5/64," Item No. 101. NSF Country File—VN, Box 4. L.B.J. Library.

13. Message, Ball to AmEmbassy Saigon, 7/10/64, "Vietnam Memos, Vol. XIII, 6/64–7/64," Item No. 32. NSF Country File—VN, Box 6. L.B.J. Library.

14. Message, Rusk to AmEmbassies, 7/10/64, "Vietnam Memos,

Vol. XIII, 6/64–7/64," Item No. 31. NSF Country File — VN, Box 6. L.B.J. Library.

15. Message, Rusk to AmEmbassy Saigon, 7/13/64, "Vietnam Memos, Vol. XIII, 6/64–7/64," Item No. 29. NSF Country File — VN, Box 6. L.B.J. Library.

16. Message, Taylor to SecState, 7/14/64, "Vietnam Memos, Vol. XIII, 6/64–7/64," Item No. 13c, p. 1. NSF Country File — VN, Box 6. L.B.J. Library.

17. *Ibid.*

18. *Ibid.*, 2.

19. Message, Taylor to SecState, 7/17/64, "Vietnam Cables, Vol. XIV, 7/64," Item No. 117. NSF Country File — VN, Box 6. L.B.J. Library.

20. Message, Taylor to SecState, 7/28/64, "Vietnam Cables, Vol. XIV, 7/64," Item No. 26. NSF Country File — VN, Box 6. L.B.J. Library.

21. Memo, Cooper to President, 12/28/64, "Vietnam Memos, Vol. XXVI, 1/10–31/65," Item No. 215. NSF Country File — VN, Box 12. L.B.J. Library.

22. Memo, Cooper to President, 12/22/64, "Vietnam Memos, Vol. XXIV, 12/19–25/64," Item No. 209. NSF Country File — VN, Box 11. L.B.J. Library.

23. Memo, Rusk to President, 6/15/64, "Vietnam Memos, Vol. XII, 6/14–27/64," Item No. 7. NSF Country File — VN, Box 5. L.B.J. Library.

24. *Ibid.*, cover letter.

25. Message, AmEmbassy Bonn to SecState, 5/9/64, "Vietnam Memos, Vol. VIII, 5/64," Item No. 104. NSF Country File — VN, Box 4. L.B.J. Library; Message, AmEmbassy Bonn to SecState, 5/11/64, "Vietnam Memos, Vol. VIII, 5/64," Item No. 100. NSF Country File — VN, Box 4. L.B.J. Library; Message, AmEmbassy Saigon to SecState, 5/19/64, "Vietnam Memos, Vol. IX, 5/13–23/64," Item No. 6. NSF Country File — VN, Box 4. L.B.J. Library; and, Message, AmEmbassy Bonn to SecState, 5/29/64, "Vietnam Memos, Vol. X, 5/24–30/64," Item No. 28. NSF Country File — VN, Box 5. L.B.J. Library.

26. Message, SecState to AmEmbassy Bonn, 6/8/64, "Vietnam Memos, Vol. XI, 6/1–13/64," Item No. 11. NSF Country File — VN, Box 5. L.B.J. Library.

27. *Ibid.*

28. *Ibid.*, 1–2.

29. *Ibid.*, 2.

30. Memo, Sullivan to Bundy, 6/24/64, "Vietnam Memos, Vol. XII, 6/14–27/64," Item No. 5. NSF Country File — VN, Box 5. L.B.J. Library.

31. Message, President to AmEmbassies, 7/2/64, "Vietnam Memos, Vol. XIII, 6/64–7/64," Item No. 78. NSF Country File — VN, Box 6. L.B.J. Library.

32. *Ibid.*, 4.

33. Message, SecState to AmEmbassies, 8/14/64, "Vietnam Memos, Vol. XV, 8/64," Item No. 140. NSF Country File—VN, Box 7. L.B.J. Library.

34. Research Memo, Thomas L. Hughes to Secretary Rusk, 8/28/64, "Vietnam Memos, Vol. XVI, 8/16–31/64," Item No. 143. NSF Country File—VN, Box 7, Cover letter & p. 1. L.B.J. Library.

35. Memo, Forrestal to President, 12/11/64, "Vietnam Memos, Vol. XXIII, 12/1–18/64," Item No. 173, p. 6. NSF Country File—VN, Box 11. L.B.J. Library.

36. Letter, President to AmEmbassy Saigon, 12/3/64, "Vietnam Memos, Vol. XXIII, 12/1–18/64," Item No. 160a, p. 4. NSF Country File—VN, Box 11. L.B.J. Library.

37. Memo, Thomson to Bundy, 12/11/64, "Vietnam Memos, Vol. XXIII, 12/1–18/64," Item No. 176. NSF Country File—VN, Box 11. L.B.J. Library.

38. Message, CINCPAC to JCS, 12/23/64, "Vietnam Memos, Vol. XXIV, 12/19–25/64," Item No. 223. NSF Country File—VN, Box 11. L.B.J. Library.

39. Memo, National Security Council (NSC) to Bundy, 12/24/64, "Vietnam Memos, Vol. XXIV, 12/19–25/64," Item No. 195. NSF Country File—VN, Box 11. L.B.J. Library.

40. Message, Rusk to AmEmbassies, 12/29/64, "Vietnam Memos, Vol. XXV, 12/26/64–1/9/65," Item No. 145. NSF Country File—VN, Box 12. L.B.J. Library.

41. Message, Rusk to AmEmbassies, 1/16/65, "Vietnam Memos, Vol. XXVI, 1/10–31/65," Item No. 153. NSF Country File—VN, Box 12. L.B.J. Library.

42. Message, Rusk to AmEmbassies, 3/5/65, "Vietnam Memos, Vol. XXX, 3/1–8/65," Item No. 163. NSF Country File—VN, Box 14. L.B.J. Library.

43. Edward Doyle, Samuel Lipsman, and the editors of Boston Publishing Company, eds., *America Takes Over: 1965–67,* the Vietnam Experience Series (Boston: Boston Pub. Co., 1982), 124.

44. Memo, World Sitrep, 5/26/65, "Vietnam Memos, Vol. XXXIV, 5/65," Item No. 311a. NSF Country File—VN, Box 17. L.B.J. Library.

45. Message, AmEmbassy Karachi to SecState, 5/23/64, "Vietnam Memos, Vol. X, 5/24–30/64," Item No. 30. NSF Country File—VN, Box 5. L.B.J. Library; and, Message, AmEmbassy Karachi to SecState, 12/23/64, "Vietnam Memos, Vol. XXIV, 12/19–25/64," Item No. 214. NSF Country File—VN, Box 11. L.B.J. Library.

46. Memo, Cooper to President, 1/28/65, "Vietnam Memos, Vol. XXVI, 1/10–31/65," Item No. 157. NSF Country File—VN, Box 12. L.B.J. Library.

47. Message, Rusk to AmEmbassy Saigon, 1/28/65, "Vietnam Memos,

Vol. XXVI, 1/10–31/65," Item No. 158. NSF Country File – VN, Box 12. L.B.J. Library.

48. Stephen T. Hosmer, *Constraints on U.S. Strategy in Third World Conflicts* (New York: Crane Russak, 1987), 90.

Chapter 3. *The Republic of Korea Commitment*

1. James Otis, "Seoul's Hired Guns," *Ramparts,* Vol. 11, No. 3 (September 1972).

2. Stanley Robert Larsen and James Lawton Collins, Jr., *Allied Participation in Vietnam* (Washington, D.C.: Department of the Army, 1975), 121.

3. Message, Ball to AmEmbassy Saigon, 7/10/64, "Vietnam Memos, Vol. XIII, 6/64–7/64," Item No. 31. NSF Country File – VN, Box 6, p. 3. L.B.J. Library.

4. Research Memorandum, Hughes to SecState, 8/28/64, "Vietnam Memos, Vol. XVI, 8/16–31/64," Item No. F143. NSF Country File – VN, p. 6. L.B.J. Library.

5. Memo, Forrestal to President, 12/11/64, "Vietnam Memos, Vol. XXIII, 12/1–18/64," Item No. 173. NSF Country File – VN, Box 11, p. 3. L.B.J. Library.

6. Message, AmEmbassy Taipei to AmEmbassy Seoul, 3/21/64, "Vietnam Memos, Vol. VI, 3/64," Item No. 79. NSF Country File – VN, Box 3. L.B.J. Library.

7. Memo, Rusk to President, 6/15/64, "Vietnam Memos, Vol. XII, 6/14–27/64," Item No. 7. NSF Country File – VN, Box 5. L.B.J. Library.

8. Message, Rusk to AmEmbassy Seoul, 7/3/64, "Vietnam Memos, Vol. XIII, 6/64–7/64," Item No. 41. NSF Country File – VN, Box 6. L.B.J. Library.

9. Message, Rusk to AmEmbassy Seoul, 7/3/64, "Vietnam Memos, Vol. XIII, 6/64–7/64," Item No. 41. NSF Country File – VN, Box 6, p. 2. L.B.J. Library; and, Memo, Rusk to President, 6/15/64, "Vietnam Memos, Vol. XII, 6/14–27/64," Item No. 7. NSF Country File – VN, Box 5, p. 5. L.B.J. Library.

10. Message, Lodge to Rusk, 5/9/64, "Vietnam Memos, Vol. VIII, 5/64," No Item No. NSF Country File – VN, Box 4. L.B.J. Library.

11. *Ibid.*

12. Message, Ball to AmEmbassy Seoul, 5/12/64, "Vietnam Memos, Vol. VIII, 5/64," Item No. 77. NSF Country File – VN, Box 4. L.B.J. Library.

13. Memo, Forrestal to President, dated 12/11/64.

14. Sungjoo Han, "South Korea's Participation in the Vietnam Conflict: An Analysis of the U.S.-Korean Alliance," *Orbis,* Vol. 21, No. 4 (Winter 1978), 893.

15. Joon Young Park, *Korea's Return to Asia: South Korean Foreign Policy, 1965–1975* (Seoul, Korea: Jin Heong Press, 1985), 102.

16. Message, Department of Defense to AmEmbassy Seoul, 12/19/64, "Vietnam Memos, Vol. XXIV, 12/19–25/64," Item No. 233. NSF Country File—VN, Box 11. L.B.J. Library.

17. Memo, Cooper to President, 12/22/64, "Vietnam Memos, Vol. XXIV, 12/19–25/64," Item No. 209. NSF Country File—VN, Box 11. L.B.J. Library.

18. *Ibid.*

19. Message, Department of Defense to Commander in Chief Pacific (CINCPAC), 12/27/64, "Vietnam Memos, Vol. XXV, 12/26–1/9/65," Item No. 147. NSF Country File—VN, Box 12. L.B.J. Library.

20. Message, AmEmbassy Seoul to SecState, 12/29/64, "Vietnam Memos, Vol. XXIV, 12/19–25/64," Item No. 208a. NSF Country File—VN, Box 11, L.B.J. Library.

21. Memo, Cooper to President, 1/5/65, "Vietnam Memos, Vol. XXV, 12/26/64–1/9/65," Item No. 120. NSF Country File—VN, Box 12. L.B.J. Library.

22. Park, *Korea's Return to Asia,* 89.

23. Larsen and Collins, *Allied Participation,* 122.

24. Message, AmEmbassy Seoul to SecState, 12/19/64, "Korean Memos, Vol. II, 7/64–8/65," Item No. 47. NSF Country File—Korea, Box 254–256. L.B.J. Library.

25. *Ibid.*

26. Message, AmEmbassy Seoul to SecState, 2/24/65. "Korean Memos, Vol. II, 7/64–8/65," Item No. 46. NSF Country File—Korea, Box 254–256. L.B.J. Library.

27. William J. Porter, as quoted in: U.S. Congress, Senate, Committee on Foreign Relations. *Republic of Korea: Hearings of the Subcommittee on United States Security Agreements and Commitments Abroad,* 91st Cong., 2d sess., 1970, Part 6: 1543–4.

28. *The United States Government Manual 1991–92* (National Archives and Records Administration: 1991), 748.

29. Memo for Mr. Bundy, 12/24/64, "Vietnam Memos, Vol. XXIV, 12/19–25/64," Item No. 195. NSF Country File—VN, Box 11. L.B.J. Library.

30. Park, *Korea's Return to Asia,* 87–8.

31. Message, Office of Strategic Development (OSD) to AmEmbassies, 1/15/65, "Vietnam Memos, Vol. XXVI, 1/10–31/65," Item No. 152. NSF Country File—VN, Box 12. L.B.J. Library.

32. Message, AmEmbassy Seoul to SecState, dated 12/19/64.

33. Message, OSD to AmEmbassies, dated 1/15/65.

34. Message, AmEmbassy Seoul to SecState, dated 2/24/65.

35. Message, AmEmbassy Seoul to SecState, 3/2/65. "Korean Memos,

Vol. II, 7/64–8/65," Item No. 45. NSF Country File — Korea, Box 254–256. L.B.J. Library.

36. Park, *Korea's Return to Asia,* 89–90; Han, "South Korea's Participation in the Vietnam Conflict," 897–8; and, Princeton N. Lyman, "Korea's Involvement in Viet Nam," *Orbis,* Vol. XII, No. 2 (Summer 1968), 563.

37. Park Chung Hee, *To Build a Nation* (Washington, D.C.: Acropolis Books, 1971), 131.

38. Kim Chun-yon as quoted in Bae-Ho Hahn's "Major Issues in the American-Korean Alliance," in *Korea and the United States,* Youngnok Koo and Dae-Sook Suh, eds. (Honolulu: University of Hawaii Press, 1984), 360.

39. Message, DOD to AmEmbassy Saigon, dated 12/19/64; and, Message, DOD to JCS, 12/23/64, "Vietnam Memos, Vol. XXIV, 12/19–25/64," Item No. 223. NSF Country File — VN, Box 11. L.B.J. Library.

40. George C. Herring, *America's Longest War: The United States and Vietnam, 1950–1975,* 2d ed. (New York: Alfred A. Knopf, 1986), 132.

41. Supplemental Memo, Rusk to President, 5/17/65, "Korea Memos, Park Visit, 5/65," Item No. 12. NSF Country File — Korea, Box 254–256. L.B.J. Library.

42. Memo, Cooper to Bundy, 1/14/65, "Korea Memos, Vol. II, 7/64–8/65," Item No. 155. NSF Country File — Korea, Box 254–256. L.B.J. Library.

43. Memo, Thomson to the President, 5/17/65, "Park Visit Briefing Book, 5/17–19/65," Item No. 2. NSF Country File — Korea, Box 254–265. L.B.J. Library.

44. Message, AmEmbassy Seoul to SecState, 5/1/65, "Korea Cables, Vol. II, 7/64–8/65," Item No. 30. NSF Country File — Korea, Box 254–256. L.B.J. Library.

45. Message, AmEmbassy Seoul to SecState, 7/29/65, "Korea Cables, Vol. II, 7/64–8/65," Item No. 10, p. 2. NSF Country File — Korea, Box 254–256. L.B.J. Library.

46. *Ibid.*

47. General Dwight E. Beach, as quoted in Larsen and Collins, *Allied Participation in Vietnam,* 125.

48. Lyman, "Korea's Involvement," 566–7; and Tae-Hwan Kwak, "U.S.-Korea Security Relations," in *U.S. Korean Relations, 1882–1982,* Tae-Hwan Kwak, ed. (Seoul, Korea: Institute for Far Eastern Studies, 1982), 227.

49. General Beach, as quoted in Larsen and Collins, *Allied Participation in Vietnam,* 125.

50. Message, AmEmbassy Seoul to SecState, dated 7/29/65, p. 3.

51. Message, AmEmbassy Seoul to SecState, dated 5/1/65, section 1 page 2, and section 2 page 2; U.S. Congress, Senate, *Republic of Korea:*

Hearings, 1569; Han, "South Korea's Participation," 898–90; Larsen and Collins, *Allied Participation in Vietnam*, 125–9; Message, AmEmbassy Seoul to SecState, 7/3/65, "Korea Cables, Vol. II, 7/64–8/65," Item No. 18. NSF Country File—Korea, Box 254–256. L.B.J. Library; and, Message, Rusk to AmEmbassy Seoul, 8/5/65, "Korea Cables, Vol. II, 7/64–8/65," Item No. 71. NSF Country File—Korea, Box 254–256. L.B.J. Library.

    52. Larsen and Collins, *Allied Participation in Vietnam*, 127.

    53. *Ibid.*

    54. U.S. Congress, Senate, *Republic of Korea: Hearings,* 1571.

    55. Message, AmEmbassy Seoul to SecState, 7/10/65, "Korea Cables, Vol. II, 7/64–8/65," Item No. 17. NSF Country File—Korea, Box 254–256. L.B.J. Library.

    56. Larsen and Collins, *Allied Participation in Vietnam*, 128.

    57. Memo, Ball to Presidential Staff, 6/29/65, "Vietnam Memos, Vol. XXXV, 6/16–30/65," Item No. 349. NSF Country File—VN, Box 19. L.B.J. Library.

    58. Message, AmEmbassy Seoul to SecState, 6/7/65, "Korea Cables, Vol. II, 7/64–8/65," Item No. 20. NSF Country File—Korea, Box 254–256. L.B.J. Library.

    59. U.S. Congress, Senate, *Republic of Korea: Hearings,* 1539.

    60. Memo of Conversation, Bundy with Korean Ambassador, 12/7/65, "Korea Memos, Vol. III, 11/65–12/66," Item No. 107. NSF Country File—Korea, Box 254–256. L.B.J. Library.

    61. Larsen and Collins, *Allied Participation in Vietnam*, 17.

    62. Han, "South Korea's Participation," 899.

    63. Chester L. Cooper, *The Lost Crusade: America in Vietnam* (New York: Dodd, Mead, 1970), 300–301.

    64. Park, *Korea's Return to Asia*, 94–5.

    65. *Ibid.*

    66. U.S. Congress, Senate, *Republic of Korea: Hearings,* 1533.

    67. U.S. Congress, Senate, *Republic of Korea: Hearings,* 1532–4.

    68. Park, *Korea's Return to Asia*, 103.

    69. U.S. Congress, Senate, *Republic of Korea: Hearings,* 1563.

    70. *New York Times,* 30 and 31 May, 1969; and, Report, Maxwell and Taylor to President Johnson, 8/5/67, "Vietnam 5D, 3/67–1/69," Item No. 44A. NSF Country File—VN, Box 85–91. L.B.J. Library.

    71. Park, *Korea's Return to Asia*, 104.

    72. *Ibid.*

    73. Message, AmEmbassy Seoul to SecState, 11/25/67, "Vietnam Allies, Vol. 5D (3), 1967–1969," Item No. 87. NSF Country File—VN, Box 85–91. L.B.J. Library.

    74. Message, AmEmbassy Seoul to SecState, 12/6/67, "Vietnam Allies, Vol. 5D (3), 1967–1969," Item No. 74a. NSF Country File—VN, Box 85–91. L.B.J. Library.

75. *Ibid.*, 2.

76. NOFORM, Status Report, no author, 12/20/67, "Vietnam 5D, 3/67–1/69," Item No. 35f. NSF Country File — VN, Box 85–91, p. 2. L.B.J. Library.

77. Message, AmEmbassy Saigon to SecState, 1/19/68, "Vietnam Allies 5D (3), 1967–1969," Item No. 45. NSF Country File — VN, Box 85–91. L.B.J. Library.

78. Message, CINCPAC to SecState, 1/19/68, "Vietnam Allies 5D (3), 1967–1969," Item No. 44. NSF Country File — VN, Box 85–91. L.B.J. Library.

79. Message, Rusk to AmEmbassy Seoul, 11/30/67, "Vietnam Allies, 5D (3), 1967–1969," Item No. 85. NSF Country File — VN, Box 85–91. L.B.J. Library; and, Memo, Rostow to President, 1/5/68, "Vietnam Allies, 5D (3), 1967–1969," Item No. 56. NSF Country File — VN, Box 85–91. L.B.J. Library.

80. Lyman, "Korea's Involvement in Viet Nam," 571.

81. U.S. Congress, Senate, *Republic of Korea: Hearings,* passim.

82. Message, White House Situation Room to Rostow, 4/17/68, "Vietnam Allies 5D (3), 1967–1969," Item No. 17. NSF Country File — VN, Box 85–91. L.B.J. Library.

83. Han, "South Korea's Participation," 107.

84. U.S. Congress, Senate, *Republic of Korea: Hearings,* 1571.

85. Park, *Korea's Return to Asia,* 113.

86. Edward Doyle, Samuel Lipsman, and the editors of Boston Publishing Company, eds., *America Takes Over, 1965–1967,* the Vietnam Experience Series (Boston: Boston Pub. Co., 1982), 132.

87. Soon, Sung Cho, "American Policy Toward Korean Unification, 1945–1980," in *U.S.-Korean Relations: 1882–1982,* Tae-Kwan Kwak, ed. (Seoul, Korea: Institute for Far Eastern Studies, 1982), 81; and, Han, "South Korea's Participation," 897.

88. Lyman, "Korea's Involvement in Vietnam," 575–6.

89. U.S. Congress, Senate, *Republic of Korea: Hearings,* 1568.

90. Message, Rusk to AmEmbassy Saigon, 1/28/65, "Vietnam Memos, Vol. XXVI, 1/10–31/65," Item No. 215. NSF Country File — VN, Box 12. L.B.J. Library; Memo, Rostow to President, 12/13/67, "Vietnam 5D, 3/67–1/69," Item No. 36. NSF Country File — VN, Box 85–91. L.B.J. Library; and, Memo, Wright to Rostow, 12/16/67, "Vietnam 5D, 3/67–1/69," Item No. 36a. NSF Country File — VN, Box 85–91. L.B.J. Library.

91. Memo, Zwick to President, 2/1/68, "Vietnam: Jan.-Feb. 1968," Item No. 18b. NSF — Walt Rostow, Box 6. L.B.J. Library.

92. Memo, President to Bunker, 2/2/68, "Vietnam: Jan.-Feb. 1968," Item No. 16. NSF — Walt Rostow, Box 6. L.B.J. Library.

93. *Congressional Record,* 90th Cong., 1st sess., 1967, Vol. 113, pt. 6: 7514.

Chapter 4. The Philippines PHILCAG Contingent

1. Stanley Robert Larsen and James Lawton Collins, Jr., *Allied Participation in Vietnam* (Washington, D.C.: Department of the Army, 1975), 52; and, Memo, Hughes to SecState, 8/28/64, "Vietnam Memos, Vol. XVI, 8/16-31/64," Item No. F143. NSF Country File—VN, Box 7, p. 5. L.B.J. Library.

2. Report of the Saigon Military Mission of General Lansdale, in *Pentagon Papers*, Gravel Edition, Vol. II (Boston: Beacon Press, 1972), 643–49; Stanley Karnow, *In Our Image: America's Empire in the Philippines* (New York: Random House, 1989), 355; and, W. Scott Thompson, *Unequal Partners: Philippine and Thai Relations with the United States 1965-75* (Lexington, Mass.: Lexington Books, 1975), 77.

3. Message, Rusk to AmEmbassies, 5/1/64, "Vietnam Memos, Vol. VIII, 5/64," Item No. 110, p. 7. NSF Country File—VN, Box 4. L.B.J. Library.

4. *Ibid.*, pp. 7–8.

5. Message, AmEmbassy Manila to SecState, 5/5/64, "Vietnam Memos, Vol. VIII, 5/64," Item No. 107. NSF Country File—VN, Box 4. L.B.J. Library; and, Message, AmEmbassy Saigon to SecState, 5/9/64, "Vietnam Memos, Vol. VIII, 5/64," No Item No. NSF Country File—VN, Box 4. L.B.J. Library.

6. Message, Rusk to AmEmbassies, dated 5/1/64, p. 7; and, Message, AmEmbassy Manila to SecState, dated 5/5/64, pp. 2–3.

7. Message, AmEmbassy Manila to SecState, dated 5/5/64, p. 2.

8. Message, Joint State-AID-Defense to AmEmbassies, 5/8/64, "Vietnam Memos, Vol. VIII, 5/64," Item No. 105, p. 1. NSF Country File—VN, Box 4. L.B.J. Library.

9. *Ibid.*, 1–2.

10. Memo, Rusk to President, 6/15/64, "Vietnam Memos, Vol. XII, 6/14-27/64," Item No. 7, p. 6. NSF Country File—VN, Box 5. L.B.J. Library.

11. Message, AmEmbassy Manila to SecState, 7/2/64, "Vietnam Memos, Vol. XIII, 6/64-7/64," Item No. 74. NSF Country File—VN, Box 6. L.B.J. Library.

12. Message, SecState to AmEmbassies Worldwide, 8/14/64, "Vietnam Memos, Vol. XV, 8/64," Item No. 140. NSF Country File—VN, Box 7. L.B.J. Library; and, Undated and unsigned report, "Vietnam Memos, Vol. XXIII, 12/1-18/64," Item No. 154a, p. 3. NSF Country File—VN, Box 11. L.B.J. Library.

13. Message, AmEmbassy Manila to SecState, 7/9/64, "Vietnam Memos, Vol. VIII, 6/64-7/64," Item No. 33. NSF Country File—VN, Box 6. L.B.J. Library.

14. *Ibid.*, 1; also, W.S. Thompson, *Unequal Partners*, 79.

15. Man Mohini Kaul, *The Philippines and Southeast Asia* (New Delhi, India: Radiant Publishers, 1978), 141.

16. Memo, Thomas L. Hughes to SecState, 8/28/64, "Vietnam Memos, Vol. XVI, 8/16–31/64," Item No. F143, p. 5. NSF Country File—VN, Box 7. L.B.J. Library.

17. Message, Rusk to AmEmbassy Manila, 10/10/64, "Vietnam Memos, Vol. XIX, 10/1–15/64," Item No. 104. NSF Country File—VN, Box 9. L.B.J. Library.

18. "President Macapagal of Philippines Visits United States," *Department of State Bulletin,* Vol. 51, No. 1323 (2 November 1964), 628–34.

19. President Diosdado Macapagal as quoted in Thompson, *Unequal Partners,* 79.

20. Message, AmEmbassy Manila to SecState, 10/26/64, "Vietnam Memos, Vol. XX, 10/15–31/64," Item No. 164. NSF Country File—VN, Box 9. L.B.J. Library.

21. Memo, Earle G. Wheeler to McNamara, 11/4/64, "Vietnam Memos, Vol. XXII, 11/16–30/64," Item No. 106b, p. 1. NSF Country File—VN, Box 10. L.B.J. Library.

22. *Ibid.*, 3.

23. Memo, Michael Forrestal to President, 12/11/64, "Vietnam Memos, Vol. XXIII, 12/1–18/64," Item No. 173, p. 2. NSF Country File—VN, Box 11. L.B.J. Library.

24. Undated and unsigned report, "Vietnam Memos, Vol. XXIII, 12/1–18/64," Item No. 154a, p. 3. NSF Country File—VN, Box 11. L.B.J. Library.

25. Message, AmEmbassy Manila to SecState, 1/8/65, "Vietnam Memos, Vol. XXV, 12/26/64–1/9/65," Item No. 143, p. 2 of sect. 1. NSF Country File—VN, Box 12. L.B.J. Library.

26. *Ibid.*, 2 of sect. 2.

27. Message, AmEmbassy Manila to SecState, 1/14/65, "Vietnam Memos, Vol. XXVI, 1/10–31/65," Item No. 151. NSF Country File—VN, Box 12. L.B.J. Library.

28. *Ibid.*

29. Message, Rusk to AmEmbassy Manila, 11/6/64, "Vietnam Memos, Vol. XXII, 11/16–30/64," Item No. 106a. NSF Country File—VN, Box 10. L.B.J. Library.

30. Instructions from President to Maxwell Taylor, 12/3/64, "Vietnam Memos, Vol. XXIII, 12/1–18/64," Item No. 160a, p. 2. NSF Country File—VN, Box 11. L.B.J. Library.

31. Note, Thomson to Bundy, 11/18/64, "Vietnam Memos, Vol. XXII, 11/16–30/64," Item No. 108a. NSF Country File—VN, Box 10. L.B.J. Library; Message, AmEmbassy Saigon to SecState, 11/18/64, "Vietnam Memos, Vol. XXII, 11/16–30/64," Item No. 108b. NSF Country File—VN, Box 10. L.B.J. Library; Memo, Bowman to Bundy, 11/19/64,

"Vietnam Memos, Vol. XXII, 11/16–30/64," Item No. 106. NSF Country File—VN, Box 10. L.B.J. Library; Memo, Forrestal to President, dated 12/11/64.

32. Message, Ball to AmEmbassy Manila, 12/13/64, "Philippine Cables, Vol. II, 6/64–6/66," Item No. 168, p. 3. NSF Country File—Philippines, Box 278. L.B.J. Library.

33. Message, OSD to AmEmbassy Saigon, 1/15/65, "Vietnam Memos, Vol. XXVI, 1/10–31/65," Item No. 152, p. 2. NSF Country File—VN, Box 12. L.B.J. Library.

34. *Ibid.*, 5.

35. Message, Rusk to AmEmbassy Manila, 2/19/65, "Philippine Cables, Vol. II, 6/64–6/66," Item No. 166. NSF Country File—Philippines, Box 278. L.B.J. Library.

36. Message, Ball to AmEmbassy Saigon, 1/28/65, "Vietnam Memos, Vol. XXVI, 1/10–31/65," Item No. 158, p. 4. NSF Country File—VN. L.B.J. Library; and, Message, Rusk to AmEmbassy Manila, dated 1/19/65, p. 3.

37. Message, AmEmbassy Manila to SecState, 3/4/65, "Philippine Cables, Vol. II, 6/64–6/66," Item No. 104. NSF Country File—Philippines, Box 278. L.B.J. Library.

38. Memo, Cooper to Bundy, 3/29/65, "Philippine Memos, Vol. II, 6/64–6/66," Item No. 194, p. 2. NSF Country File—Philippines, Box 278. L.B.J. Library.

39. World Sitrep, Aid to Viet-Nam, 5/26/65, "Vietnam Memos, Vol. XXXIV, 5/65," Item No. 311a, p. 6. NSF Country File—VN, Box 17. L.B.J. Library.

40. Message, Rusk to AmEmbassy Manila, 7/2/65, "Philippine Memos, Vol. III, 7/66–7/67," Item No. 154, p. 2. NSF Country File—Philippines, Box 278. L.B.J. Library.

41. Message, Blair to SecState, 7/6/65, "Philippine Cables, Vol. II, 6/64–6/66," Item No. 69. NSF Country File—Philippines, Box 278. L.B.J. Library.

42. Thompson, *Unequal Partners,* 79.

43. Ferdinand Marcos as quoted by Man Mohini Kaul, *The Philippines and Southeast Asia,* 143.

44. Message, Rusk to AmEmbassy Manila, 12/3/65, "Philippine Cables, Vol. II, 6/64–6/66," Item No. 137. NSF Country File—Philippines, Box 278. L.B.J. Library; Message, AmEmbassy Manila to SecState, 12/16/65, "Philippine Cables, Vol. II, 6/64–6/66," Item No. 26. NSF Country File—Philippines, Box 278. L.B.J. Library.

45. Kaul, *The Philippines and Southeast Asia,* 144–5.

46. *Ibid.*, 146.

47. Thompson, *Unequal Partners,* 107.

48. Message, AmEmbassy Manila to SecState, 2/26/66, "Philippine

Cables, Vol. II, 6/64–6/66," Item No. 13, p. 2. NSF Country File—Philippines, Box 278. L.B.J. Library.

49. Thompson, *Unequal Partners,* 81.

50. Memo, Kintner to Rostow, 9/7/66, "Confidential File," Item No. CO235, pp. 2–3. Confidential File CO206–CO300, Box 11. L.B.J. Library.

51. Memo, McNamara to President, 9/9/66, "Philippine Memos, Vol. III, 7/66–7/67," Item No. 132. NSF Country File—Philippines, Box 278. L.B.J. Library; and, Memo, Rostow to Ball, 9/11/66, "Philippine Memos, Vol. III, 7/66–7/67," Item No. 135. NSF Country File—Philippines, Box 278. L.B.J. Library.

52. Thompson, *Unequal Partners,* 81–2.

53. "President Marcos of the Philippines Visits the United States," *Department of State Bulletin,* Vol. 55, No. 1424 (10 October 1966): 533.

54. U.S. Congress, Senate, *Republic of the Philippines: Hearings,* 31.

55. Thompson, *Unequal Partners,* 97.

56. Message, AmEmbassy Manila to SecState, 7/13/67, "Philippine Cables, Vol. III, 7/66–7/67," Item No. 7. NSF Country File—Philippines, Box 278. L.B.J. Library.

57. *Ibid.,* 103.

58. Message, AmEmbassy Manila to SecState, 8/17/67, "Philippine Cables, Vol. IV, 8/67–11/68," Item No. 77. NSF Country File—Philippines, Box 279. L.B.J. Library; Memo, Benjamin H. Read to Rostow, 9/20/67, "Vietnam 5D, 3/67–1/69," Item No. 43. NSF Country File—VN, Box 85–91. L.B.J. Library; Memo, Rostow to President, 2/27/68, "Vietnam 5D, 3/67–1/69," Item No. 31. NSF Country File—VN, Box 85–91. L.B.J. Library; Talking Paper, Meeting with G. Mennen Williams, 5/1/68, "Philippine Cables, Vol. IV, 8/67–11/68," Item No. 157a. NSF Country File—Philippines, Box 279. L.B.J. Library; and, Memo, Rostow to President, 5/18/68, "Vietnam 5D, 3/67–1/69," Item No. 68. NSF Country File—VN, Box 85–91. L.B.J. Library.

59. Larsen and Collins, *Allied Participation in Vietnam,* 73.

60. Loren Baritz, *Backfire: A History of How American Culture Led Us into Vietnam and Made Us Fight the Way We Did* (New York: William Morrow, 1985), 183.

61. Stephen R. Shalom, *The United States and the Philippines* (Philadelphia: Institute for the Study of Human Issues, 1981), 109.

62. Kaul, *The Philippines and Southeast Asia,* 147.

63. Thompson, *Unequal Partners,* 96.

64. Message, AmEmbassy Manila to SecState, dated 2/26/66, p. 2.

65. Larsen and Collins, *Allied Participation in Vietnam,* 73–4.

66. Memo, Bell to President, 2/20/65, "Philippine Memos, Vol. II, 6/64–6/66," Item No. 195e, p. 2. NSF Country File—Philippines, Box 278. L.B.J. Library.

67. Message, AmEmbassy Manila to SecState, 12/19/64, "Vietnam Memos, Vol. XXIV, 12/19–25/64," Item No. 234. NSF Country File—VN, Box 11. L.B.J. Library.

68. Memo, Cooper to President, 12/28/64, "Vietnam Memos, Vol. XXV, 12/26/64–1/9/65," Item No. 127, p. 1. NSF Country File—VN, Box 12. L.B.J. Library.

69. Memo, Allen Claxton to Cooper, 4/18/65, "Philippine Memos, Vol. II, 6/64–6/66," Item No. 195b. NSF Country File—Philippines, Box 278. L.B.J. Library.

70. Message, AmEmbassy Manila to SecState, dated 7/6/65, p. 2; Message, AmEmbassy Manila to SecState, dated 7/13/67, p. 1 sect. 2; Memo, Read to Rostow, 12/13/67, "Vietnam 5D, 3/67–1/69," Item No. 43, p. 6. NSF Country File—VN, Box 85–91. L.B.J. Library; Memo, Rostow to President, 12/13/67, "Vietnam 5D, 3/67–1/69," Item No. 36, p. 1. NSF Country File—VN, Box 85–91. L.B.J. Library; Memo, Wright to Rostow, 12/16/67, "Vietnam 5D, 3/67–1/69," Item No. 18, p. 1. L.B.J. Library; also, U.S. Congress, Senate, *Republic of the Philippines: Hearings,* 286–7.

Chapter 5. The Thai Troop Commitment

1. John L.S. Girling, *Thailand: Society and Politics* (Ithaca, N.Y.: Cornell University Press, 1981), 92.

2. David K. Wyatt, *Thailand: A Short History* (New Haven, Conn.: Yale University Press, 1982), 287.

3. Girling, *Thailand: Society and Politics,* 110–3.

4. U.S. Congress, Senate, Committee on Foreign Relations. *The Kingdom of Thailand: Hearings Before the Subcommittee on United States Security Agreements and Commitments Abroad,* Part 3, 91st Cong., 1st sess., 1969: 744.

5. Ganganath Jha, *Foreign Policy of Thailand* (New Delhi, India: Radiant Publishers, 1979), 54.

6. Adulyasak Soonthornrojana, "The Rise of United States–Thai Relations, 1945–1975" (Ph.D. diss., University of Akron, 1986), 200–1.

7. Wyatt, *Thailand: A Short History,* 287.

8. Girling, *Thailand: Society and Politics,* 237–8.

9. *Ibid.*, 235–6.

10. Message, Rusk to AmEmbassies, 5/1/64, "Vietnam Memos, Vol. VIII, 5/64," Item No. 110. NSF Country File—VN, Box 4, p. 7. L.B.J. Library.

11. Stanley Robert Larsen and James Lawton Collins, Jr., *Allied Participation in Vietnam* (Washington, D.C.: Department of the Army, 1975), 27.

12. Jha, *Foreign Policy of Thailand,* 102; Wyatt, *Thailand: A Short*

History, 288; Memo, Hughes to SecState, 8/28/64, "Vietnam Memos, Vol. XVI, 8/16–31/64," Item No. F143. NSF Country File—VN, Box 7, p. 6. L.B.J. Library.

13. Memo, Rusk to President, 7/14/64, "Thailand Memos, Vol. I, 11/63–11/64," Item No. 61B. NSF Country File—VN, Box 281–282. L.B.J. Library; and, Memo, Rusk to President, 7/23/64, "Thailand Memos, Vol. 1, 11/63–11/64," Item No. 64A. NSF Country File—VN, Box 281–282. L.B.J. Library.

14. Instructions from President to Taylor, 12/3/64, "Vietnam Memos, Vol. XXIII, 12/1–18/64," Item No. 160a. NSF Country File—VN, Box 11. L.B.J. Library.

15. Memo, Forrestal to President, 12/11/64, "Vietnam Memos, Vol. XXIII, 12/1–18/64," Item No. 173. NSF Country File—VN, p. 4. L.B.J. Library.

16. World Sitrep on Free World Assistance to Viet-Nam, 3/11/65, "Vietnam Memos, Vol. XXXI, 3/12–31/65," Item No. 200A. NSF Country File—VN, Box 15, p. 6. L.B.J. Library.

17. Wyatt, *Thailand: A Short History*, 289; Jha, *Foreign Policy of Thailand*, 102.

18. Girling, *Thailand: Society and Politics*, 93.

19. Memo, Ball to Bundy, 6/29/65, "Vietnam Memos, Vol. XXXV, 6/16–30/65," Item No. 349. NSF Country File—VN, Box 19, p. 16. L.B.J. Library.

20. Wyatt, *Thailand: A Short History*, 285.

21. Message, AmEmbassy Bangkok to SecState, 7/21/65, "Thailand Cables, Vol. III, 4/65–12/65," Item No. 102. NSF Country File—Thailand, Box 283–284, p. 1. L.B.J. Library.

22. Girling, *Thailand: Society and Politics*, 113.

23. Message, Rusk to AmEmbassy Bangkok, 7/29/65, "Thailand Cables, Vol. III, 4/65–12/65," Item No. 21. NSF Country File—Thailand, Box 283–284, p. 1. L.B.J. Library.

24. Message, AmEmbassy Bangkok to SecState, 7/31/65, "Thailand Cables, Vol. III, 4/65–12/65," Item No. 108. NSF Country File—Thailand, Box 283–284, p. 1. L.B.J. Library.

25. *Ibid.*

26. *Ibid.*, 2.

27. W. Scott Thompson, *Unequal Partners: Philippine and Thai Relations with the United States, 1965–1975* (Lexington, Mass.: Lexington Books, 1975), 83; and, Message, Rusk to AmEmbassies, 12/3/65, "Negotiating and International Actions Concerning Vietnam, Vol. III, 4/65–12/65," Item No. 40. NSF Country File—VN, Box 213. L.B.J. Library.

28. U.S. Congress, Senate, *Kingdom of Thailand: Hearings*, 624.

29. Memo, Hughes to SecState, dated 8/28/64, p. 6.

30. Thompson, *Unequal Partners*, 83–4.

31. Message, AmEmbassy Bangkok to SecState, 1/6/67, "Thailand Cables, Vol. V, 10/66–2/67," Item No. 20. NSF Country File—Thailand, Box 283–284, p. 1. L.B.J. Library. Thanom's notification to Washington is contained in: Memo, Rostow to President, 1/3/67, "Thailand Cables, Vol. V, 10/66–2/67," Item No. 121. NSF Country File—VN, Box 283–284. L.B.J. Library.

32. Soonthornrojana, "The Rise of United States–Thai Relations," 201.

33. Larsen and Collins, *Allied Participation in Vietnam*, 32.

34. Report, Clark M. Clifford and Maxwell D. Taylor to President Johnson, 8/5/67, "Vietnam 5D, 3/67–1/69," Item No. 44a. NSF Country File—VN, Box 85–91. L.B.J. Library.

35. Norman B. Hannah, *The Key to Failure: Laos and the Vietnam War* (New York: Madison Books, 1987), 232.

36. Thompson, *Unequal Partners*, 85.

37. Foreign Minister Thanat Khoman speaking before the American Chamber of Commerce in Thailand, July 15, 1970; as quoted in Thompson, *Unequal Partners*, 84.

38. U.S. Congress, Senate, *Kingdom of Thailand: Hearings*, 895.

39. As quoted in Thompson, *Unequal Partners*, 86.

40. Memo, Rostow to President, 10/6/67, "Vietnam Allies 5D, 1967–1969, Korea-U.K.," item No. 124. NSF Country File—VN, Box 85–91, p. 2. L.B.J. Library.

41. U.S. Congress, Senate, *Kingdom of Thailand: Hearings*, 706.

42. *Ibid.*, 842–3.

43. *Ibid.*, 844.

44. Jack Shulimson, *U.S. Marines in Vietnam: An Expanding War 1966* (Washington, D.C.: History and Museums Division, Headquarters, U.S. Marine Corps, 1982), 344–6.

45. Larsen and Collins, *Allied Participation in Vietnam*, 42.

Chapter 6. The Australian and New Zealand Contributions

1. Gregory Pemberton, *All the Way: Australia's Road to Vietnam* (Sydney, Australia: Allen & Unwin, 1987), 205–7.

2. *Ibid.*, 207.

3. *Ibid.*, 207–8.

4. Dennis L. Cuddy, "Australian Involvement in the Vietnam War," *Australian Journal of Politics and History*, Vol. 28, No. 3 (1982), 341.

5. Glen St. John Barclay, *Friends in High Places: Australian-*

American diplomatic relations since 1945 (Oxford, England: Oxford University Press, 1985), 126.

6. *Ibid.*, 127.

7. Cuddy, "Australian Involvement," 341.

8. K.J. Holyoake, as quoted in Malcolm McKinnon, "Costs and Continuity: New Zealand's Security and the United States," *Political Science,* Vol. 30, No. 1 (July 1978), 33.

9. Barclay, *Friends in High Places,* 127.

10. Barclay, *Friends in High Places,* 140; Cuddy, "Australian Involvement in the Vietnam War," 342.

11. Glen St. John Barclay, *A Very Small Insurance Policy: The Politics of Australian Involvement in Vietnam, 1954–1967* (St. Lucia, Australia: University of Queensland Press, 1988), 50.

12. Message, AmEmbassy Canberra to SecState, 6/8/64, "Vietnam Memos, Vol. XI, 6/1–13/64," Item No. 10. NSF Country File—VN, Box 5. L.B.J. Library; Memo, McGeorge Bundy to President, 6/24/64, "Vietnam Memos, Vol. XII, 6/14–24/64," Item No. 2. NSF Country File—VN, Box 5. L.B.J. Library; and, Pemberton, *All the Way,* 200–1.

13. Roger Hilsman, as quoted in Pemberton, *All the Way,* 202–3.

14. Barclay, *Friends in High Places,* 140–1.

15. Barclay, *A Very Small Insurance Policy,* 54.

16. Cuddy, "Australian Involvement in the Vietnam War," 351.

17. Barclay, *Friends in High Places,* 145.

18. Ian McNeill, *The Team: Australian Army Advisers in Vietnam, 1962–1972* (New York: Hippocrene Books, 1984), 5.

19. Pemberton, *All the Way,* 198.

20. Memo, Rusk to President, 6/15/64, "Vietnam Memos, Vol. XII, 6/14–27/64," Item No. 7. NSF Country File—VN, Box 5. L.B.J. Library.

21. Message, Ball to AmEmbassy Canberra, 5/30/64, "Vietnam Memos, Vol. X, 5/24–30/64," Item No. 27. NSF Country File—VN, Box 5. L.B.J. Library.

22. McKinnon, "Costs and Continuity," 34–5; and, Memo, Hughes to SecState, 8/28/64, "Vietnam Memos, Vol. XVI, 8/16–31/64," Item No. F143. NSF Country File—VN, Box 7, p. 4. L.B.J. Library.

23. Pemberton, *All the Way,* 212.

24. *Ibid.*, 213.

25. Memo, Forrestal to President, 12/11/64, "Vietnam Memos, Vol. XXIII, 12/1–18/64," Item No. 173. NSF Country File—VN, Box 11. L.B.J. Library; Message, AmEmbassy Saigon to SecState, 1/19/65, "Vietnam Memos, Vol. XXVI, 1/10–31/65," Item No. 154. NSF Country File—VN, Box 12. L.B.J. Library; and, World Sitrep, 3/11/65, "Vietnam Memos, Vol. XXXI, 3/12–31/65," Item No. 200a. NSF Country File—VN, Box 15. L.B.J. Library.

26. Barclay, *Friends in High Places,* 147.

27. Paul Hasluck, as quoted in Pemberton, *All the Way,* 217.

28. *Ibid.,* 260.

29. Barclay, *Friends in High Places,* 148.

30. Pemberton, *All the Way,* 270.

31. *Ibid.,* 270–1.

32. Message, AmEmbassy Wellington to SecState, 5/27/64, "New Zealand Cables, Vol. 1, 11/63–11/68," Item No. 124. NSF Country File – New Zealand, Box 277. L.B.J. Library; and, Message, AmEmbassy Wellington to SecState, 5/28/64, "New Zealand Cables, Vol. 1, 11/63–11/68," Item No. 123. NSF Country File – New Zealand, Box 277. L.B.J. Library.

33. Alan S. Watt, *The Evolution of Australian Foreign Policy: 1938–1965* (Cambridge, England: Cambridge University Press, 1968), 352.

34. "Why New Zealand Aids South Vietnam," *Vietnam Perspectives,* Vol. 1, No. 2 (November 1965), 56.

35. Harold Holt, as quoted in Paul Rodan, "Harold Holt's Foreign Policy, 1966–67," *Australian Journal of Politics and History,* Vol. 25, No. 3 (1979), 313.

36. U.S. Congress, Senate, Committee on Foreign Relations. *The Republic of the Philippines: Hearings Before the Subcommittee on United States Security Agreements and Commitments Abroad,* Part 1, 91st Cong., 1st sess., 1969: 276.

37. Stanley Robert Larsen and James Lawton Collins, Jr., *Allied Participation in Vietnam* (Washington, D.C.: Department of the Army, 1975), 14–5.

Chapter 7. "More Flags": The Final Years

1. Message, AmEmbassy Saigon to AmEmbassy Tehran, 7/18/64, "Vietnam Cables, Vol. XIV, 7/64," Item No. 111. NSF Country File – VN, Box 6. L.B.J. Library.

2. Louis Heren, *No Hail, No Farewell* (New York: Harper & Row, 1970), 184.

3. Ambassador George C. McGhee, "The Tasks of the Free-World Community," *Department of State Bulletin,* Vol. 53, No. 1365 (23 August 1965), 329.

4. Memo, Cooper to President, 1/12/65, "Vietnam Memos, Vol. XXVI, 1/10–31/65," Item No. 184. NSF Country File – VN, Box 12. L.B.J. Library.

5. Message, Rusk to AmEmbassies, 12/29/64, "Vietnam Memos, Vol. XXV, 12/26/64–1/9/65," Item No. 145. NSF Country File – VN, Box 12, p. 1. L.B.J. Library.

6. U.S. State Department, *World Sitrep on Free World Assistance*

to Viet-Nam, 5/26/65, "Vietnam Memos, Vol. XXXIV, 5/65," Item No. 311a. NSF Country File—VN, Box 17. L.B.J. Library.

7. Secretary of State Rusk in CBS Interview with Secretary Rusk and Secretary McNamara, "Political and Military Aspects of U.S. Policy in Viet-Nam," *Department of State Bulletin,* Vol. 53, No. 1366 (30 August 1965), 352.

8. U.S. State Department, *Support of Other Governments for U.S. Position re Viet-Nam,* 6/3/65, "Vietnam Cables, Vol. XXXV, 6/1–21/65," Item No. 213. NSF Country File—VN, Box 18, p. 2. L.B.J. Library.

9. Robert J. Donovan, *Nemesis: Truman and Johnson in the Coils of War in Asia* (New York: St. Martin's/Marek, 1984), 80.

10. Memo, Ball to SecState, 6/29/65, "Vietnam Memos, Vol. XXXV, 6/16–30/65," Item No. 349. NSF Country File—VN, Box 19, p. 19. L.B.J. Library.

11. Howard B. Furer, ed., *Lyndon B. Johnson 1908– : Chronology—Documents—Bibliographical Aids* (Dobbs Ferry, N.Y.: Oceana, 1971), 55.

12. "Secretary Rusk Interviewed for Japanese Magazine," *Department of State Bulletin,* Vol. 58, No. 1513 (24 June 1968), 822.

13. World Sitrep on Free World Assistance to Viet-Nam, 3/11/65, "Vietnam Memos, Vol. XXXI, 3/12–31/65," Item No. 200a. NSF Country File—VN, Box 15, p. 2. L.B.J. Library.

14. U.S. Congress, Senate, Committee on Foreign Relations. *Republic of China: Hearings of the Subcommittee on United States Security Agreements and Commitments Abroad,* 91st Cong., 2d sess., Part 4: 965.

15. Memo, Forrestal to President, 12/11/64, "Vietnam Memos, Vol. XXIII, 12/1–18/64," Item No. 173. NSF Country File—VN, Box 11, p. 4. L.B.J. Library.

16. Memo, Hughes to SecState, 8/28/64, "Vietnam Memos, Vol. XVI, 8/16–31/64," Item No. F143. NSF Country File—VN, Box 7, p. 10–14. L.B.J. Library.

17. Harold Wilson, *Harold Wilson, A Personal Record: The Labour Government 1964–1970* (Boston: Little, Brown, 1971); Craig V. Wilson, "Rhetoric, Reality, and Dissent: The Foreign Policy of the British Labour Governments 1964–1970" (Ph.D. diss., Washington State University, 1982); John Baylis, *Anglo-American Defense Relations 1939–1984: The Special Relationship,* 2nd ed. (New York: St. Martin's, 1986); J.L. Granatstein, "Cooperation and Conflict: The Course of Canadian-American Relations since 1945," in *Canada and the United States: Enduring Friendship, Persistent Stress,* eds. Charles F. Doran and John H. Sigler (Englewood Cliffs, N.J.: Prentice-Hall, 1985).

18. Memo, Cooper to Bundy, 12/21/65, "Vietnam Memos, Vol.

XLIII, 12/15–31/65," Item No. 221. NSF Country File—VN, Box 24–25. L.B.J. Library.

19. "Vice President Humphrey Reports to President on Asian Trip," *Department of State Bulletin,* Vol. 54, No. 1396 (28 March 1966), 489–94; "Mr. Clifford and General Taylor Report on Talks on Viet-Nam with Allied Leaders," *Department of State Bulletin,* Vol. 57, No. 1470 (28 August 1967), 256–60; and, Report, Clark M. Clifford and Maxwell D. Taylor to President Johnson, 8/5/67, "Vietnam 5D, 3/67–1/69," Item No. 44a. NSF Country File—VN, Box 85–91. L.B.J. Library.

20. Stanley Robert Larsen and James Lawton Collins, Jr., *Allied Participation in Vietnam* (Washington, D.C.: Department of the Army, 1975), 22–3.

21. *Vietnam Information Notes,* Office of Media Services, Bureau of Public Affairs, Department of State, Number 4, December 1967; *Vietnam Review 4A: Free-World Assistance to South Vietnam,* Armed Forces Information Service, Department of Defense, April 1968; and, Memo, Read to Rostow, 6/3/68, "Vietnam Memos 5D, 3/67–1/69," Item No. 10a. NSF Country File—VN, Box 85–91. L.B.J. Library.

22. Glen St. John Barclay, *A Very Small Insurance Policy: The Politics of Australian Involvement in Vietnam, 1954–1967* (St. Lucia, Australia: University of Queensland Press, 1988), 55–6.

Chapter 8. Conclusions

1. Jay Mallin and Robert K. Brown, *Merc: American Soldiers of Fortune* (New York: Macmillan, 1979), 1–5.

2. Immanuel Kant, *Grounding for Metaphysics of Morals,* translated and analyzed by H.J. Paton (New York: Harper & Row, Publishers, 1964).

3. Memo, Read to Rostow, 12/13/67, "Vietnam 5D, 3/67–1/69," Item No. 38. NSF Country File—VN, Box 85–91, p. 5. L.B.J. Library.

4. Memo, Rostow to President, 12/13/67, "Vietnam 5D, 3/67–1/69," Item No. 36. NSF Country File—VN, Box 85–91 L.B.J. Library.

5. *Ibid.,* 2.

6. Memo, Wright to Rostow, 12/16/67, "Vietnam 5D, 3/67–1/69," Item No. 36a. NSF Country File—VN, Box 85–91. L.B.J. Library.

7. Memo, Rostow to President, 1/5/68, "Vietnam 5D, 3/67–1/69," Item No. 34. NSF Country File—VN, Box 85–91. L.B.J. Library.

8. Memo, Wright to Rostow, dated 12/16/67.

Bibliography

Primary Sources
Lyndon Baines Johnson Library Holdings

NSF Country File — VN

Box 3

"Vietnam Memos, Vol. VI, 3/64." Item No. 79. Memo, Forrestal to President, 3/21/64.

Box 4

"Vietnam Memos, Vol. VIII, 5/64." Item No. 110. Message, Rusk to AmEmbassies, 5/1/64.

"Vietnam Memos, Vol. VIII, 5/64." Item No. 107. Message, AmEmbassy Manila to SecState, 5/5/64.

"Vietnam Memos, Vol. VIII, 5/64." Item No. 105. Message, Joint State-AID-Defense to AmEmbassies, 5/8/64.

"Vietnam Memos, Vol. VIII, 5/64." Item No. 104. Message, AmEmbassy Bonn to SecState, 5/9/64.

"Vietnam Memos, Vol. VIII, 5/64." No Item No. Message, Lodge to Rusk, 5/9/64.

"Vietnam Memos, Vol. VIII, 5/64." Item No. 101. Message, AmEmbassy London to SecState, 5/11/64.

"Vietnam Memos, Vol. VIII, 5/64." Item No. 100. Message, AmEmbassy Bonn to SecState, 5/11/64.

"Vietnam Memos, Vol. VIII, 5/64." Item No. 77. Message, Ball to AmEmbassy Seoul, 5/12/64.

"Vietnam Memos, Vol. IX, 5/13–23/64." Item No. 6. Message, AmEmbassy Bonn to SecState, 5/19/64.

Box 5

"Vietnam Memos, Vol. X, 5/24–30/64." Item No. 30. Message, AmEmbassy Karachi to SecState, 5/23/64.

189

"Vietnam Memos, Vol. X, 5/24–30/64." Item No. 28. Message, AmEmbassy Bonn to SecState, 5/29/64.

"Vietnam Memos, Vol. XI, 6/1–13/64." Item No. 11. Message, Rusk to AmEmbassy Bonn, 6/8/64.

"Vietnam Memos, Vol. XI, 6/1–13/64." Item No. 10. Message, AmEmbassy Canberra to SecState, 6/8/64.

"Vietnam Memos, Vol. XII, 6/14–27/64." Item No. 7. Memo, Rusk to President, 6/15/64.

"Vietnam Memos, Vol. XII, 6/14–27/64." Item No. 5. Memo, Sullivan to Bundy, 6/24/64.

"Vietnam Memos, Vol. XII, 6/14–27/64." Item No. 2. Memo, McGeorge Bundy to President, 6/24/64.

Box 6

"Vietnam Memos, Vol. XIII, 6/64–7/64." Item No. 78. Message, President to AmEmbassies, 7/2/64.

"Vietnam Memos, Vol. XIII, 6/64–7/64." Item No. 74. Message, AmEmbassy Manila to SecState, 7/2/64.

"Vietnam Memos, Vol. XIII, 6/24–7/64." Item No. 41. Message, Rusk to AmEmbassy Seoul, 7/3/64.

"Vietnam Memos, Vol. XIII, 6/24–7/64." Item No. 33. Message, AmEmbassy Manila to SecState, 7/9/64.

"Vietnam Memos, Vol. XIII, 6/64–7/64." Item No. 31. Message, Ball to AmEmbassies, 7/10/64.

"Vietnam Memos, Vol. XIII, 6/64–7/64." Item No. 32. Message, Ball to AmEmbassy Saigon, 7/10/64.

"Vietnam Memos, Vol. XIII, 6/64–7/64." Item No. 29. Message, Rusk to AmEmbassy Saigon, 7/13/64.

"Vietnam Memos, Vol. XIII, 6/64–7/64." Item No. 13c. Message, Taylor to SecState, 7/14/64.

"Vietnam Cables, Vol. XIV, 7/64." Item No. 117. Message, Taylor to SecState, 7/17/64.

"Vietnam Cables, Vol. XIV, 7/64." Item No. 111. Message, AmEmbassy Saigon to AmEmbassy Tehran, 7/18/64.

"Vietnam Cables, Vol. XIV, 7/64." Item No. 26. Message, Taylor to SecState, 7/28/64.

Box 7

"Vietnam Memos, Vol. XV, 8/64." Item No. 140. Message, SecState to AmEmbassies, 8/14/64.

"Vietnam Memos, Vol. XVI, 8/16–31/64." Item No. F143. Memo, Hughes to Secretary Rusk, 8/28/64.

Box 9

"Vietnam Memos, Vol. XIX, 10/1–15/64." Item No. 104. Message, Rusk to AmEmbassy Manila, 10/10/64.

"Vietnam Memos, Vol. XX, 10/15–31/64." Item No. 164. Message, AmEmbassy Manila to SecState, 10/26/64.

Box 10

"Vietnam Memos, Vol. XXII, 11/16–30/64." Item No. 106b. Memo, Wheeler to McNamara, 11/4/64.

"Vietnam Memos, Vol. XXII, 11/16–30/64." Item No. 106a. Message, Rusk to AmEmbassy Manila, 11/6/64.

"Vietnam Memos, Vol. XXII, 11/16–30/64." Item No. 108a. Note, Thomson to Bundy, 11/18/64.

"Vietnam Memos, Vol. XXII, 11/16–30/64." Item No. 108b. Message, AmEmbassy Saigon to SecState, 11/18/64.

"Vietnam Memos, Vol. XXII, 11/16–30/64." Item No. 106. Memo, Bowman to Bundy, 11/19/64.

Box 11

"Vietnam Memos, Vol. XXIII, 12/1–18/64." Item No. 154a. Unsigned and undated report.

"Vietnam Memos, Vol. XXIII, 12/1–18/64." Item No. 160a. Letter, President to Taylor, 12/3/64.

"Vietnam Memos, Vol. XXIII, 12/1–18/64." Item No. 176. Memo, Thomson to Bundy, 12/11/64.

"Vietnam Memos, Vol. XXIII, 12/1–18/64." Item No. 173. Memo, Forrestal to President, 12/11/64.

"Vietnam Memos, Vol. XXIV, 12/19–25/64." Item No. 170. Message from National Military Command Center, 12/15/64.

"Vietnam Memos, Vol. XXIV, 12/19–25/64." Item No. 234. Message, AmEmbassy Manila to SecState, 12/19/64.

"Vietnam Memos, Vol. XXIV, 12/19–25/64." Item No. 233. Message, DOD to AmEmbassy Seoul, 12/19/64.

"Vietnam Memos, Vol. XXIV, 12/19–25/64." Item No. 209. Memo, Cooper to President, 12/22/64.

"Vietnam Memos, Vol. XXIV, 12/19–25/64." Item No. 223. Message, CINCPAC to JCS, 12/23/64.

"Vietnam Memos, Vol. XXIV, 12/19–25/64." Item No. 214. Message, AmEmbassy Karachi to SecState, 12/23/64.

"Vietnam Memos, Vol. XXIV, 12/19–25/64." Item No. 195. Message, NSC to Bundy, 12/24/64.

"Vietnam Memos, Vol. XXIV, 12/19–25/64." Item No. 208. Message, AmEmbassy Seoul to SecState, 12/29/64.

Box 12

"Vietnam Memos, Vol. XXV, 12/26/64–1/9/65." Item No. 147. DOD to CINCPAC, 12/27/64.

"Vietnam Memos, Vol. XXV, 12/26/64–1/9/65." Item No. 127. Memo, Cooper to President, 12/28/64.

"Vietnam Memos, Vol. XXV, 12/26/64–1/9/65." Item No. 145. Message, Rusk to AmEmbassies, 12/29/64.

"Vietnam Memos, Vol. XXV, 12/26/64–1/9/65." Item No. 120. Memo, Cooper to President, 1/5/65.

"Vietnam Memos, Vol. XXV, 12/26/64–1/9/65." Item No. 143. Message, AmEmbassy Manila to SecState, 1/8/65.

"Vietnam Memos, Vol. XXVI, 1/10–31/65." Item No. 184. Memo, Cooper to President, 1/12/65.

"Vietnam Memos, Vol. XXVI, 1/10–31/65." Item No. 151. Message, AmEmbassy Manila to SecState, 1/14/65.

"Vietnam Memos, Vol. XXVI, 1/10–31/65." Item No. 152. Message, OSD to AmEmbassies, 1/15/65.

"Vietnam Memos, Vol. XXVI, 1/10–31/65." Item No. 153. Message, Rusk to AmEmbassies, 1/16/65.

"Vietnam Memos, Vol. XXVI, 1/10–31/65." Item No. 158. Message, Rusk to AmEmbassy Saigon, 1/28/65.

"Vietnam Memos, Vol. XXVI, 1/10–31/65." Item No. 157. Memo, Cooper to President, 1/28/65.

Box 14

"Vietnam Memos, Vol. XXX, 3/1–8/65." Item No. 163. Message, Rusk to AmEmbassies, 3/5/65.

Box 15

"Vietnam Memos, Vol. XXXI, 3/12–31/65." Item No. 200a. World Sitrep on Free World Assistance to Viet-Nam, 3/11/65.

Box 17

"Vietnam Memos, Vol. XXXIV, 5/65." Item No. 311a. Memo, World Sitrep, 5/26/65.

Box 18

"Vietnam Cables, Vol. XXXV, 6/1–21/65." Item No. 213. United States State Department, *Support of Other Governments for U.S. Position re Viet-Nam*, 6/3/65.

Box 19

"Vietnam Memos, Vol. XXXV, 6/16–30/65." Item No. 349. Memo, Ball to Presidential Staff, 6/29/65.

Box 24–25

"Vietnam Memos, Vol. XLIII, 12/15–31/65." Item No. 221. Memo, Cooper to Bundy, 12/21/65.

Box 85–91

"Vietnam 5D, 3/67–1/69." Item No. 44a. Report, Maxwell and Taylor to President, 8/5/67.

"Vietnam 5D, 3/67–1/69." Item No. 43. Memo, Read to Rostow, 9/20/67.

"Vietnam Allies, Vol. 5D, Korea-U.K., 1967–1969." Item No. 124. Memo, Rostow to President, 10/6/67.

"Vietnam Allies, Vol. 5D (3), 1967–1969." Item No. 87. Message, AmEmbassy Seoul to SecState, 11/25/67.

"Vietnam Allies, Vol. 5D (3), 1967–1969." Item No. 85. Message, Rusk to AmEmbassy Seoul, 11/30/67.

"Vietnam Allies, Vol. 5D (3), 1967–1969." Item No. 74a. Message, AmEmbassy Seoul to SecState, 12/6/67.

"Vietnam 5D, 3/67–1/69." Item No. 36. Memo, Rostow to President, 12/13/67.

"Vietnam 5D, 3/67–1/69." Item No. 38. Memo, Read to Rostow, 12/13/67.

"Vietnam 5D, 3/67–1/69." Item No. 36a. Memo, Wright to Rostow, 12/16/67.

"Vietnam 5D, 3/67–1/69." Item No. 35f. Status Report (no author), 12/20/67.

"Vietnam Allies, Vol. 5D (3), 1967–1969." Item No. 56. Memo, Rostow to President, 1/5/68.

"Vietnam Allies, Vol. 5D (3), 1967–1969." Item No. 54. Memo, Rostow to President, 1/5/68.

"Vietnam Allies, Vol. 5D (3), 1967–1969." Item No. 45. Message, AmEmbassy Saigon to SecState, 1/19/68.

"Vietnam Allies, Vol. 5D (3), 1967–1969." Item No. 44. Message, CINCPAC to SecState, 1/19/68.

"Vietnam 5D, 3/67–1/69." Item No. 31. Memo, Rostow to President, 2/27/68.

"Vietnam Allies, Vol. 5D (3) 1967–1969." Item No. 17. Message, White House Situation Room to Rostow, 4/17/68.

"Vietnam 5D, 3/67–1/69," Item No. 68. Memo, Rostow to President, 5/18/68.

"Vietnam 5D, 3/67–1/69." Item No. 10a. Memo, Read to Rostow, 6/3/68.

"Vietnam 5D, 3/67–1/69." Item No. 2. Message, Rusk to all Diplomatic and Consular Posts, 1/7/69.

Box 213

"Negotiating and International Actions Concerning Vietnam, Vol. III, 4/65–12/65." Item No. 40. Message, Rusk to AmEmbassies, 12/3/65.

NSF Country File — Republic of Korea

Box 254–256

"Korea Memos, Vol. II, 7/64–8/65." Item No. 53. Message, AmEmbassy Seoul to SecState, 12/19/64.

"Korea Memos, Vol. II, 7/64–8/65." Item No. 155. Memo, Cooper to Bundy, 1/14/65.

"Korea Memos, Vol. II, 7/64–8/65." Item No. 46. Message, AmEmbassy Seoul to SecState, 2/24/65.

"Korea Memos, Vol. II, 7/64–8/65." Item No. 45. Message, AmEmbassy Seoul to SecState, 3/2/65.

"Korea Memos, Vol. II, 7/64–8/65." Item No. 30. Message, AmEmbassy Seoul to SecState, 5/1/65.

"Korea Memos, Vol. II, 7/64–8/65." Item No. 30a. Message, AmEmbassy Seoul to SecState, 5/1/65.

"Park Visit Briefing Book, 5/17–19/65." Item No. 2. Memo, Thomson to President, 5/17/65.

"Korea Memos, Park Visit, 5/65." Item No. 12. Memo, Rusk to President, 5/17/65.

"Korea Cables, Vol. II, 7/64–8/65." Item No. 20. Message, AmEmbassy Seoul to SecState, 6/7/65.

"Korea Cables, Vol. II, 7/64–8/65." Item No. 18. Message, AmEmbassy Seoul to SecState, 7/3/65.

"Korea Cables, Vol. II, 7/64–8/65." Item No. 17. Message, AmEmbassy Seoul to SecState, 7/10/65.

"Korea Cables, Vol. II, 7/64–8/65." Item No. 10. Message, AmEmbassy Seoul to SecState, 7/29/65.

"Korea Cables, Vol. II, 7/64–8/65." Item No. 71. Message, Rusk to AmEmbassy Seoul, 8/5/65.

"Korea Memos, Vol. III, 11/65–12/66." Item No. 107. Memo of Conversation, Bundy with Korean Ambassador, 12/7/65.

NSF Country File—Republic of the Philippines

Box 278

"Philippine Cables, Vol. II, 6/64–6/66." Item No. 168. Message, Ball to AmEmbassy Manila, 12/13/64.

"Philippine Cables, Vol. II, 6/64–6/66." Item No. 166. Message, Rusk to AmEmbassy Manila, 2/19/65.

"Philippine Memos, Vol. II, 6/64–6/66." Item No. 195e. Memo, Ball to President, 2/20/65.

"Philippine Cables, Vol. II, 6/64–6/66." Item No. 104. Message, AmEmbassy Manila to SecState, 3/4/65.

"Philippine Memos, Vol. II, 6/64–6/66." Item No. 194. Memo, Cooper to Bundy, 3/29/65.

"Philippine Memos, Vol. II, 6/64–6/66." Item No. 195b. Memo, Claxton to Cooper, 4/18/65.

"Philippine Memos, Vol. III, 7/66–7/67." Item No. 54. Message, Rusk to AmEmbassy Manila, 7/2/65.

"Philippine Cables, Vol. II, 6/64–6/66." Item No. 69. Message, Blair to SecState, 7/6/65.

"Philippine Cables, Vol. II, 6/64–6/66." Item No. 137. Message, Rusk to AmEmbassy Manila, 12/3/65.

"Philippine Cables, Vol. II, 6/64–6/66." Item No. 26. Message, AmEmbassy Manila to SecState, 12/16/65.

"Philippine Cables, Vol. II, 6/64–6/66." Item No. 13. Message, AmEmbassy Manila to SecState, 2/26/66.

"Philippine Memos, Vol. III, 7/66–7/67." Item No. 132. Memo, McNamara to President, 9/9/66.

"Philippine Memos, Vol. III, 7/66–7/67." Item No. 135. Memo, Rostow to Ball, 9/11/66.

"Philippine Cables, Vol. III, 7/66–7/67." Item No. 7. Message, AmEmbassy Manila to SecState, 7/13/67.

"Philippine Cables, Vol. IV, 8/67–11/68." Item No. 77. Message, AmEmbassy Manila to SecState, 8/17/67.

"Philippine Cables, Vol. IV, 8/67–11/68." Item No. 157a. Talking Paper, Meeting with G. Mennan Williams, 5/1/68.

NSF Country File — Kingdom of Thailand

Box 281–282

"Thailand Memos, Vol. I, 11/63–11/64." Item No. 61b. Memo, Rusk to President, 7/14/64.
"Thailand Memos, Vol. I, 11/63–11/64." Item No. 64a. Memo, Rusk to President, 7/23/64.

Box 283–284

"Thailand Cables, Vol. III, 4/65–12/65." Item No. 102. Message, AmEmbassy Bangkok to SecState, 7/21/65.
"Thailand Cables, Vol. III, 4/65–12/65." Item No. 21. Message, Rusk to AmEmbassy Bangkok, 7/29/65.
"Thailand Cables, Vol. III, 4/65–12/65." Item No. 108. Message, AmEmbassy Bangkok to SecState, 7/31/65.
"Thailand Cables, Vol. V, 10/66–2/67." Item No. 121. Memo, Rostow to President, 1/3/67.
"Thailand Cables, Vol. V, 10/66–2/67." Item No. 20. Message, AmEmbassy Bangkok to SecState, 1/6/67.

Miscellaneous L.B.J. Library Files

NSF — Walt Rostow. Box 6. "Vietnam: Jan-Feb 1968." Item No. 18b. Memo, Zwick to President, 2/1/68.
NSF — Walt Rostow. Box 6. "Vietnam: Jan-Feb 1968." Item No. 16. Memo, President to Bunker, 2/2/68.
NSF — Confidential File. Box 11. "Confidential File CO206-CO300." Item No. CO235. Memo, Kintner to Rostow, 9/7/66.

Other Primary Sources

Congressional Record. 90th Cong., 1st sess., 1967. Vol. 113, pt. 5, 5870.
Congressional Record. 90th Cong., 1st sess., 1967. Vol. 113, pt. 6, 7514.
Department of State Bulletin.
    Vol. 50, No. 1294 (13 April 1964). Secretary of Defense Robert S. McNamara, "United States Policy in Vietnam," 562–70.

Vol. 51, No. 1323 (2 November 1964). "President Macapagal of Philippines Visits United States," 628–34.

Vol. 53, No. 1365 (23 August 1966). Ambassador George C. McGhee, "The Tasks of the Free-World Community," 324–332.

Vol. 53, No. 1366 (30 August 1966). CBS Interview with Secretary of State Rusk and Secretary of Defense McNamara, "Political and Military Aspects of U.S. Policy in Viet-Nam," 342–374.

Vol. 54, No. 1396 (28 March 1966). "Vice President Humphrey Reports to President on Asian Trip," 489–491.

Vol. 55, No. 1424 (10 October 1966). "President Marcos of the Philippines Visits the United States," 526–34.

Vol. 57, No. 1470 (28 August 1967). "Mr. Clifford and General Taylor Report on Talks on Viet-Nam with Allied Leaders," 256–260.

Vol. 58, No. 1513 (24 June 1968). "Secretary Rusk Interviewed for Japanese Magazine," 821–844.

New York Times. 1969. 30, 31 May.

Pentagon Papers. Gravel Edition, Vol. III. Boston: Beacon Press, 1972.

U.S. Congress. Senate. Committee on Foreign Relations. *The Republic of the Philippines: Hearings Before the Subcommittee on United States Security Agreements and Commitments Abroad.* Part 1. 91st Cong., 1st sess., 1969.

U.S. Congress. Senate. Committee on Foreign Relations. *The Kingdom of Thailand: Hearings Before the Subcommittee on United States Security Agreements and Commitments Abroad.* Part 3. 91st Cong., 1st sess., 1969.

U.S. Congress. Senate. Committee on Foreign Relations. *Republic of China: Hearings Before the Subcommittee on United States Security Agreements and Commitments Abroad.* Part 4. 91st Cong., 2d sess., 1970.

U.S. Congress. Senate. Committee on Foreign Relations. *Republic of Korea: Hearings of the Subcommittee on United States Security Agreements and Commitments Abroad.* Part 6. 91st Cong., 2d sess., 1970.

United States Government Manual 1991–92. National Archives and Records Administration, 1991.

U.S. President. *Public Papers of the Presidents of the United States.* Washington, D.C.: Office of the *Federal Register,* National Archives and Records Service, November 22, 1963 to June 30, 1964. Lyndon B. Johnson, 1965.

Vietnam Information Notes. Washington, D.C.: Office of Media Services, Bureau of Public Affairs, Department of State, December 1967.

Vietnam Review 4A: Free World Assistance to South Vietnam. Washington, D.C.: Armed Forces Information Service, Department of Defense, April 1968.

Secondary Sources

Barber, James D. *The Presidential Character.* Englewood Cliffs, N.J.: Prentice-Hall, 1972.

Barclay, Glen St. John. *Friends in High Places: Australian-American diplomatic relations since 1945.* Melbourne, Australia: Oxford University Press, 1985.

————. *A Very Small Insurance Policy: The Politics of Australian Involvement in Vietnam, 1954–1967.* St. Lucia: University of Queensland Press, 1988.

Baritz, Loren. *Backfire: A History of How American Culture Led Us into Vietnam and Made Us Fight the Way We Did.* New York: William Morrow, 1985.

Baylis, John. *Anglo-American Defense Relations 1939–1984: The Special Relationship,* 2d ed. New York: St. Martin's, 1986.

Bell, Jack. *The Johnson Treatment.* New York: Harper & Row, 1965.

Bornet, Vaughn Davis. *The Presidency of Lyndon B. Johnson.* Lawrence: University Press of Kansas, 1983.

Bowman, John S., ed. *The Vietnam War: An Almanac.* New York: Bison Books of World Almanac Publications, 1985.

Brodie, Bernard. *War and Politics.* New York: Macmillan, 1973.

Cho, Soon Sung. "American Policy Toward Korean Unification, 1945–1980." In *U.S. Korean Relations: 1882–1982,* ed. Tae-Kwan Kwak. Seoul, Korea: Institute for Far Eastern Studies, 1982.

Clifford, Clark M. "Viet Nam Reappraisal." *Foreign Affairs* 47 (July 1969), 601–22.

Conkin, Paul K. *Big Daddy from the Pedernales: Lyndon Baines Johnson.* Boston: Twayne, 1986.

Cooper, Chester L. *The Lost Crusade: America in Viet-Nam.* New York: Dodd, Mead, 1970.

Cuddy, Dennis L. "The American Role in Australian Involvement in the Vietnam War." *Australian Journal of Politics and History* 28 (1982), 340–53.

Dallek, Robert. *Lone Star Rising: Lyndon Johnson and His Times 1908–1960.* New York: Oxford University Press, 1991.

Davies, Michael. *L.B.J.: A Foreign Observer's Viewpoint.* New York: Duell, Sloan and Pearce, 1966.

Destler, I.M., Leslie H. Gelb and Anthony Lake. *Our Own Worst Enemy: The Unmaking of American Foreign Policy.* Updated and rev. ed. New York: Simon & Schuster, 1984.

Divine, Robert A. "The Johnson Revival: A Bibliographical Appraisal." In *The Johnson Years, Volume Two: Vietnam, the Environment, and Science,* ed. Robert A. Divine. Lawrence: University Press of Kansas, 1987.

Donovan, Robert J. *Nemesis: Truman and Johnson in the Coils of War in Asia.* New York: St. Martin's/Marek, 1984.

Doyle, Edward, Samuel Lipsman, and the editors of Boston Publishing Company, eds. *America Takes Over: 1965-67.* The Vietnam Experience Series. Boston: Boston Pub. Co., 1982.

Evans, Roland and Robert Novak. *Lyndon B. Johnson: The Exercise in Power.* New York: New American Library, 1966.

Furer, Howard B., ed. *Lyndon B. Johnson 1908- : Chronology — Documents — Bibliograhical Aids.* Dobbs Ferry, N.Y.: Oceana, 1971.

Girling, John L.S. *America and the Third World: Revolution and Intervention.* London: Routledge & Kegan Paul, 1980.

_____. *Thailand: Society and Politics.* Ithaca, N.Y.: Cornell University Press, 1981.

Goodwin, Richard N. *Remembering America: A Voice from the Sixties.* Boston: Little, Brown, 1988.

Granatstein, J.L. "Cooperation and Conflict: The Course of Canadian-American Relations since 1945." In *Canada and the United States: Enduring Friendship, Persistent Stress,* eds. Charles F. Doran and John H. Sigler, 45–68. Englewood Cliffs, N.J.: Prentice-Hall, 1985.

Hahn, Bae-Ho. "Major Issues in the American-Korean Alliance." In *Korea and the United States,* eds. Youngnok Koo and Dae-Sook Suh, 91–110. Honolulu: University of Hawaii Press, 1984.

Han, Sungjoo. "South Korea's Participation in the Vietnam Conflict: An Analysis of the U.S.-Korean Alliance." *Orbis* 21 (Winter 1978), 893–912.

Hannah, Norman B. *The Key to Failure: Laos and the Vietnam War.* New York: Madison Books, 1987.

Heath, Jim F. *Decade of Disillusionment.* Bloomington: Indiana University Press, 1975.

Hee, Park Chung. *To Build a Nation.* Washington, D.C.: Acropolis Books, 1971.

Heren, Louis. *No Hail, No Farewell.* New York: Harper & Row, 1970.

Herring, George C. *America's Longest War: The United States and Vietnam, 1950–1975.* 2d ed. New York: Alfred A. Knopf, 1986.

Hosmer, Stephen T. *Constraints on U.S. Strategy in Third World Conflicts.* New York: Crane Russak, 1987.

Jha, Ganganath. *Foreign Policy of Thailand.* New Delhi, India: Radiant Publishers, 1979.

Kant, Immanuel. *Grounding for Metaphysics of Morals.* Translated and analyzed by H.J. Paton. New York: Harper & Row, 1964.

Karnow, Stanley. *In Our Image: America's Empire in the Philippines.* New York: Random House, 1989.

Kattenburg, Paul M. "Viet Nam and U.S. Diplomacy, 1940–1970." *Orbis* 15 (Fall 1971), 818–41.

Kaul, Man Mohini. *The Philippines and Southeast Asia.* New Delhi, India: Radiant Publishers, 1978.

Kearns, Doris. "Lyndon Johnson's Political Personality." *Political Science Quarterly* 91 (Fall 1976): 385–410.

King, Larry L. "Machismo in the White House: L.B.J. and Vietnam." *American Heritage* 27 (August 1976): 8–13, 99–101.

Kwak, Tae-Hwan. "U.S.-Korea Security Relations." In *U.S.-Korean Relations, 1882–1982,* ed. Tae-Kwan Kwak, 223–43. Seoul, Korea: Institute for Far Eastern Studies, 1982.

LaFeber, Walter. "Consensus and Cooperation: A View of United States Foreign Policy, 1945–1980." In *United States Foreign Policy at the Crossroads,* ed. George Schwab, 3–26. Westport, Conn.: Greenwood Press, 1982.

Larsen, Stanley Robert and James Lawton Collins, Jr. *Allied Participation in Vietnam.* Washington, D.C.: Department of the Army, 1975.

Lyman, Princeton N. "Korea's Involvement in Viet Nam." *Orbis* 12 (Summer 1968), 563–81.

McCarron, William E. "On Machiavelli and Vietnam." In *Military Ethics: Reflections on Principles—the profession of arms, military leadership, ethical practices, war and morality, educating the citizen soldier,* eds. Malham Wakin, Kenneth Wenker, and James Kempf, 193–202. Washington, D.C.: National Defense University Press, 1987.

McKinnon, Malcolm. "Costs and Continuity: New Zealand's Security and the United States." *Political Science* 30 (July 1978), 29–44.

McNeill, Ian. *The Team: Australian Army Advisers in Vietnam 1962–1972.* New York: Hippocrene Books, 1984.

Mallin, Jay and Robert K. Brown *Merc: American Soldiers of Fortune.* New York: Macmillan, 1979.

Morgenthau, Hans J. "Vietnam and the National Interest." In *Viet Nam: History, Documents, and Opinions on a Major World Crisis,* ed. Marvin E. Gettleman, 365–76. Greenwich, Conn.: Fawcett, 1965.

Olson, James S., ed. *Dictionary of the Vietnam War.* Westport, Conn.: Greenwood Press, 1987.

Otis, James. "Seoul's Hired Guns." *Ramparts* 11 (September 1972): 18–20, 56–57.

Park, Joon Young. *Korea's Return to Asia: South Korean Foreign Policy, 1965–1975.* Seoul, Korea: Jin Heong Press, 1985.

Porter, Gary. "Globalism—The Ideology of Total World Involvement." In *The Vietnam Reader,* eds. Marcus G. Raskin and Bernard B. Fall, 322–327. New York: Vintage Books, 1965.

Roberts, Chalmers M. "The Day We Didn't Go to War." *The Reporter* 14 (September 1954), 31–5.

Rodan, Paul. "Harold Holt's Foreign Policy 1966–1967." *Australian Journal of Politics and History* 25 (1979), 310–8.

Shalom, Stephen R. *The United States and the Philippines.* Philadelphia: Institute for the Study of Human Issues, 1981.

Shulimson, Jack. *U.S. Marines in Vietnam: An Expanding War 1966.* Washington, D.C.: History and Museums Division, Headquarters, U.S. Marine Corps, 1982.

Soonthornrojana, Adulyasak. "The Rise of United States–Thai Relations, 1945–1975." Ph.D. diss., University of Akron, 1986.

Steinberg, Alfred. *Sam Johnson's Boy: A Close-up of the President from Texas.* New York: Macmillan, 1968.

Summers, Harry G., Jr. *Vietnam War Almanac.* New York: Facts on File, 1985.

Thompson, Kenneth W. "The Johnson Presidency and Foreign Policy: The Unresolved Conflict between National Interest and Collective Security." In *Lyndon Baines Johnson and the Uses of Power,* eds. Bernard J. Firestone and Robert C. Vogt, 289–96. New York: Greenwood Press, 1988.

Thompson, W. Scott. *Unequal Partners: Philippine and Thai Relations with the United States 1965–75.* Lexington, Mass.: Lexington Books, 1975.

Turley, William S. *The Second Indochina War: A Short Political and Military History, 1954–1975.* New York: New American Library, 1986.

Turner, Kathleen J. *Lyndon Johnson's Dual War: Vietnam and the Press.* Chicago: University of Chicago Press, 1985.

Valenti, Jack. *A Very Human President.* New York: W. W. Norton, 1975.

Watt, Alan Stewart. *The Evolution of Australian Foreign Policy 1938–1965.* Cambridge, England: Cambridge University Press, 1968.

White, Ralph K. *Nobody Wanted War.* Garden City, N.Y.: Doubleday, 1968.

"Why New Zealand Aids South Vietnam." *Vietnam Perspectives* 1 (November 1965), 55–6.

Wilson, Craig V. "Rhetoric, Reality, and Dissent: The Foreign Policy of the British Labor Governments 1964–1970." Ph.D. diss., Washington State University, 1982.

Wilson, Harold. *Harold Wilson, A Personal Record: The Labour Government 1964–1970.* Boston: Little, Brown, 1971.

Wyatt, David K. *Thailand: A Short History.* New Haven, Conn.: Yale University Press, 1982.

Index

DATE DUE